THE SNOWFLAKE ON THE BELFRY

OTHER BOOKS BY ANNA BALAKIAN

Literary Origins of Surrealism
Surrealism: The Road to the Absolute
The Symbolist Movement: A Critical Appraisal
André Breton, Magus of Surrealism
The Fiction of the Poet from Mallarmé to the Post-Symbolist Mode

EDITED BY ANNA BALAKIAN

The Symbolist Movement in the Literature of European Languages (with introductory and concluding essays)
André Breton Today (co-edited by Rudolf E. Kuenzli; with an introductory essay)
Eva the Fugitive by Rosamel del Valle (translated from the Spanish, with an introductory essay)

THE SNOWFLAKE ON THE BELFRY

Dogma and Disquietude in the Critical Arena

ANNA BALAKIAN

INDIANA UNIVERSITY PRESS
Bloomington and Indianapolis

© 1994 by Anna Balakian

All rights reserved

No part of this book may be reproduced or utilized in any form or by any means, electronic or mechanical, including photocopying and recording, or by any information storage and retrieval system, without permission in writing from the publisher. The Association of American University Presses' Resolution on Permissions constitutes the only exception to this prohibition.

The paper used in this publication meets the minimum requirements of American National Standard for Information Sciences—Permanence of Paper for Printed Library Materials, ANSI Z39.48-1984.

Manufactured in the United States of America

Library of Congress Cataloging-in-Publication Data

Balakian, Anna Elizabeth, date.
   The snowflake on the belfry : dogma and disquietude in the critical arena / Anna Balakian.
     p.   cm.
   Contains several lectures presented at Indiana University in Oct. 1991 as well as a collection of her previously presented essays and lectures.
   Includes index.
   ISBN 0-253-31132-2
   1. Literature—Philosophy. 2. Criticism. 3. Modernism (Literature) 4. Experimental poetry—History and criticism. I. Title.
PN45.B24   1994
801'.95—dc20   93-7762

1 2 3 4 5   99 98 97 96 95 94

CONTENTS

PREFACE vii
INTRODUCTION xi

Part I

I. By Way of Entry into the Fray: The Critics and Their Authors 3
II. The Snowflake on the Belfry: The Aesthetic Dimension in Literary Criticism 9
III. Problems of Modernism 24
IV. Interartifactuality 44
V. Hermeneutical Criticism and the Surrealists 63
VI. Toward a New Aesthetics 81
VII. Scientific Relativism and the Arts 97
VIII. Multiculturalism: The Case of Surrealism 119

Part II

IX. Influence and Literary Reception: The Equivocal Junction of Two Methods 135
X. Of Origins and Originality 149
XI. Mallarmé as Subversive Theorist 158
XII. The Monolith of Romania: Myth or Reality? 171
XIII. At the Frontiers between Poetry and Theology According to Jacques Maritain 180
XIV. *Anicet*, or the Search for Beauty 199
XV. A Triptych of Modernism: Reverdy, Huidobro, and Ball 214

XVI.	The Unfamiliar Literatures	236
XVII.	Quality Control in the Teaching of Literature	241
XVIII.	Canon Harassment	249
XIX.	Literary Theory and Comparative Literature	258

NAME INDEX   267

PREFACE

In October 1991 I had the savory (I can still feel it on my tongue) experience of spending three weeks as a Visiting Fellow at the Institute for the Humanities of Indiana University.

There, without any special assignment, I was left to roam over the comprehensive campus, enjoy the magnificent library, and attend some of the performances in the arts that could challenge the cultural centers of our largest cities. Indiana University appeared to me immense, not only physically but in the multitudinous disciplines it offers. I had dialogue and conversation on a one-to-one basis, with several at a time, and with many on an intelligent level devoid of political bias. We got to the core of what joins the concerns of academics and every thinking man or woman in the world of learning. We also sometimes verged on the Socratic with other Fellows far afield, particularly in the physical sciences and Hebrew Biblical studies. We were amazed at the similarity at the core of our incentives to reach a workable philosophy of our position in the universe utilizing the new ways to discover data which would affect not only our perceptions of the cosmos but our behavior and expression of an altered humanism through our university work.

Although I was offered an apartment, I chose to live in a dormitory and to have breakfast each morning in the common cafeteria. There I met and talked with a cross section of students, undergraduate and graduate, majoring in a variety of subjects. A New Yorker in Middle America, generationally wide apart from these young and surprisingly avid seekers of knowledge, I wondered what we would have in common; not much, I thought, judging from the multitude of lecture announcements posted on the walls along the flight of stairs that took me up to my modest room. I made no overture unless and until the regular residents approached me. The miracle was that we had so much to talk about that was not in their special fields of interest or my expertise but demonstrative of a cohesive ingredient that filters through the specific to the general.

All the Humanities Center had asked me to do was give several lectures. The last one was not on the official schedule but at the request of the students at the residence hall. I talked to a packed house about the unconventional ideas I sustained on modernism (some of which had already circulated around campus from my official lectures). As I talked, there were nodding heads of approval and brows with perplexed frowns, but all on faces brightly awake and ready to bombard me with questions at the end of the lecture. My politically incorrect attitudes were matched by creative affront on their part, and I enjoyed as I have not in some time both the positive and the negative responses about literature and its meaning for our time without once mentioning gender, race, or sexual orientation. Instead we questioned notions of communication and interpretations of human and cosmic perspectives. Those who came to talk to me individually after the lecture expressed agreement and disagreement, but the remark I cherished most and which rang in my ears all the way to New York was the repeated "You made a difference." As I was coming to the last part of my visit I was approached by colleagues and students with requests for copies of my lectures. But my texts were in rough drafts and had been enlivened with extemporaneous remarks; they were not ready to be handed out. My former student, Professor David Hertz, who had become my mentor on the Indiana campus, suggested that I collect the lectures in a publication. Mysteriously, one day Joan Catapano, a sponsoring editor with Indiana University Press, found her way to my office at the Institute, and we were able to discuss a tangible volume that would bring together the Indiana lectures and others which I thought belonged beside them. Among the essays I selected from more than a hundred there were two that were originally written in French. One of these, "Of Origins and Originality," is included because it was seminal although it comes from my early days. The other, "Toward a New Aesthetics," is a very recent one delivered in Amiens the summer before. I discovered that translating oneself is the hardest type of translation and found myself rewriting the pieces.

I warned the editors at Indiana University Press that in publishing my essays they were dealing with outright subversion both in relation to the climate currently created by the intelligentsia in its academic infiltrations and to the Press's own catalogue, which so comprehensively represents the current zeitgeist. But they have been so brave as to accept on their list this small but persistent voice of dissent against what I think is the unthinkable intention by a militant minority to destroy our cultural heritage. I trust the reader will not hold my editors or publisher responsible for the content of this volume but instead will praise them for supporting free speech.

This volume is dedicated to the students of Indiana University who demonstrated inquisitive and open attitudes toward me and my literary positions. My deepest gratitude to David Hertz for his role in making this volume possible.

INTRODUCTION

The theory of literature is a misnomer, whereas the theory of criticism is a viable practice that reflects the critic's choice of approach to literary works. To identify one's work as criticism is a presumptuous declaration, supported by a conscious or unconscious belief that one has something to say about the work beyond what the creative writer has already communicated. The critic's response to the work of the artist-writer is at the junction where the analytical mind meets the creative mind's synthesis. The disquietude occurs when the critic tries to justify the critical response as a value-added enlargement of the creative act. From the point of view of the self-defining work of the creative writer—and all great works are self-defining—the critical engagement is precarious and fittingly characterized by the Heideggerian image of the featherweight snowflake's effort to activate the bell in the belfry.

Before the current era, critics were satisfied to limit their roles to teacher and retriever. They took pride in the power of the great teacher to select and to throw light on the qualities of the work and establish criteria whereby the general reader would be directed to select qualitatively from the quantities of works impossible to absorb in a single lifetime. And since it takes an immense exposure to the ever-increasing growth of the literary miscellany, the notion and practice of specialization emerged whereby concentration and delimitation endowed the critic's performance with authority.

The retriever function was equally important, because the loss of a significant work is as tragic as losing something cherished and irreplaceable in the rubble of a burning edifice. Many of the works resulting from the regular productivity of professional writers are indeed replaceable and renewable with succeeding generations. There is nothing so sobering as to gauge the general lifespan of a piece of writing by scanning the pages of an issue of the *New York Times Book Review* of several decades past. The popular *Anthony Adverse*s are easily forgotten, and the spirit that created them in the first place passes into the works of succeeding generations. But the critic's function is to retrieve the jewel from the conflagration. Constantly on the lookout, a relentless sleuth engaged in an exciting, exploratory adventure in pursuit of discoveries in dusty recesses of libraries, in dreary bibliographies, in old periodicals, forgetting all else, forgotten by all others—such is the scholarly, critical retriever.

Teaching literary values on the basis of authority gained through exposure and teaching experience, and retrieving the lost from accident or circumstantial neglect, were considered legitimate purposes for a productive and self-renewing activity until a new breed of critics came along to intrude into the anthologies, to invade the classroom, to compound the reference books as manipulators rather than sponsors of the creative writers, not to highlight the intrinsic qualities that explained the survival of great works but to superimpose their own ideologies. When the work (opus) became a text, it turned into a beast of burden carrying some other person's dogma. The critic had turned from the role of mediator to that of entrepreneur, from explorer to exploiter, and the relation of retriever to retrieved turned into investor and return.

The selected essays in Part I represent my confrontation of the ever-more-pervasive dogmatic use of literature in criticism and my disquietude over the fate not only of criticism but even more of literature itself, which needs the snowflake, not to ring the bell to any particular tune but to maintain a seasonal balance in the literary climate. In Part II I give illustrations of my own activities as retriever and teacher particularly of poetic works.

The analytically oriented dogmatic critics have most often chosen as their frame of reference writers such as Rousseau, Flaubert, Mallarmé, Henry James, and Proust, who, by bringing a marked degree of analytic consciousness to their work, created a comfortable meeting ground with these critics. I am perplexed that these critics have bypassed the surrealist theories on life and artistic process in developing their critical thinking. My guess is that most of the initial group of dogmatic critics were ignorant of this important phenomenon of the twentieth century because they came to maturity at a time when most schools in Europe had not yet admitted surrealism into the academic curriculum.

My own thinking has been permeated with the surrealist factor because I was an explorer of surrealism and found it the most exciting channel of reference in my own critical quest, which became also part of my spiritual quest to find and teach works that can make a difference in the life of the reader.

The last four essays especially address readers teaching or studying Comparative Literature. It took half a century to establish this discipline in the university curriculum, and many ideological and professional assaults to ward off in order to keep it alive and growing. But at the end of the century its growth is becoming alarming rather than elating.

To qualify as a Comparatist it was presumed that the prospective candidate had to acquire a certain command of several languages so that perceptions of literary works would be direct, precise, and pristine. The imperative was not only the acquisition of the cultural background but the linguistic form of its communication. It was also considered that only by comparative knowledge of several literatures historically grouped together was the Comparatist qualified to give relative evaluation of literary merit.

With the addition of "the other arts" and the more recent entry of a very powerful faction of philosophy, sociology, and clinical psychology, Comparative Literature has virtually turned into comparative studies. The only justification for overflow into these other disciplines would be if they could contribute aesthetic values to a relationship whose centerpiece is literature; instead, the more recent results of such "comparisons" have become ideological and political, whereby the literary work plays an assisting rather than commanding role, and even in that subsidiary position it is subject to a watering down and almost a dismissal of the very specificity and rigor of the methodology that distinguished Comparative Literature from General Literature on the one hand and cultural history on the other.

The process that stretches the boundaries of the discipline and narrows the need for linguistic capabilities has left the doors wide open for all manner of theoreticians to take over. The resulting products are too often monolingual in approach, too vast in scope to have pertinence, and too restricted in political positions and in their scholarly referential radius to add substance to our knowledge of literature.

There is such a vast field of unexplored literature of merit world wide that beckons to the Comparatist "to get on with it." It is pitiful that the increase in the number of Comparatists has become a bad omen. A comment made by Denis Donoghue in the *New York Review of Books* in a reference to theoretical writings in the field of English and American literature can apply even more appropriately to the practitioners of Comparative Literature: "Theory tends to become the primary means of postponing, perhaps forever, the labor of reading works of literature: or of ensuring that the reading of a particular work of literature will merely fulfill the theory that precedes it." (Vol. XI, no. 6, March 25, 1993) Donoghue consoles himself with the impression that nonetheless procedures and substance in the classroom continue to be propitiously classic.

If such is the situation, professors are constantly widening the gap between what they write and what they teach, and they must beware of abolishing the image of the university as a structure of communicating vessels whereby scholarship filters into teaching and teaching catalyzes scholarship.

Part I

I

BY WAY OF ENTRY INTO THE FRAY
THE CRITICS AND THEIR AUTHORS

Arriving in France at a nontouristic moment, I was able to attend a noninternational colloquium on the new novel, held in Strasbourg in the last few days of April 1970. I was there as a nonparticipant, a mere observer—and I observed a pure case of the exercise of tyranny in the realm of letters.

According to the program, the current state of the novel was the subject of the meeting, and the participants could be grouped variously as novelist-critics, journalist-critics, and professor-critics, criticism being the common denominator. The age spectrum ranged from the mid-thirties to the mid-sixties. The generation gap did not seem to be determined by chronological age as oldsters rushed to jump on the youth caravan and some younger participants intoned their speeches in a manner reminiscent of their fathers.

This heterogeneous group was to take inventory of the accomplishments of that hybrid form of writing loosely called the new novel. As the period in which something can remain new had not been taken into consideration in its appellation, the new novel had in the meantime grown older, and the meaning of "new" remained undefined after three days of examination.

Actually, it soon became apparent that the new novel had been a pretext for the practice of the new criticism, and the non-new novelist-critics and professor-critics had been summoned there to serve as targets for the new critic's cannon.

The first speaker, Robert Sabatier (who knew the publishing business from both ends of the production line, as author of a best-seller, *Les Allumettes suédoises,* and as an editor of a well-known publishing house) announced in foreboding tones the end of literary journals; the invasion of fake books, which he defined as writings produced to exploit newspaper headlines and personalities, such as a new political leader, a sensational criminal, an astronaut, a movie star, a heart surgeon, etc.; and the deplorable plight of the professional writer with his scandalously meager royalties. Having been put in a mood to receive the news of the death of all literature, we were next called upon to listen to Vercors, the erstwhile hero of the French Resistance of World War II, on THE NOVEL WHAT FOR? He answered his question by first declaring that he was not a novelist, then making the suggestion that there was no reason to write unless one had to relate some deep and/or towering adventure or experience in life.

That is when the first blast of cannon occurred.

The devil's disciple came in the form of a youngish man, wearing very dark glasses, who kept on his black spectacles throughout the three days although there was no suggestion of sunshine either inside or outside during that tardy spring season. I shall not mention his name since he stuck to his strong contention during the whole time that *there is no such thing as an author;* there is only writing.

To identify him, suffice it to say that he belongs to the lineage of the *structuralists,* more recently called *semiologists,* for whom literature's only reason for existence is to provide language with its "maximum possibilities of functioning." They take literary works away from their authors as in the early stages of communism the state was said to take children away from their parents. The name of their magazine, *Tel Quel,* suggests the orphaned state of the literary work, cut off from its biographical and biological tree, floating around like

By Way of Entry into the Fray 5

a message in a bottle to be deciphered like the Rosetta stone or some inscription in an ancient cave.

After the man in the dark glasses had annihilated Vercors and a few others with his disdain and stamped under foot such old-fashioned ideas as "a born writer," "literary heritage," "linguistic style," etc., he proceeded to apply his deciphering tactics to a novel of the "new" novelist Claude Simon. After spending the next forty-five minutes tracking down the color yellow and all its aphorisms in the said book, he gave his own critique of his critique by declaring that he had just endowed the book with unity by weaving together the network of yellow motifs in it.

That his yellow focus might be news to the author of the work is no problem because the work is collective property and the author was merely the medium through whom the work was written. The work has written itself *(s'est écrit)* through the author, and the readers, i.e., the intelligent ones like the men around *Tel Quel,* exercise their power to read by using the book as a gymnasium where they can strengthen their reading muscles.

All books are not for reading in this manner. In fact, some are for burning, those of incorrigible individualists who keep intruding their narcissistic egos into their writing or who, in asides, take the reader into their confidence and tell him exactly where to look for their message.

The writers whose works fall on the autopsy tables of the new critics are the self-disciplined ones, those who went to a lot of trouble choosing the right word, who made a careful collection of components to construct their narrative, who managed to keep their egos as unobtrusive as possible: people like Flaubert, Mallarmé, the seventeenth-century French classicists, and in later times such novelists as Proust, James, and Kafka.

What the new critics do to these writings is to dismantle them as one would dismantle a clock but with no concern about putting it back together again. Some of the caste is happy just to reduce the work to debris and transform it into an abstract formula carefully clothed in heavy pseudo-scientific terminology and accompanied with mathematical charts:

	Destinateurs	Dons	Destinaires
Situation 1	M——	E(+)—	——C
	C——	A(−)—	——E
Situation 2	M——	C(−)—	——A
	A——	E(+)—	——M

Others have ulterior motives: out of the fragments they can code messages particularly compatible with their own ideology, which is predominantly Marxist-oriented. In their manipulations, authors we considered pious become iconoclasts and those we have taken to be spokesmen of their society become its enemies, suddenly buried in revolutionary verbiage. Were they to rise from their graves and protest that they are being misinterpreted, their categorical answer would be that each reader has the right to find his own message. But such is the cunning of the new critic that in his writing it reads as if Racine had in truth turned against the Establishment rather than simply in the critic's semiotic reading of him.

One by one the people who had come to Strasbourg to read a paper on the intended topic of the colloquium were acidly put in their places by the young man in the dark glasses and his aides. They were accused of bringing a literary approach to literature; they were informed that the novel before 1945 could be reduced to Flaubert, Proust, and Kafka. Anything else was redundant. But then, actually, even in 1945 what was there? Camus? But nobody over fourteen would find Camus of any interest! Nothing of any consequence really happened before 1955!

The wonder of it was that although time was always running short and the audience, with its large contingent of students, rarely got a chance to put in a word, the young man with the dark glasses was allowed to intervene after every paper like an executioner wielding the ax.

The other astonishing aspect was the lack of any form of resistance to the flagrant dogmatism and arrogant repartee. One after the other the regular critics or novelist-critics who had given seriously documented, informative papers capitulated without much more than a whimper. Others, as if to be thought younger than their years, seconded and applauded the semiotic intruder.

Sitting next to me was a pale professor from the north of France whose caved-in chest and tired eyes suggested a lifelong preoccupation with teaching and meditation. He confessed to me that this was it—he had to erase all his previous methodology; none of it could survive.

All or nothing! Nothing for the past, all for the present! History is suspect, sociology is caving in. No source, no code, no system is to survive from the past. With the new society comes a new way of reading, with writing that is to be functionally adapted to the new way of reading!

It might have been fun, this discussion between the old and the new, between the values tested and found imperfect and the values not yet tested; the process of testing the new might even have started. Instead, the deadpan faces of attackers and the equally deadpan faces of apathetic defendants—and no humor evident on either side!

Actually, Strasbourg was an ideal location to observe the schismatic state of the critics and their favorite authors. In Strasbourg, as in the new writing, there is no melding of the new with the old; here is the old city with its quaint buildings and steeples, and then there is the new city with its uniform, bland, functional structures.

The last morning of the colloquium I woke up with an alexandrine of Racine ringing in my ears. How marvelous is the human unconscious; it had found a parallel to my disquietude in one of the great source works of French literature. Let me pin it down before the citation is relegated to outer, noncontingent space. It comes from *Athalie*, a play based on the Biblical story of a descendant of David who overcomes the pagan woman-ruler Athalia. The young boy, Eliacin, has been reared in the worship of his God in the seclusion of the Temple. Finally he is discovered and confronted by the pagan queen, who questions him. What gods do you worship, young man? Do you know my gods? And the little boy answers with all the candor of his simplistic dogmatism:

> Le mien est tout, Madame, et le vôtre n'est rien.
> (Mine is everything, Madam, and yours is nothing.)

NOTE

This essay first appeared in *The American PEN*, vol. 2, no. 1 (Summer 1970), 38–42.

II

THE SNOWFLAKE ON THE BELFRY
THE AESTHETIC DIMENSION IN LITERARY CRITICISM

The new methodologies threaten the pursuit of aesthetic knowledge in literature. The presumption one detects from the reading of analytical, empirical, formalistic criticism is that the objectives of literature are not very remote from those of scientific inquiry and that, therefore, the literary text can be submitted to the same methods of analysis and commentary, and with similar terminology. Having spent more than four decades in the study of literature and criticism, and traced the histories of permanence versus impermanence in modes and conventions of aesthetics, I deplore the neglect of the aesthetic factor which arouses sensitivity, expands the imagination of the reader as it reveals states of consciousness in the writer—all elements which cannot identify directly with psychological, social, or ideological truths.

The history of literary criticism has corresponded rather closely to that of literature itself. In fact, criticism flourishes like the parasitical mistletoe on the oak tree. Instead of feeding on life and its realities, as does literature, it derives its substance from the front-line response to life, which literature is. The literary critic's gradual sophistication has paralleled that of the writer of what we call literature. In rising societies when literature consisted of direct communication with the reader in the form of ideas, narration, description, or expression of emotions, the function of the critic consisted primarily in clarifying meaning. He helped to popularize the work and played a game of lottery in picking the winners. If literature is experience once removed from life, criticism is twice removed from it, creating a double transformation of reality into artifice. In the past century what we have come to designate as avant-garde has consisted in a form of writing which gradually widened the gap between literature and standard notions of communication, and in the past several decades we might say that there has emerged an avant-garde of criticism which in the same spirit of sophistication has widened the gap between the nonprofessional reader of literature and the critic's response to literature.

If there has developed an interaction between the personality of the original author and that of the critic, the confrontation is becoming progressively a dialogue between the critic and the text, cut off from the author, in which the critic's own attitudes relate to those perceived in the text. There occurs an *interference* between author and reader in the form of a metatext of preconceived social attitudes or philosophical orientations to the work of art whose dimensions are limited neither to a sociology nor to a philosophy.

These critics bring to the aesthetic work a terminology borrowed from other disciplines and a set of meanings unrelated to the literary work. They adapt to the literary commentary procedures from sociologists, linguists, psychiatrists whose preoccupations are remote from literature and who are in no way to blame for these unsolicited applications.

What precisely separates these other disciplines from literature is the aesthetic factor, and therefore their terminologies remain incapable of dealing with the work of art. As Wolfgang Iser aptly put it, "an analysis of text processing requires more than just a linguistic model."[1] I would be happier with this supportive statement if it did not contain the word "processing," which immediately implies that what you do to literature passes through the same activity as what you do to all other data!

It is assumed by these recent processors of literature that the work of art is a phenomenon endowed with an independent existence; it is an object distinct from the personal life course of its author. The work presumably has no personal past but is a product of a collective unconscious going far and deep into the past of the group. Having no personal past, it has an immediacy for the reader. According to Gaston Bachelard, a referee of the new critics, "You must be in the presence of the image in the instant of the image." If situated in a historical background, the *now*-character of the text would be obliterated. If the background is viewed, instead, as part of the collective genes, the text's living heritage would ever be manifest. So the history of the work is replaced by the biology and anthropology of the text. The critic's point of view is a scientific hypothesis and admitted as such. As Todorov stated in 1966 in his review of Benveniste's *Problèmes de linguistique générale:* "Criticism today can only be hypothetical, partial and provisional." Critical texts inspired by him have indeed remained hypothetical, for over the years they have not led to total, unified critical works but at most to "collected" essays. The hypothetical precludes the exercise of judgment in criticism. And in "Activité structuraliste," Roland Barthes averted concern for the literary factor even in his definition of an aspect of aesthetics most intimately connected with literary writing, that of the *image:* "The image is intellect added to the object and this addition has an anthropological value in the fact that it is man himself, his history, his situation, his liberty and the very resistance that nature creates to his mind."[2]

If the author's personal and literary history was to be replaced by that of Man, designated in general terms, one more layer had to be stripped to deliver him to this anonymity: that of style. Style, once thought to be the highest state of art, comes to be considered a subterfuge, a "prestige seeking" device, a stigma, an artificial embellishment that often hides the true nature of the work, according to Barthes's view. It is presumably a barrier to meaning, imposed by the author to block our way to the primal structure and significance of the work. Of course, putting Barthes in context, we can readily realize that he was reacting to his French secondary education, to those classes in "lectures expliquées" where he was confronted with texts studied as the epitome of "high style" consisting almost exclusively of neoclassical and Romantic literature.

The truth about style for anyone who has followed the history of modernism is that instead of being superfluous to the text it has become more and more soluble with the thought process of the creative writer and integral to the meaning of meaning. Consider what would happen to Mallarmé if he were stripped of style. The question that is not asked is what must we think of authors such as Faulkner, Hemingway, Joyce, and more recently Beckett and Burroughs and a host of others who make use of style not for prestige but actually to diminish prestige. What is blatantly overlooked is the modern writer's *negative* use of style through the practice of demotic language below his own cultural level to authenticate and validate the level of reality of his narrative and its truth claim.

Thus the work of art, stripped of its biography, history, and style, floats around like a message in a bottle seeking its recipient. The critic treats it like the Rosetta stone or some inscription in an ancient cave; its importance is determined by its contemporary significance so that reception becomes closely connected with a hermeneutic process which renders its meaning enigmatic to correspond to a world convinced of the relativity and indeterminacy of values and truth claims.

The work's constancy then is merely in its myth-bearing character participating in the elemental patterns of human existence. The focus on the perennial or universal significance of the literary text brings it into the orbit of myth culture as interpreted by Claude Lévi-Strauss. If, sociologically speaking, the myth is a deviation stemming from natural reality and from collective taboos, then what we call literary writing, stripped of style, is in essence presumed to be an extension of myth or folklore. Freed of its aesthetic ingredients, the work can be processed to reveal its social character. Instead of being placed in the framework of a *known* history (presumed to be biased), its history is now revealed inductively from the interior of the work. A botanical analogy is to the point. Whereas previous methodologies deemed deterministic, such as Sainte-Beuve's, would begin with the analysis of the soil and the tree to understand the kind of fruit it could bear, in a reversed process the actual fruit is asked to manifest its soil, tree, and climate. The critic's function would be, consequently, to create a second time the reality which the writer had recreated originally to determine its culture.

Such defoliation of literature leaves raw language as the only source of history, personality, society. The presupposition is that language liberated from style reveals unmitigated truth. If, therefore, the orientation of the critical text is anthropological and sociological, the substance to be analyzed is linguistic. The language of thought, free of its aesthetic dimensions, allegedly provides true semiotic data, both environmental and behavioral. It is in this context that references are made to Lacan's quotation of the German writer von Kleist: "Idea does not exist before language, it is formed with it." In other words, thought tends toward expression in its fulfillment. Language then is the purest index of the unconscious, nourished by its collective memory box of prejudices, taboos, patterns of thought, all of which combined produce the human psyche of which the literary text is a revelation. The study of literature via its language would demonstrate a fundamental shift of critical focus. According to Michel Foucault, emphasis was placed in the past on the element which he calls "the super-revelation of the transcendental"; whereas, in a reversal of approach, what interests the human scientist are the nonconscious aspects of the language which shaped the text.

Linguistics, then, ironically relying on the probe and conclusions of psychologists, tends to eliminate the so-called psychological approach to criticism, which was based on interpretations of the author's behavior extraneous to the text and as gleaned also through an analysis of the behavior of his characters *in* the text. Lacan, in the wake of Freud, impressed by the interpretations of Freud, exploring his patients' behaviors through their spontaneous verbalizations, came to believe that literary writing can also become its own psychological document. What is overlooked again is the aesthetic factor. Language used by the creative writer does not necessarily betray the biography either of the author or of his characters; *parole* occurs as a very conscious activity resulting from the interplay of natural automatism and eclectic rejection of certain verbal data. This voluntary choice turns *parole* into something artificial, and that artificial element is identifiable with aesthetics. Certainly literary *parole*, a contrived fiction, has no connection with the induced spontaneity of the psyche in a patient under clinical hypnosis or under the autosuggestion of a therapist. And the search for anagrams, homonymic double talk, and paradigms in the language of the literary text is an arbitrary emphasis having more to do with the critic's predisposition than the author's. When Lacan tried to apply his clinical methodology to the *parole* of Rimbaud, the poet emerged from this process as merely a mental patient. If the psychoanalytic methodology were applied widely to literary writers, a gallery of mental cases would emerge instead of artists, paradoxically reverting to the challenged proposition that the text reflects the author.

The structuralism-oriented critic, then, arrives at what he considers *constants* in literature, after having suspended judgment, by establishing verities about social and psychological behavior in literature through the description of the basic structures of literary language after he has discarded its *literary* qualities. He fulfills Barthes's blunt assertion that "literature is itself a science, or at least knowledge, no longer of the 'human heart' but of human language." Out of the dregs he arrives at common denominators, approaching the type of knowledge one can glean from myth, archetypes, or paradigms.

But in taking his cues from scientific inquiry, has he fulfilled the scientific goals at least if not the literary ones? Not according to Emile Benveniste, who was taken as a model by many of the structuralists and neostructuralists; he forewarned them that the prober has not really done anything significant or scientific unless he goes on to show how the structure functions: "The worst danger is to believe that in describing the facts you are a scientist." In other words, you reach scientific respectability only by showing the function, i.e., in revealing a system. We might answer that when, after having shown how the author has constructed the work, you show how the structure functions, your target automatically becomes *meaning*, and you are back to interpretation, even though the point of departure was diametrically opposed to previous forms of interpretation. The difference, then, is that in search of function a system is superposed on the consecutive structures discovered. The result for those who proceed from individual structure to the creation of systems is to produce a reductive effect on the work itself. The systems that emerge are often ingenious, sometimes even revelatory. But they tend to spotlight one facet of the work to the detriment or omission of other aspects. And since those writers whom we tend to identify as "great" are in fact very complicated individuals, the systematization seems more appropriate for simpler and less prominent writers. The critic's ability to organize and classify often bypasses the ambiguities, complexities, and contradictions which torment the artistic mind and are willfully injected into the work of art. The critical expertise, therefore, can actually work against the work of art by overlooking the ambivalences of the artist's temperament. Gérard Genette declared: "The defect of modern criticism lies perhaps less in its psychologies than in its too individualistic conception of psychology."[3]

Instead of this individualism, he proposed the study of clusters of structures that reveal codes applicable to the group; this form of criticism "can find the message in the code, discerned through the analysis of immanent structures, and no longer imposed from outside by ideological prejudices."[4] But in truth, what occurs is that, too often, instead of uncovering a system in the author studied, we discover the prejudices and operational system of the critic himself. Under the guise of scientific objectivity there lurks the danger of arbitrary, weighted statements conveyed as absolute, scientifically proven truths.

What distinguishes a social document from a work of art is precisely the fact that the individual intervenes in the work of art *deforming* the set patterns, codes, syndromes on which the work is based. Some of the very trimmings that seem to be reducible and irrelevant to the empirical critic are factors in distinguishing a literary work from a document, a literary persona from a case study, a masterpiece from an aesthetically faulted work. The will of the author alters the common knowledge inherent in stereotyped language and in the collective archetypes. If the criterion of worth were to be determined by the degree of direct reflection of social conditions or psychological norms, the very notion of *masterpiece* would have to be completely revised and to the designations of ethnography, historiography, would have to be added the term "literariography." As the Thomist philosopher Jacques Maritain said many years ago, if art were a means to knowledge, it would be furiously inferior to geometry.

The structuralist or poststructuralist critic has not been able to handle the question of aesthetic quality. The artist establishes criteria in a universe of his own over which he has autonomous control commensurate with his talents, and he invites comparison. If the text in question is considered in isolation from other texts, there can be no comparison, and therefore no gauge of the aesthetic factor. Isolated textual analysis provides opportunities for intellectual gymnastics to veer from aesthetic appraisals and too often it omits recognition of the role of aesthetics in the reality of the text. Even most so-called stylistic analyses are performed as means to arrive at concepts remote from the imaginative factor or affective intensity that nurture the use of style. This oversight forewarns of the eventual annihilation of the notion of literature as a separate form of writing from the informative. In response to the criticism that empirical methodologies might be leading to sterility, Jacques Derrida said: "I believe that the risk of sterility and sterilization has always been the price of lucidity."[5] The further question might be: "Is it even lucid?"

Literature is not always conveniently representative of a society or conveniently representative even of rebellion against that society. It is often unpredictable, problematic, even prophetic. It provides a battleground for the struggle between instinct and the human will. If it is representative of anything, it is representative of the nonrepresentative; it is the resistance against the norm.

Too often the work of art is being used as a vehicle on which the critical mind gallops away. Many a literary specialist would have liked to have been a philosopher but, failing that, he infiltrates the literary text with his philosophical perceptions. Whereas the critic used to spend his time simplifying philosophy, now he tries to turn literature into philosophy, adding to the burden of deciphering meaning the further one of fabricating terminology as he goes along. Obscurity is not always a sign of profundity. One is reminded of Claude Mauriac's observation: "There is no blindness worse than that of an exacerbated intelligence digging away where there is no depth."[6] If one examines closely some of the statements of heavy-handed critics who approach literature, one can find beneath the appearance of a supremely lucid mind confusion and contradiction. For instance, in his essay "Signature, Event, Context," Jacques Derrida, the most applauded pseudophilosopher of his time, elaborates on the contention, categorically accepted by his followers, that there is no context because every utterance, oral or written, is essentially separable from the original text and able to engender new contexts. In other words, authorship and the intentions of the author are presumably irrelevant to future meanings that the work or any parcel of it can achieve. To quote him: "A written sign contains a power to break away (rupture) from its context, i.e., from the totality of the presences which organize the moment of inscription."[7] And then Derrida goes on to say that the meaning can be grafted on other chains. Notice the mixed metaphors! The first one is borrowed from cosmology, suggesting the power of earthquakes; the next—the isolation of the inscription—suggests archaeological discovery after the totality of a social structure has vanished; the last starts with botanical terminology, suggesting grafting from one tree to another—and that would have been an internally consistent metaphor if separated from the first two. But unfortunately the grafting is not done on "chêne" (oak tree) but on "chaîne," meaning chain in the scientific sense of system, and how someone grafts something on a chain becomes quite befuddled and incongruous to me, particularly since "chain" suggests continuity and not interruption, and upon examination we find the author's vocabulary constantly betraying his passion for historical discontinuity.

The dark philosophers of modern criticism have been attempting the tabula rasa that Locke and Descartes threatened but did not carry out. A history that let them down arouses in them a silent anger aimed at destroying that very history, its network of relationships, accumulation of cultural references, to be replaced by a vision of contingencies in which Man himself becomes a haphazard figment of his own power of communication. Armed by an erudite language of their own, they pronounce the death of history and predict the doom of Man himself. History deceived Man according to Foucault into believing that he was progressing in a coherent structure and according to a timetable. He responds to this so-called disillusion by stressing on the contrary the finitude and imminent disappearance of Man as a determinant of events. The pseudoproofs of this "dispersion" of Man are presumably evident in literature, chosen in fragmented pieces that give the semblance of inscriptions on tombstones—which explains the association Foucault constantly has made between literature and archaeology.

The overall intent is to undermine Western culture by deleting the validity of its referential role in literature. Literature becomes a double-edged weapon. On the one hand, positivist methodologies arrive at absolute generalizations about the official history of Western civilization; on the other hand, as if to make their case stronger, the theoreticians postulate on the indeterminacy principle to turn literature into shifting sands of semiotic ambiguity. Negation of obvious meaning to substitute alternate and often contradictory meaning through the manipulation of rhetorical devices and arbitrary assumptions of irony on the part of the author undermines the universal continuity of the communication and leaves the impression that the critic is wiser than the author of the text.

Theories of hermeneutics and reader-reception rely on deterministic methods to prove the indeterminacy of the deepest values associated with the work of art: its sincerity, its power to convey and share emotions, and identify a code of ethics.

But here, as in the creation of systems, what is again overlooked is the aesthetic factor. Because literature is not primarily a document to give information, it is by the same token immune to misinformation. It aims at its best to cultivate the imagination and expand the affective range, whereas it is only those elements not intrinsic to the literary factor that may be subject to indeterminacy and to Derrida's "Différance." Fear is fear from time immemorial, so is anger, jealousy, ecstasy, or grief: if the reasons that stir these emotions may change with succeeding eras, the manifestations are universally recognizable. A text may be subject to relative perceptions as to its meaning, but if, regardless of its historical moment, it creates a deep feeling in the reader, stimulates aesthetic pleasure, extends the sense of temporal and spatial dimensions, then it meets the test of the absolute qualities of literature. None of the empirical approaches to criticism has given new measurements to test a text's intoxicating power or literary blood pressure, what in lay language we call "inspiration." When, instead, critics try to discover strategies in the author's creative process, they give the impression that all artists are chess players. The truth of the matter is that Marcel Duchamp was the only avowed chess player of the league, and he would have been the last to claim that the power to put one over on the reader was a prime gauge of literary merit.

The many texts that have been resuscitated from oblivion as worthy of critical attention, such as *S/Z*, prove that the neglect was justified, and their main virtue may have been to serve as a vehicle to demonstrate the critic's intelligence rather than the author's achievement. The literary power of a text is a constant rather than a variable. The critic's mission in the world of the arts is to point the way to the emotional and imaginative stimulation inherent in literary texts.

In dealing with ideological communication, the processes of hermeneutics can serve only to search for the differential that can arise out of the intellectual attitudes that occur in the course of historical time and permeate languages and alter connotations. The hermeneutics relating to imaginative communication is of a totally different metal and has to do with the density of the literary text.

In naive societies, where emotions were explicit and the leaps of the imagination were not restrained or repressed, the creator of the literary text would communicate *directly* to achieve its affects and impact. In our more reticent, reserved societies, hermeneutic devices, used by the artists in all the media, are more likely to reach the broader variability of the scale of sensibilities and imaginative resources of the reader. Indirect discourse (such as in symbolism, surrealism, collage narratives, and word-plays) has opted for ambiguity of communication to allow a broader range of affective and imaginative interpretation or identification by the reader. The hermeneutic activity of the critic in this respect is to gauge the range of the polyvalence of the author.

Now, when the privileged reader (critic) reduces ideologically the hermeneutic meaning to a single track, he destroys the polysemy of the writing and limits its literary power. Along with the delimitation, the process diminishes the literary experience, and unilateral understanding is not apt to compensate, no matter how analytically expert, for the loss of the affective elements which make for the pleasure of the reading. The critic, whose interest in the arts is purely intellectual, finds the pleasure of the text in his own hermeneutic exercises in deciphering. Barthes explains the process very aptly in *Le Plaisir du texte*. Aesthetic pleasure is of a totally different caliber. It consists of emotional reception, enlargement of the experience of reality, self-illumination, as constant factors of that pleasure. In that light, variabilities of "production" and "consumption" in terms of the ideological comprehension of art, no matter how large they may be proved in the course of time, are totally irrelevant and indeed insignificant to the appreciation of the arts.

Other disciplines are better suited to the search for truth and its inconstancies. The arts are not reflections of facts, but if they do not meet standards of accuracy, they break down the polarization of the famous antinomies between the verifiable realities and the imaginary world, between measured time and timelessness, chance and necessity.

It is the challenge of the modern critic to discern the degrees of attainment of the unity of the work of art in the face of the complexities of the human psyche and in defiance of the indeterminacy of ideas and of the gratuitous character of phenomena.

The threats to the aesthetic differential of literature, rather than the relativity of meaning, bring into focus the ambiguous position of the critic and scholar of literature. It is not a very tenable one. The critic is a performer with an ingrained desire to be a creator. He is not really satisfied with

Heidegger's suggestion that he has as little power to affect the work of art as a snowflake has to make the church bell ring. Those who have been creating a mythology of criticism turn the tables around, view the author as a performer, as an interpreter of the social reality, and make the critic into the creator because writing a subtext that develops a system is indeed a form of creation.

But the general philosophical conclusions of these creative systems to the reading of literature are in the long run destructive of the substance of what we call literature: they are a fortiori incongruous in relation to the most modern discipline of literary scholarship, Comparative Literature, which has as its objective the discovery of new relationships in literature through the breakdown of the national and ideological barriers that separate literary figures. In the face of formidable energies dedicated to the de-historization and dismemberment of literature, the Comparatist faces a fearful challenge: to establish contacts, connections, and continuity within the spectrum of a universal cultural history, to be the frontliner in the coming struggle for the survival and expansion of literary scholarship, having its own autonomy and developing methodologies that consider of central concern the dimension of aesthetics.

NOTES

This essay, which appeared in the *Stanford Literature Review*, vol. 4, no. 1, 47–58, is an elaboration and extension of a previous statement, "Comparative Literature and Aesthetic Value," which appeared in *Neohelicon* 12 (1983), Budapest, Akademiai Kaido.

1. Wolfgang Iser, *The Act of Reading* (Baltimore: Johns Hopkins University Press, 1980), 32.
2. Roland Barthes, "Activité structuraliste," *Essais critiques* (1963), 215.
3. Gérard Genette, *Figures I* (Paris: Seuil, 1965), 163.
4. Ibid., 150.

5. Jacques Derrida, "Structure, Sign and Play in the Discourse of the Human Sciences," in *The Structuralist Controversy,* ed. R. Macksey and E. Donato (Baltimore: Johns Hopkins University Press, 1970), 271.
6. Claude Mauriac, *L'alittérature* (1958; Paris, 1969), 223.
7. Jacques Derrida, "Signature, événement, contexte," *Marges de la philosophie* (Paris: Minuit, 1972), 377.

III

PROBLEMS OF MODERNISM

Each generation of writers had the habit of reacting against the past by declaring itself "modern." The quarrel of the Ancients and the Moderns used to be a cyclical phenomenon. "New" is in itself empty of meaning, a connective word between what was and what is to come. In early uses the word had a pejorative meaning, implying that what was new and modern could not be as good as what had the prestige of approval over a period of time.

Baudelaire as both poet and critic was one of the first to splice the meaning of "modern" in a modest article relating to his viewing of the art of his time. In his piece called "La Modernité" he first gives the image of a little man running around searching for the modern and expresses the normally accepted derogatory meaning: "the transitory, the fugitive, the contingent," but then adds "that which is capable of drawing the eternal from the transitory."

Since the middle of the nineteenth century critics as well as artists in the broader sense of the word have compounded ambiguities on "modern" by using it in both senses. Succeeding generations have been calling themselves modern and allowing the word to lose gradually its defensive tone and instead assume an attitude of contestation and even arrogance. It has become in many cases a cry of rebellion, and sometimes what the late Renato Poggioli called agonism, no longer apologetic but rather challenging. Others have claimed the label "modern" in the Baudelairian sense that while reflecting the passing climate of the time, what is modern has caught "the eternal and the immutable." Critic-readers have learned to distinguish between these two definitions by calling the protesters avant-garde and have retained for the latter the label "modern" and even "high modern"* cast in solid gold.

In both cases there has emerged an added aspect of the confusion. There has developed a tradition of the antitraditional, and the label of "modern" has been retained for works of the past. Let me explain. With the passage of time each era claiming the advantage of a little distance used to delimit what had passed with a more precise label and claim for its own rebellion or renewal in the arts its own modernity. Ours is the first era on record in which succeeding waves of moderns carry on their backs the memorabilia of their ancestors and sustain the myth that modernism, proclaimed and acknowledged at a moment in time for a group of works, forever retains that label in reference to those works, that it survives in a cumulative form, generation after generation, and that avant-gardes as well as golden-seal moderns can follow each other without a posteriori appraisal, which might result in a more permanent label than the temporal one of "modern."

Seen from the Anglo-American perspective, Joyce, Proust, Ezra Pound, D. H. Lawrence, Virginia Woolf, all so different from each other, remain under the label of "modern" on the basis of their capability of retrieval of the eternal from the transitory, and writers as different from each other as Henry Miller, Gertrude Stein, André Breton remain "modern" from the avant-garde angle of protest and rebellion. The French, more pedagogical in their classifications, have adhered to Baudelaire's definition in one sense but, unable to define their own modernism, have virtually abandoned the label itself and created newer "ism" labels. The Spanish still cling to "modernismo" with its special reference to Rubén Darío and his particular brand of Symbolism. They

---

*Cf. Matei Calinescu, *Faces of Modernity: Avant-garde, Decadence, Kitsch* (Bloomington: Indiana University Press, 1977), on "high modernism."

complicate the chronological problem by following up with "postmodernismo," which is not of the vintage of the Anglo-American postmodernism. The Germans associate modern with Expressionism and Dada, the Russians hang on to Futurism as the ultimate modern before the curtain came down on any further movement in the arts. The common agreement among all of them is to call a certain moment in time modern and surrender the word to it for eternity. In calling the past modern the commentators would let their elders retain the label and in amazing timidity would relegate to their own era the rank of rear-garde, paradoxically labeling the contemporary scene "postmodern." Then the sometime literary critic, sometime philosopher Jean-François Lyotard comes along to usher us into the post-postmodern in his book entitled *The Postmodern Condition.* Has there ever been such ancestor worship recorded on the part of writers and artists themselves or of critics and literary historians? In terms of literary criticism the ambiguity simply tells us that out of the plethora of books on the market on "modernism" or "the avant-garde" there is very little chance that they are discussing the same artists or writers or the same period in literary history.

Jean Weisgerber, in structuring his two volumes on modernism in the twentieth century for the monumental project of the *Comparative History of Literature in European Languages,* tried to eliminate the problem by using the collective title *Les Avant-gardes littéraires.* But thereby he raised a new problem; in borrowing a term metaphorically from military terminology one expects the garde itself after the avant-garde. For more than two decades in the course of various communications I have been asking, "Where is the garde of the avant-garde?" I have heard no answers. Instead we observe in studies of theories of the avant-garde such terms as "old avant-garde," "the return of the avant-garde," "post-avant-garde" (although I can't quite see how you can be out front and at the tail end simultaneously), "academy of the first avant-garde," "other avant-garde," "the twilight of the avant-garde," and most recently "the neo-avant-garde." The implications of these two labels, the meaningful and meaningless one of "modern" and the uncomfortable one of "avant-garde," suggest the inability of the current moderns to provide self-determination or in retrospect attribute to past "moderns" more precise and discrete qualifications. It is no solution to suggest, as Ihab Hassan has in relation to Surrealism, that "these movements have all but vanished now, Modernism has proved more stable." Existentialism and Minimalism, the two most recent efforts at group classification, have already outlived their recentness. The end of the century that has had in its existence so many ruptures with the past has not yet had the vision and the courage to proclaim the past moderns as *pre-something* that would define changes in literature and art in our era reflecting our society and at the same time preserving those of its qualities that may have resilience and permanence.

The reason that one sometimes denigrates a phenomenon or task is the realization that one cannot cope with it. That is perhaps why literary history is a bad term these days and the practice of analysis has priority over attempts at synthesis. We have dwelt on the most comfortable assumption that ruptures in the realm of arts can be paralleled with political revolutions, but in doing so we may be overlooking the fundamental cohesions that existed beneath the many "isms" of the first half of our century, alternately called modern and avant-garde.

My perspective tells me that there is something else that is understressed: throughout the century all literature and art that could be termed modern in its time and that laid the foundations of what exists today as "the arts" and qualifies as our modernity is related to radical concepts, not politically radical but scientifically so, that have altered our philosophy of existence and thereby reshaped our notions of aesthetics, mimesis, representation, and creativity. Such are the drastic changes in concepts of reality, time, nature, causality and chaos, indeterminacy, and above all, in terms of all the arts, the notion of communication and reception.

As the spectrum of reality enlarges, replacing the old opposition between real and supernal, a progressive distinction is perceived between mimesis and more sophisticated representations of the relative notion of reality. And we have gradually understood that the unconscious is not simply the opposite of the conscious but part of a continuum within the totality of human experience. The old and sage dichotomies between the real and the unreal, the conscious and the unconscious, simply no longer hold, and the dialectics involving them have been run into the ground. The famous phrase of the early decades of the century, "the juxtaposition of distant realities," so often cited as the basis of daring associations created in poetry and paintings by the still so-called moderns and a governing principle of so many works of art and poetry, has lost much of the meaning it had at its inception because we know now that distance exists only in the eye of the beholder, and that if the creative artist has brought two entities together, it is because on some level of sensorial lucidity a connection was made.

In the same way, disordinate perceptions—such as what Rimbaud called the reasoned disorder of the senses—and their representation reflect disorder only if the natural world is perceived as a network of determinable and tested physical laws producing predictable results. But we have discovered that every law of physics does not have a Newtonian regularity or if it does it is not yet within our capacity to grasp, and we have also learned that there are phenomena which cripple at least temporarily our perception of a logical, precise universe. And in accepting these facts we, as a society, have had to develop the ability to express with mathematical precision the indeterminacies of the material world. Because this ambiguity or presumed randomness is part of our reality, it can be said that the writers or painters who once were considered avant-garde because they performed in an unrealistic or irrational way are from a more educated view no longer avant-garde because they are still holding the mirror up to nature when they represent this indeterminacy: it is not that the mirror is distorted but that nature is discovered to have parameters beyond those previously known and areas of the unknown but not unknowable realities. In other words, the perceived disorder is part of the system of laws whose supposed randomness may be only an appearance manifested in our partial knowledge of the totality.

Early in the twentieth century, Guillaume Apollinaire, whose voice was more European than French, said in his essay *Les Peintres cubistes:* "Great poets and great artists have the social function to renew unceasingly the appearance that nature assumes in the eyes of humans." Obviously even then he did not consider nature a constant but an ever changeable factor.

From hard ground to soft terrain, the writer moves with the scientists, stunned by his own ignorance, which he characterizes as indeterminacy, replacing previous attitudes of positivism and determinism. In his isolation and sense of loss of control, he drifts into a nonanthropocentric universe. And whereas most observers of the strong element of alienation in the literature of our century may continue to attribute it to psychological disturbances and social maladjustments, the alienation may more correctly be explained by cosmic causes.

The sense of dispersion emphasized by neophilosophers such as Derrida and Foucault is not new to modernism. All self-named moderns have had it. An early avant-gardist, Hugo Ball, often too exclusively associated with Dada but closer in reality to Rimbaud, described the condition of the modern man of his time in an article on Kandinsky in 1917 during a devastating war. Curiously, his apocalyptic fresco is not politically inspired but reflects a metaphysical anxiety: "The world showed itself to be a blind juxtaposition and opposing of uncontrolled forces. Man lost his divine countenance, became matter, chance, an aggregate. He became a particle of nature . . . no more interesting than a stone: he vanished into nature . . . a world of abstract demons swallowed the individual . . . psychology became chatter."

If, in responding to the effect of this condition on the arts, Ortega y Gasset coined the phrase "dehumanization of the arts," "dehumanization" means something quite different today from what it meant in the early part of the century. We can each select a cast of characters to reflect this dehumanization from the annals of literary and art history of the seventy-five years since Hugo Ball's statement and Ortega y Gasset's definition: from Marcel Duchamp's mockery of art in his ready-mades to the latest involutions of abstract art, from the boldness of collage to the whimperings detected in the techniques of fragmentation in all the arts, from the suddenly meaning-stripped world of Sartre's then modern, now classic character Roquentin in *La Nausée* to the nameless soldier in Alain Robbe-Grillet's *In the Labyrinth,* from destruction of time-perspective in John Hawkes's novels to the randomness of images in William Burroughs's writings. All were "modern" in a moment in time, and all can be said to hold the mirror up to nature as nature was perceived at that moment in time. In that sense, in each case the classical dictum of a Boileau or a Pope was applicable to his aesthetics and in that sense his forms of representation are from our vantage point mimetic. If his expression of nature is being called antirealistic by some contemporary critics it is so only in terms of previous definitions of reality and nature. The minute one considers our changed perception of reality, such writings and art expressions fit the changed definitions of reality. The disparity between the perception of the critics and the artists is due to the fact that critics are clinging to the older notions of reality and nature, and they are not as agile in grasping the ontological changes. They are bridging the gap between their superannuated notion and the artist's more updated one with the convenient use of the label "modern."

One of the most important transitions—oh so gradual but so irreversible once it is made—in the changing characterization of "modern" is the manner in which the "modern" artists are reacting to the passing of a centrality of purpose and of a supernal presence. Instead of mourning they are accepting the plurality of the universe, of which their predecessors had been warned three centuries earlier but had not seriously implemented, that changes their perspective in their art forms. There was to be a giant difference between the Nietzschean proclamation that God was dead and the proposition that God never existed. As the poet-artist Jean (or Hans) Arp observed, "Dada was the revolt of the nonbelievers against the disbelievers." The concept was there, but not many practitioners in the arts were implementing that view. It had not yet been ingrained. The revolution in the arts that I would call a postapocalyptic posture is a more radical one than reactions to the kind of sociopolitical events that are generally attributed to avant-garde manifestations and their reflections on the arts. I would suggest that modernism today, responding primarily to passing political winds and ideologies, is modern only in terms of the first part of Baudelaire's definition, "transitory, fugitive, contingent," or in my own words I would call them contemporary works dependent on circumstantial events, reserving the label "modern" for those which anchor their vision on phenomena relating to decentralization and decontrol in what is perceived to be an indifferent universe.

Among those who share these deeper disquietudes there are some who reject the continuity more generally perceived between themselves and earlier moderns; instead they sense grave schisms separating them from their predecessors. Nathalie Sarraute has expressed this distance with some irony: "The works of Joyce and Proust already loom in the distance like witnesses of a closed era. It will not be long before we shall be taking guided tours of these historic monuments in the company of schoolchildren in silent respect and in somewhat mournful admiration." By habit and respect, Joyce, Yeats, Thomas Mann, Proust, and others of their generation may still be called modern, particularly from the Anglo-American perspective because neither England nor the United States had an early-century onslaught of "isms." But the fact is that in terms of their works, the signifier "modern," still applied to them, has subsequently acquired another set of signifieds. These great writers of the recent past are indeed part of what Mallarmé called an interregnum; they are waiting for literary historians to give them a more permanent classification than the temporary and provisional "modern" can sustain, and if such a designation does not come forth they will simply join the ranks of the classics without any special label of their own.

Even if we isolate the writers and artists who gave form as well as expression to their sense of the decentralization and instability of the dimensions of reality and apply to them the label of "modern" in our time, we will find great disparities in the ways they reject or represent their adjusted vision of human and physical nature according to Freud and according to Einstein (just to mention two of the many shakers of our reality).

From this angle it is now possible to view as premodern some of those who are still being called modern in literary history and in books on modernism. Such are the makers of Symbolism and Dada and other refugees into language. Of the Symbolists, an early twentieth-century critic, Raoul Hausman, denigrated their resistance to a drastically changing world; he called their act a "naive nostalgia to see the world through human will as if it was imagined by man." The symbolist nihilism, and in some countries it was called aestheticism, was quiet and introverted. In man's quicksand entrapment, the literary icon was able to create an artificial world to serve as the vitalizing power of the writer's slipping individuality. The second mode of the premodern was a direct attack on the growing notion of a nonanthropocentric world. It was a much more hostile and sometimes teasing reaction in verbal terms. It was flamboyantly represented as we know by Dada: "Dada wants nothing, it is a sure thing that they will achieve nothing, nothing, signed by Francis Picabia who knows nothing, nothing." This was a modernism of rupture, asserting that the assumption of a meaning-free cosmos reduces the perceiver to an equally meaning-free status. Simultaneous with a rejection of language expressed in such structures as phonetic poems was the development of a language of rejection. This rejection was paralleled in the plastic arts with a challenge of the objects to which aesthetic qualities had been attributed.

If the rejection of language developed a language of rejection, it is also true that in the reality of language others sought their sole comfort and strength, a replacement of the divine Logos by a new confidence in language which would equate naming with the act of creation. Stephen Hawking, an eminent popularizer of science, suggests in *A Brief History of Time* that neophytes viewing the changes catalyzed by recent scientific activities take the advice of the philosopher-mathematician Wittgenstein and in their perplexities seek refuge in language. Earlier poets had done that in a premodern era. Vicente Huidobro, Pierre Reverdy, James Joyce, the early surrealists had perceived language as an armor and a staff in the resistance to chaos. To quote Hugo Ball again, "You may laugh, language will one day reward us for our zeal, even if it does not achieve any directly visible results. We have loaded the word with strengths and energies that helped us to rediscover the evangelical concept of the word (logos) as a magical complex image" (see essay 15). And a number of years later, Octavio Paz: "Against silence and noise I invent the Word, freedom that invents itself and invents me every day." To this day language has had a main hold both on poets and in major areas of philosophy.

But I see three other modes directly confronting the decentralized universe, modes in which language is not an end in itself but a means of making responses to the cosmos. They are the modernisms dealing with identification, representation, and revision, all responding to the expanded definition of nature.

Identification (or imitation) with the decontrolled universe is expressed by simulation of it, signaling direct involvement with it. This form of mimesis is demonstrated in the random spirit of collage, in happenings theatrically staged, connective structures suggesting sequence replaced by gaps suggestive of dark holes in thought, action, or human perception of time, in the fragmentation of language or object in text or canvas or celluloid to suggest correspondences between the dislocated narrator and his incohesive surroundings, wherein anger and indifference are personalized not in pathos but through irony and complacency, as if the joke were not on man but on the universe. If life is a travesty, let art be a game! In adopting an amorphous structure and discarding even the elementary codes of art, it is as if the writer or artist were confirming that nothing short of the negation of art can be the symbol of a terminal era. It is this involvement of the perceiver with the perceived chaos, using irony as the only weapon against total dissolution and silence, that has become the literary fortune of Dada among those modernists of today, self-identified as postmodern.

If indeed there are many evidences of authors and painters who identify with flotsam and chaos through their subjective and lately minimalist response, there is also in evidence the *representation* of human dispersion in the form of personas who are *not identified* with the narrator but are his cast of characters in a dramatic narrative, creating a distance that protects the narrator from pathos and self-entrapment. I view as such the works of Samuel Beckett, Marguerite Duras, John Hawkes, Günter Grass, Alain Robbe-Grillet, and many so-called neorealists or antirealists in British, Italian, and South American literature. When Molloy, and not Beckett, says "I listen and the voice is of a world collapsing endlessly, a frozen world under a faint and untroubled sky," we, the readers, are joining the author in the act of observing his characters struggling with a redefined notion of reality, and in sharing the detachment of the author we are immune to the element of the tragic. (The voice is not necessarily that of the author; why do critics assume that every somber utterance must necessarily represent the author's attitude?)

It is significant that some of the most prominent writers who have taken the decontrolled, decentralized universe in their stride use the myth of the labyrinth.

Molloy searches for the lost center in the metaphor of the return to the Mother. Robbe-Grillet's nameless, faceless character searches out his memory-stripped consciousness in a void. In neither case is there an Ariadne in sight. These new Theseuses are engaged in what Robbe-Grillet calls "an interminable walk through the night," going nowhere, dying everywhere. A situation of impasse is very structurally staged, the decor is selected, landmarks on the journey are consciously chosen; the central character pirouetting has no recourse to human support, or reliance on a benevolent nature or outside force. There is no possibility of battle or an act of courage at the end; because no single danger can be identified, there is no opportunity for risk and no need to manifest resistance.

Robbe-Grillet's unidentified protagonist copes with the ambiguities not only of space but also of time. We have the excellent example here of architectonic form without a content of supplied meanings. There is the structure of allegory, explicit in the title and implemented in the geometric engineering of the composite events, but the author warns us that there is no allegory of values implied; if no interpretation is invited, then all meaning is exterior and polysemous. If human memory is emblematically present in a box that the protagonist carries around in an eternally present moment, there are no questions as to where or why. The loss of identity is spelled out in a series of maneuvers, compounding each other, and yet the character never says "I am lost." This is not an imitation of the randomness perceived in nature or a thrusting of the author into the whirlpool of nothingness but *a staging of it*.

Similarly, in Claude Simon's *The Grass* the author tackles the age-old theme of the devastations caused by the passage of time; the metaphor of the grass is used as the emblem for the imperceptibility of the passage of time, as a measure of growth whether on a physical or a psychological basis. To demonstrate the difference between Proust's handling of time and the newer manipulations of the time dimension, let us presume that Proust views the past as a contained package of memories that he can retrieve according to the power of the faculty of remembering: voluntary memory, involuntary flashback, association memory, etc. The newer novelists represent not so much hindsight as the degree of clarity of their troubled eyes, which are not at all sure that anything remains; they believe only in the centrality of the moment. In describing the precarious quality of the moment, man's meager and sole possession, Octavio Paz sees it as a form of instantaneous eternity in his meditative essay "The Dialectics of Solitude," included in *The Labyrinth of Solitude*.

Previous novelists, modern in their time, have presented alienated heroes. Famous among them are Kafka's protagonists, Dostoevsky's underground man, and Sartre's nauseated Roquentin. But it is important to note that in the case of Kafka and Dostoevsky the social rather than the ontological factor underlies the alienation; in the case of Sartre's hero, there is strong author identification rather than objective representation of character, and at the end there is a therapeutic solution to the malaise with autobiographical overtones.

Characters not judged, time deprived of continuity, space used circularly, objects distanced from their functional associations, characters unidentifiable with their creators, acceptance of inconsistencies in personality attributed to the normal interplay of degrees of consciousness, use of verbal and phenomenal chance as acceptable factors of life as of art: these features prevalent in recent modernist writings separate them from earlier concepts of the modern and necessitate newer classification for *past* moderns.

I have referred to identification and representation. The other mode, that of modernism, of revision, is the mode of those who, instead of representing a changed perception of the universe, take artistic control of it. André Breton's most important contribution of the groundwork of the literature of modernism as it is shaping up today was his earlier adjustment to the new factors in a way to make literature and art and their need for determined absolute values viable in a relativist world. He called upon a moral rather than an aesthetic motivation to free the various forms of art from engulfment in the unreliable. The so-called moral value of such willed revision would make both writer and painter, as well as reader and beholder, better able to cope with daily life, as he thought. Such an objective contains a philosophy directed to a concrete and pragmatic achievement rather than to abstract levels of dialogue.

Viewing surrealism in the context of realism—a correction Breton made in his definition as he proceeded from the First Manifesto to *Surrealism and Painting*—he explained that there can exist a process of transformation of the real into the artifact. The primary function he demanded of himself and of his fellow surrealists was to recuperate the random and the senseless, the automatic and the fortuitous, and to submit them to the control of the artist. The artistic universe need not be decontrolled to match a decontrolled universe. Beauty, for instance, can survive the demolished canon of an art representative of an orderly world only if it is made to correspond to an unpredictable universe: it has to be convulsive in order to suggest that convulsive nature the poet or artist accepts; but here we have a process neither of imitation nor of representation; instead the surrealists resort to subterfuges of controls to recreate the turbulence on their own terms: not through breaks in grammar or ruptures of syntax but through self-referential associations opening up limitless meanings and interpretations, not the destruction of familiar objects but their dislocation or recycling. It is not an attempt to represent the indeterminacy of nature but a creation of indeterminacies in those very aspects of nature that are presumed to have remained constants. But expecting neither sympathy nor meaning in nature, the poet or painter began to project his own countenance onto the world around him.

The poets and painters acted according to consorted theories that brought about great understanding of each other's work. But the painters' manifestations, as it turned out, can be more graphically perceived: the defiances of the laws of gravity painstakingly manifested in the paintings of René Magritte; the dislocations of familiar objects, their change of function in Dali and his imitators; the annihilation of the barriers between the kingdoms of the animal, vegetable, and mineral in the spectacular amalgams of Max Ernst; the efforts to create new objects and new horizons in the case of Yves Tanguy; the surrealist signets such as the Minotaur and the Mandragora that suggest a correction of nature's separation of man and animal. All these manifestations can be summarized as the poet-painter's effort to engender purpose where we can outwardly perceive none. The ultimate question proposed to modernisms of the future is whether human desire can give direction to objective chance. In their self-referential structures the best of surrealists appeared to think so.

The prophetic Apollinaire had foreseen two kinds of artists in modern time. One instinctively and intuitively lets the representation of modern humanity seep through him into the work of art; in that respect the postmoderns are justified in claiming that there is a touch of everyman in the so-called work of art and that it is therefore a collective possession. The other category, in which Apollinaire named Picasso as the original force, recreates a universal model, an aggregate of stylized projection to what might be called a cosmic scale of naturalism. Picasso has been much more recognized of course than his counterpart in literature, Breton. But even in Picasso's case, I wonder whether that admiration has been sufficiently focused on that moment of epiphany when he slipped out of his blue period into the stream of light coming from the depths and the edges of night.

A fundamental argument emerges among moderns concerning the destiny of the metaphor. Robbe-Grillet declared some twenty-five years ago that in view of the absence of human meaning in the universe, the practitioners of the arts should eliminate analogy in their works and thereby suppress the metaphor. But the neosurrealists, particularly the poets of Hispano-America, have increasingly sharpened the image as the sole device to guard what Breton had recognized as the creative spirit in its efforts to overcome what would otherwise be a solipsistic existence "when the primordial connections have been broken." The aim would then be to readjust and conciliate the apparatus of the poetic analogy to the new materialistic data. To quote Breton again: "For me the only *evidence* in the world is controlled by the spontaneous relationship, extra-lucid, and insolent, which becomes established under certain conditions, between such and such things which common sense would avoid confronting. . . . I am hopelessly in love with all that adventurously breaks the thread of discursive thought, takes off suddenly into a stream of light, illuminating a life of extremely fertile relationships." In fact Breton and those who have followed him into today's modernism are compelled to inquire into the nature of nature, which is the ultimate subject of modern inquiry.

As we know, the element of rebellion, which is an essential feature of any and all modernism, can be expressed—and indeed was spectacularly expressed early in this century—by deconstructions in perceptions of aesthetics and in sociopolitical activisms. But the rebellion involved in the moral concerns of any serious artist penetrates a deeper level of the art of expression.

Apollinaire described the evolution of Picasso as the calm after the frenzy; "calm" in that context means mastery of process as an answer to unilateral, belligerent attitudes toward the conditions of life in the twentieth century. What Apollinaire perceived in the development of the art of Picasso is the transformation of circumstantial rebellion into the multitiered image of subversion in painting, in poetry, in film, whereas frenzy is the overt exercise of uncontrolled, unsparing movement. One of the great changes in subsequent manifestations of modernism is the channeling of these energies of rebellion so that they are no longer the outer garment of the artist but assume through shocking analogies the double-edged meaning of reconstruction, constructing while deconstructing, espousing no single issue but catalytic of any issue.

It is too early to take inventory of all the avant-gardes that constitute the self-perpetuating modernism of the twentieth century. What matters for the moment is to proceed beyond the attempt to understand motivations, beyond tolerance of each and every one, because indeed to love the avant-garde has become as popular and trendy as it previously was to shun it. Instead it may well be time to go beyond tolerance to critical discrimination. The distinctions between modes should be helpful in discerning the degree of craftsmanship in any such modes. If there emerges what appears to be sloppy composition, is it because the artist wants to represent a sloppy state of existence or is it simply a sloppy state of composition for lack of technical and aesthetic expertise? If the plot dissolves, if character remains flat, is the structure an intentionally reductive form of art, an act of artistic minimalism, or is it due to a lack of imaginative resourcefulness or a unilateral desire to shock and nothing more? If there is no ending, is it because the author believes that the elimination of a sense of ending suggests the quagmire in which humanity is engulfed or does it betray on his part a lack of inventiveness or a weakness in the mastery of the particular art? When does the excremental image lose its power of analogy to return to its original signification of waste? When does erotic language and its objectification lose its luxurious quality to become standard pornography? Are awkwardly shaped figures on a canvas or tedious repetitions of geometric lines a statement about the destruction of human form or a sign of haphazard bluff? Is it time to ask at what point even the most flamboyant avant-garde artist gets repetitious, tired, boring? Or, on the other hand, when do minimal linguistic discourse and gaps of total silence, hailed as achievements of the most recent examples of modernism, become merely indicative of clinical aphasia or verbal deficiencies?

One of the greatest powers of the modernisms of the past has been the overtone of sincerity and commitment; how far can the ironic element of author distancing from reality be carried out without bringing about reader-spectator distancing as well from the work declared as art?

The time has come, I think, when answers to this type of questioning may have to replace the more current, simplistic responses to the avant-garde—which have consisted either of rejecting it totally and in principle or accepting it and embracing it totally and without reservation and without even recognizing that in a single writer or artist there are better and lesser degrees of achievement. I bought some time ago at a book fair the latest work of a very personable playwright whose fame as a "neo-avant-garde" is fast rising. The title was "Burn This," and after reading it I had the feeling that the title was very appropriate. But this piece of trash received acclaim and an award. Audiences used to be too resistant to the avant-garde; now either they have become pushovers if the work is overt or they run away if it is a bit subtle—and the artists are becoming too eager to please.

Renato Poggioli, whose *Theory of the Avant-Garde* has become a universal reference in any serious discussion of the question of modernism in spite of the availability of many books subsequently written on the subject, thought that it was too early to evaluate. He therefore made his classifications according to the sociological factors involved. But his book is of 1950 vintage. It is hard to believe that we are designating moderns in the same way more than forty years later. Political protest and social negativism are still being rated as the basic elements of modernism and it is no longer too early to begin evaluation. It is time to look empirically at achievements rather than intentions. There is good and bad avant-garde no matter what standards of evaluation we use. A torso on canvas hanging on the wall may shock the viewer. Maybe it is a protest against violence and as such it is perhaps a sociological document, but it has to fulfill certain other criteria to be classified as art, and to be judged as modern it has to have a quality that extracts out of the transient something of the eternal. I have suggested certain categories of the modern. My distinctions are arbitrary and have to do with my own reading lists and philosophy of art. My intention is not to impose them on anyone else but to indicate that it is time to establish values, or at least guidelines, whereby we can regroup the moderns of the past with a good triage in the bargain, and gauge what to expect in current and even future moderns as eventually viable classics. With the ever-changing political and social scene, it is time to minimize the element of protest as a signal of the modern and to ask, what else is there? It is time to scrutinize the various powers of construction rather than be overwhelmed by the destructive intensity of the work. It no longer matters who shouted loudest, who shocked most widely. The question now is who shaped a permanent ticker tape of pleasure behind the instant notoriety, who went beyond talk about the unconscious to really give verbal approximation of unconscious or dream discourse, who conveyed the power of reality in the midst of concurrent processes of awareness and unawareness, whose work nourished the works of others instead of cloning itself endlessly?

Underlying the great variety of forms and attitudes loosely grouped and retained under the provisional title of "modernism" there emerge new encodings in search of new classifications. Writers and artists have had to make choices between identifying with new challenges to new notions of time, space, chance, consciousness, and reality and distancing their art from these factors, revising the parameters of the arts accordingly. The transitory label of "modern" must be passed along to new editions of modernism while the great work of separating the chaff from the wheat is carried out as we weigh the viability and degree of meaning and change of meaning of previous modernisms.

I am concerned as I read from the pen of scholars with solid reputations such subservient remarks as "from Lacan we know," "from Foucault we learn," "Derrida tells us." Academic scholars acquiesce too much and thereby plant in their disciples dangerous seeds of docility. Has it occurred to some that Lacan, Foucault, and Derrida could learn a few things from those of us who have been reading literature rather than psychology, archaeology, and philosophy?

As the post, post, post accumulate they seem to announce the ultimate end. Whereas some commentators on our era are eager to proclaim the death of literature, others obsessed with the prefix "post" are laboring under the assumption that we are witnessing the inevitable afterglow of a setting sun. How discouraging this attitude must be both to young writers and to their prospective critics! The paradox is that with the radical changes in the meaning of meaning, the broadening of the channels of communication, and the multiplication of the inner and outer aspects of nature, there has never been such an auspicious moment for the creator as well as the receiver to discover the imminent modern.

IV

INTERARTIFACTUALITY

The field encompassing the relationship of literature and art has become very fertile in the past three decades. As poets and painters have gravitated more and more toward each other, critics have been drawn out of curiosity and fascination toward this phenomenon, and critical observation of the interaction has turned out to be a steady sustenance, particularly for comparatists. Yet those who practice this interdisciplinary research and writing do not agree on its meanings and goals.

In studying surrealism at the dawn of my career as a scholar, I was not aware that I was engaged in an interdisciplinary pursuit, nor that I had thereby become a comparatist. All I knew was that I had touched an aspect of contemporary aesthetics that made a strong case for the holistic nature of human expression, extended the parameters of poetry to the practice of all the arts, and overflowed into daily living—all subject to the powers of the imagination.

The various relationships of image and object have prevailed in several of my books and essays, but I have ventured on the road from praxis to theory only in the past decade. Professor Ulrich Weisstein, for many years a member of the Indiana University faculty, has a comprehensive article, "Literature and the Visual Arts," in the Modern Language Association publication *Interrelations of Literature* that should serve as background for anyone venturing into the field. If Wallace Stevens found thirteen ways of looking at a blackbird, Weisstein found at least sixteen channels through

Interartifactuality

which one can move in the study of the relationship of literature and the visual arts.

I am not about to add a seventeenth category but to highlight six that I have been proposing in a series of lectures and have gathered into a text entitled "Theoretical Assumptions of Interartifactuality" for a Festschrift in honor of Professor Owen Aldridge of the University of Illinois under the general title *Aesthetics and the Literature of Ideas*. My work in progress took me from ideas to agents, particularly to philosophical writers who were attempting to analyze paintings in terms of verbal communication, and I ventured to *read* art before several audiences more interested in art than in literature, audiences accustomed to hearing or reading descriptive art criticism. The reaction has been a pleasant surprise. Finally, remembering Guillaume Apollinaire's early avant-garde contention that one can be a poet in any domain, I speculated on what it would take for critics to become poets in this extended meaning of the word, a link between poetry and painting.

My current reflections on this problematic subject, whose boundaries are as undefined as free-form art, are not to be construed as definitive. I am musing like a latter-day Balboa (in stance, not in conquest) gazing upon the expanse of the Pacific Ocean.

If intertextuality has become a current practice in critical theory related to literatures of different eras or areas, I propose that we use the term "interartifactuality" in establishing relationships between literature and the visual arts.* The critical process involved becomes the positioning of any art object (painting, sculpture, ready-mades, poem-objects, and creations on celluloid) with the literary work that is dominated by verbal images in all forms of writing except expository prose. Also in this context should be examined the unhyphenated work of ambidextrous creators in the

---

*Music videos on MTV are a manifestation of interartifactuality in the popular culture and should be a subtext of inquiry.

verbal and visual field, who are also painters–art critics or poets–art critics, and poet-painter theoreticians. Finally to be included are works in which the juxtaposition has been done for us, the two media having been integrated as the canvas houses writing and the writing contains drawings and paintings.

Although there are six categories that I deem to be most prevalent in the field of interartifactuality, the sixth interests me most and seems the most pertinent to creative criticism.

The most common category, the darling of literary historians, consists in situating a literary work in terms of the inspirations it enjoyed, among them the viewing of a painting. There are an infinite number of examples of such studies. But the process becomes critically more interesting when the reader/viewer makes an arbitrary choice of such confluences to study the effect of the inspirer on the inspired. Two media (or more), the literary and the visual, can turn the establishment of a simple literary fact into an opportunity for critical mediation between the two forms of expression.

A three-tiered example is widely known: Mallarmé, not yet a declared symbolist, sees a painting by Boucher, by pure chance, that represents a faun and some nymphs after whom the faun is lusting. Mallarmé is inspired to write a poem, and sometime later his friend the painter Manet illustrates the poem. I would venture to say that the first scholar who established this connection and had nothing more to say about it was not engaging in interartifactual activity, unless of course the study pointed out how the contiguity functioned in aesthetic terms. One would have to follow the communication from the pictorial to the verbal and then from the verbal back to the pictorial and then juxtapose the first and second visual expressions to see what if anything had happened because of the intervention of the poem. One also could follow the path of subsequent illustrations and transformations of the visual techniques implying changing perceptions of the verbal. And one could gauge the distance Mallarmé had traveled in the art of representation, then see if his symbolist techniques had any effect on Manet and others inspired by his poem, and finally how much distance there was between Boucher and the later painters because of Mallarmé. Aesthetic rather than historical considerations would be the basis of the exercise of interartifactuality.

A second category can be made of willed relationships, when the canvas becomes the source and the catalyst of a poem and not a random or fortuitous occurrence. The poem then becomes the representation not of a natural object, figure, or landscape but of an artifact. Leonardo da Vinci observed that the affinity of painting and poetry lay in the function of mimesis which both arts exercised, as Weisstein reports in the aforementioned reference. But in many cases the poem becomes in fact a re-presentation of nature by first being distanced through the grill of another artifact that deprives it of its organic mobility, releasing it to imaginative artificiality. Thus the poet is reinforcing the notion that a poem need not be bound to an imitation of nature but can be the result of a second-degree mimesis producing a new artifact that rises out of the original one.

In this respect the practice of interartifactuality can have a field day with Baudelaire, so many of whose poems are born of his viewing of a painting or statue. In many cases the poem becomes a perverted representation of the visual as it moves into the verbal. In "A une madone" he responds to a Spanish-style statue of the Virgin Mary with the verbal portrait of a woman on whom he commits linguistic sadism. Elsewhere he turns the penitent Don Juan of a Delacroix painting— Don Juan on his way to Hell—into an audacious portrait of an undaunted rebel.

Other examples can be gleaned from the poetry of Rilke, who had close connections with painters. I know of no commentary on his fifth elegy that does not mention that the representation of the saltimbanques had a connection with Picasso's painting of that name. What that reference did for us, the readers of the poem, or initially what the exposure did to Rilke has not to my knowledge been shown. An exercise in interartifactuality would consist of an interpretation of the poem without knowledge of a connection with Picasso and, in contrast, a study of the succinct Picasso referentiality that becomes a factor in the vision or expression of the poem.

The third classification is the one Helmet Hatzfelt identified a long time ago which involves primarily the illustrators of the literary texts of their contemporaries. To recall his famous quotation: "Each epoch has its zeitgeist that if understood can be brought to bear upon the problems of form in any of the arts." Such illustrations or simultaneous representations can illuminate styles and archetypes identifiable with certain periods or literary movements. They can reinforce or highlight characteristic traits, verbal and pictorial signets and *écritures*. Professor Frederick Garber of the State University of New York at Binghamton has had much success in this area, particularly in crystallizing Romanticism. Subjects like the treatment of the Napoleonic Wars and representations of the Salome figure are still open for subtle analysis of interartifactual reflections dealing with a particular climate or milieu.

The fourth category consists also of coexistences but with the contention that more than one zeitgeist can exist in the same place at the same time and reflect more than one mode. And even works collectively grouped under the same label in the separate arts may not be representative of the same climate or the same mode of expression. Though dealing with the same subjects and themes, they may demonstrate big gaps in aesthetic performance and philosophical overtones.

These coexistences of zeitgeist create grave pitfalls for interpretations and invite future studies of interartifactuality. For instance, the Belgian dramatist Maurice Maeterlinck, who was widely identified as a symbolist, made his heroine Mélisande muse: "I don't know where I come from or where I am going." And the painter Gauguin, an artist of the same era, reiterates virtually the same utterance as a title of a fresco: "Where do we come from, what are we, where are we going?" Is Gauguin a symbolist because he uses the same expression and uncertainty about existence as Maeterlinck? Gauguin's graphic characters are far removed from the symbolist style of representation: one shadowy, the other bright and colorful; one decadent, the other almost primitive. And the figure of Orpheus as perceived by Gustave Moreau in contrast with the Orpheus that is intrinsic in the series of Rilke's poems entitled *Sonnets to Orpheus* do in no way echo each other although both the artist and the poet are often characterized as symbolist.

The whole relationship between symbolist poetry and so-called symbolist painting is moot and invites studies in interartifactuality. The label "symbolist" was not a self-identification for the painters as it was for the writer. The label "symbolist painting" was attributed a posteriori to works of the late nineteenth century based on similarities of subject matter and not of form, or of a collaborative poetics. In a later period, Apollinaire associated the cubist painters with the avant-garde poets of the time without revealing a common aesthetics. In *Les Peintres cubistes* he poeticized the artists in regard to what he called their "metaphysical paintings." His commentary could better be characterized as *his* metaphysical approach to cubist painting.

I like to call my fifth category the co-naissance, or born together, of those nurtured consciously in the same theories of poetics, with mutual agreement in philosophy and goals and desirous of mutual transfers. These do not *reflect* a zeitgeist but create one of their own, often in common resistance to the general climate of their time. They cross barriers with audacity; on the part of those using verbal expression there is revealed an attempt to substitute images for each other to convey simultaneous reception of sensations, to avoid linear reception of meaning. On the part of visuals, there was an effort to set in concrete form theoretical abstractions held in common.

It is mostly in the twentieth century that one finds this kind of interrelations, between Hugo Ball and Kandinsky early in the century and in spectacular ways in the parallel development of surrealist painters and poets. In many cases the artists became critics as well; Dali was an art critic as well as a poet; Marcel Jean, unmatched as an artist, is also an extraordinary historian and critic who, because he has lived a normal life, has not been sufficiently noticed by those who expect and look for a spectacular lifestyle. It would be hard to choose between the artist and the poet in Jean Arp and Henri Michaux, and the list is long of interartifactual artist-poets and their need for interartifactual criticism.

My sixth category encompasses conscious collaborations, works emerging not simply from a common aesthetics but from situations in which poet and artist agree to work together and a work in one medium catalyzes a response in another. The distinction between illustration and collaboration lies in the very roots of these two words. In illustrating, one brings "light" to the work, whereas in a collaboration the work uniting the verbal and visual creations is a double creative labor in which identification and responsibility are shared. In such a collaboration as *Les Chants de Maldoror* by Lautréamont and Dali, the poet, dead for many years, was of course not aware of Dali's intentions, but when Dali was catalyzed to add his work to the poet's it became a new work, the old transformed by the new. More often, as in the case of the surrealists, the interspecies communication occurs with the full awareness and consent of the collaborators involved. There were such understandings between Breton and Max Ernst, between Breton and Miró, between Eluard and Miró, between Picasso and Eluard, to name but a few.

In viewing these collaborations interartifactually, one realizes that understanding is a relative concept. The nonrational comprehension of coexisting art forms can replenish linear communication without restricting us to it. This group of correspondences between the verbal and the visual arts is to me the most intriguing. It puts the critic on the spot, challenging him to find a new meaning for what we call interpretation and in a sense to become obliged to participate in the creative act.

The essential agreement on the part of poets and painters in this category is that the image-generating voltage of objects or words is to be measured according to the degree to which they can endow the readers or viewers with the power to envision in their turn without being bound to the visions of the artists/poets. The communication is indirect, and the reception is evidenced in the receiver's own medium. It is as if one asked a question in English and received the answer in French. In their apperception of each other's works the poet and the painter shall not try to identify the meanings that they may be able to share with each other but have as their target the range of possibilities for figurations that are representationally unrelated. This attitude is a recognition that the dimensions of poetry are extended into the domain of the arts in all their ramifications and that the artist in the twentieth century is acting or has to act as a poet to become something more than a mere technician in the skills of representation. Moreover, the critic becomes himself a poet when he intrudes into this complicity between the poet and the painter.

This poetic perspective that brings together the creators in this particular category of artistic works and those who aspire to respond to them creatively was widely espoused not only by the *cénacle* of the surrealists but by those who passed out of surrealist ranks for political or personal reasons, for the mark remained on them even when they disavowed allegiance. And a second and third generation assumed this kind of collaborative art internationally.

Here is one striking example of the critico-poetic repertory of Paul Eluard from his collaboration with Picasso in a work called *Donner à voir,* i.e., to give not sight but the power to see (Eluard, *Pléiade,* I, 945).

> All men communicate through their vision of things and this vision of things will serve to express the point they have in common, they, things, they as things, things in relation to them. That day a truly visionary quality will have integrated the universe with man, i.e., man with the universe.

Among the more spectacular ambidextrous artists, Ludwig Zeller, the Chilean poet-artist now settled in Canada, is currently very productive. The erotic and the dream are the double focus of his attention, particularly as they interrelate. The dream remains one of the human states constantly discussed in modern literature and psychology, simulated in painting and film, stated rather than conveyed in literature. But the consistency and the sustained character demanded in conscious representation of it have been faulted for several generations. Because Zeller practices very skillful interartifactuality, he complements the script with the visual images, reinforcing the vision from one form as it begins to wane with the other, lending through the combination an added depth he could not otherwise command. And if he has two hands working for him in his own person, there are two more right behind him in the person of Susana Wald, his wife and collaborator. A complex work such as *Woman in Dream* would give much challenge and intellectual nourishment to an interartifactual critic. Unfortunately Zeller and his equally talented wife do not command in the Anglo-American world the kind of public they deserve.

In the joining of the arts in our time we are really witnessing a manifestation not of metaphysics but of the enlargement of the vistas of the physical world, an activity parallel to that of the physical scientists. This hypothesis raises intricate questions about mimesis, referentiality, the nature of meaning, and ultimately the nature of what we call physical nature. If the most serious poets and artists are disturbing the frontiers of time and space, can we continue to analyze their correlated works in terms of concepts more appropriate to the comprehension of narrative prose texts?

Some of the questions raised by the artists (in the wide connotation of the word) have been pondered much more widely by recent philosopher-critics than by the conventional critics of art and literature. But unfortunately when such philosophic critics as Michel Foucault, Jacques Derrida, Yuri Lotman, Robert Weimann, and others approach these questions, they draw their supportive illustrations from the novel form of the past rather than from art and poetry of twentieth-century vintage, or if they refer to poets it is to rear-garde ones such as Ezra Pound and T. S. Eliot. And, ironically, when Foucault takes on an art work of a contemporary of his, he shoots himself in the foot. His essay on René Magritte, *Ceci n'est pas une pipe*, is indeed an exception in the philosophical medley of references to poetry and art, but it misses its mark because of the attitudes and positions he and his confrères have taken.

Theoretical critics have been clinging to words as vehicles to convey their thoughts. The idea is there first; the search is for convenient examples to support it. Their philosophy, their zeitgeist, shines through the artifact used as corroborative testimony. The ideas themselves, after the reading of a few of their texts, are transparent and predictable. But contemporary poets and artists demand responses lying outside the hierarchies of the referentially acceptable world of codes and conventions. References to older works and practices in the interartifactuality of the past are so much more comfortable. In tackling the recent products, the critics would have to create encounters between the art work and the verbal image that is evoked in them, thereby relating them to a nonrestrictive universe and an interiority they cannot fathom. They would have to avoid duplicating verbally the artifact, just as the painter has abstained from representing the outer or even the inner object that may have catalyzed his work of art. In both cases the works that have established a contact between the verbal image and the visual one are representative neither of a common reality nor of each other's dislocation of it.

Representation is what has primarily disappeared from current art, giving way to presentation, or staging. And in the realm of poetry that was precisely what distinguished surrealism from other writing. When in critical response the commentator presumes to suggest this or that explanation, he is hanging on to that ultimate vestige of recognition the artist or poet has left in his work as he has passed on to a semantic or plastic transcendence.

When Baudelaire observed that poets could become critics but that critics were not likely to become poets, he was making a strict separation between the mind that routinely deals in abstractions and even reduces the concrete to abstraction and the poetically inclined person who can convey even abstractions in concrete expression. Baudelaire did not foresee the long education that was to take place whereby even the critic would learn—through immense exposure—to experience a new way of perceiving existence and thence works of art. The conventional critic, who does not pretend to be a poet while practicing art criticism, finds abstractions all around him, and when he is at a loss to identify the subject as we generally understand the word, he assumes that the artifact he views or verbally imagines is bereft of subject matter. When on the contrary he admits that there is no such thing as abstract art or poetry, he has indeed caught up with the orientation of the poet and the painter without having to practice the writing of verse or undertaking his own configurations on canvas.

The fact is that when the poet and the painter have effected a joint input, their collaboration has affected their response to the outside world. This conspirational change of perspective might have been expected to have made a greater impact on popular criticism and general readership since World War II than it has actually made. But surrealism and its succession as a theory of aesthetics has had a bad press, although surrealist art has become a highly valued commodity.

Traditionally the poet's and artist's work consisted in representing the universe and its perceived order from which their work was removed only by a light barrier. It is hard to break such a habit, harder for the critic than for the artist. The opposite of reality was irreality or fiction, and it was expressed by reference to either a supernal world or a fantastic one; or else it was said to reflect the inner world considered as disorderly rather than incoherent. Critical writing responding to works based on either the reality or antirealist assumption could not qualify as being in itself a poetic act. The critic explained, described, classified, interpreted, and even simulated the particular mood, all age-old critical functions.

The critic was satisfied to share the referential system of the writer or artist whether in the presence of a commonly acceptable reality or an equally accepted negation or absence of such reality. Even myths are based on recognized realities, as anthropologists have in recent times demonstrated. No matter how broad the base, there are in legendary figurations references which provide common recognition on the part of the reader or viewer, and which the critic, with his broader knowledge of sources, can confirm and in so doing exercise an authority that favors acceptance of his judgment. Referentiality raises questions of source, of levels of originality, of the techniques of resemblance, substitution, connivance, perspective, etc. These are all serious intellectual maneuvers worthy of the practice of criticism whether of literature or art.

The critic is well aware, however, of the ontological changes in perception in the world of the arts. He has also realized that the position of "critic" has become perilous since the middle of the twentieth century. Philosophers, linguists, and anthropologists have developed a new language that critics of literature and the visual arts find protective and convenient to adopt as their own. And in becoming overimpressed (the French word *épater* is more expressive of the state) by the direction the human sciences have taken, critics have tried to join these other disciplines. It is a marriage of convenience. These critics-philosophers have method but not too many subjects of critical discourse applicable to the field of literature, whereas the critics who aspire to interartifactual goals have substantive targets but lack method or a language of their own. They can never again assume that they are practicing interartifactual criticism by making vague statements such as this one to prove a relationship between a piece of writing and a painting: "In both these prints *we sense the atmosphere* of Honoré de Balzac's *Chef-d'oeuvre inconnu*, the novella Picasso illustrated in 1927."

So in a time that is being hailed as the age of criticism, we find a big gap. On one side, the literary critics have separated themselves more and more from aesthetic texts as they are drawn to philosophy, which reduces the text to the role of illustrative material serving an idea, while the art critics lose sight of the aesthetic issues and retreat into historical description. On the other side of the gap, the artist and the creative writer have been closing their ranks so that they in parallel fashion separate themselves from expository and narrative prose.

To close the gap there has to occur a transfer of language to characterize a change in perception. Whereas for a long time now we have become accustomed to the use of the word "paint" in discussing verbal images in poetry and even in some types of prose, now we have been put in a position to learn to use the word "read" in viewing the visual arts and writing about them. It takes a certain turn of mind to read a text as if we were looking at a painting; now we may have to put ourselves in a position to read a canvas.

When Magritte wrote under the image of a pipe, "Ceci n'est pas une pipe," he was not being facetious; he was daring to demolish the concept of referentiality and to challenge the viewer or critic to respond through a poetic act by redirecting his vision. Exposure to the work of Magritte gave the non-poet Foucault a rare opportunity to respond as a poet, as mentioned earlier. But the critical response got derouted, although Magritte and Foucault were no strangers to each other's work. Foucault recognized the shocking withdrawal of referentiality in Magritte's work, and he tried to explain it as a theoretician, making distinctions between resemblance and similitude, similitude being, to quote him, "freed from its old complicity with representation." So far the statement remains serenely theoretical. But then Foucault observes the tantalizing effect of concrete but frightfully dislocated precisions on Magritte's canvases in general and, falling back on his more usual references to the human sciences, he attributes Magritte's unusual art expression to manifestations of "heterotopia," a disorder deemed by psychiatrists to cause the inappropriate linking together of things. Thereby he completely missed the point. He betrayed his incompatibility with what in surrealist terms is a creative encounter of distant realities. The nihilistically oriented philosopher could not conceive of the leaps of imagination that determine for the artist the distance between words and objects on a canvas, whereby the standard is lost in the proximity that the poet or artist can create between them. This act of communication is symptomatic not of heterotopia but of euphoria on the part of those who have succeeded in rearranging the material entities to suit their needs and create their own settings and landscapes.

As existentially conditioned modern inhabitants of planet Earth, we accept the fact that ambiguity and indeterminacy have become legitimate subjects of scientific and philosophical speculation, but we seem less inclined to link them with art except as indicative of mental derangement in the clinical sense of the word. In responding to the interartifactuality factor, the critic has to accept this parallel as a positive and binding factor among writers and artists who can induce juxtapositions that demolish the conventional associations. With multiple referentiality these combinations are grounded in concrete physical properties but evade interpretation on conceptual terms. The human experience caught in that ambiguity is presumed to be enriched and therefore utopian rather than heterotopic. In Eluard's words, art would promote "confidence in that existence." The intellect that is not open to such presentations and cannot overcome the habit of relying on a single reference system will qualify this unrelatedness as "abstract" or even go so far as to call it absurd. Such a mentality is bound by what separates the arts and what governs the differences rather than searching for the goals they may share. But repetitive exposures to such presentations create an interreferentiality, from one canvas to another or from one series of verbal images to the next. This process makes them tolerable to the general public and thence to the critic, whose function is presumed to be a descriptive reportage rather than an analytical exercise. In Foucault's case it is precisely an intricate analytic procedure but still not a responsive act of the imagination. With works such as Dali's, Tanguy's, Miró's, Magritte's, and a host of others', criticism can enter the register of creative writing only when the critic discusses neither referentiality nor nonreferentiality as a device to promote discussion but appropriates the power of analogy that makes images gravitate toward each other or dwell in each other, the two dominant methods whereby surrealists and those derivative of their style have replaced both the mimetic and the antimimetic and have rejected the very notion of any but self-generating references. The critic who recognizes this intention dismisses any connection of the title with the independent reality of the artifact.

This brings us to the factor of meaning. What is meaning in the art forms of the twentieth-century innovations? Modern theoretical writings have labored long over signifiers and displaced signifieds, over differences in meaning that arise out of the passage of time and the emergence of new connotations representing new ideologies and perceptions. But no matter what fluctuations there have been in such interpretations of meaning, what all these analyses agree to accept is the notion that there is an original constant factor in meaning in terms of which they negotiate their variations or even their negations.

In poetry, the first in modern times to probe the meaning of meaning beyond anagrammatic, calligrammatic, or phonemic word play was Mallarmé. Scrutinizing the work of linguists of his day, he learned to put to poetic use several revelations about language. He went beyond the original arbitrariness of the sign in the realization that the signifiers do not simply change meaning, that words do not simply pick up multiple connotations as they move along in time in the use and disuse we make of them, but that the poetic project can capitalize on the fact that words have many meanings to begin with. If then the artist even as the poet proceeds from no predetermined meaning or function in the object named and then moves to several tiers of meaning, he blocks any possibility of unilateral deciphering of his own meaning by another and thereby shakes off the analytical critic. Instead he provokes what Dali has called "a delirium of interpretations" or better still reveals to the critic who would turn his criticism into a subgenre of poetry that the powerful artifact does not carry meaning at all in the accepted sense of the word but creates a *climate* saturated with accrued meanings. (Using banking terminology, we might say "compounded daily.") The liberation of the signifier from the signified was part of a fundamental revolution against conventions and the artistic canon. In the application of this concept to art and literary criticism we could say that the critic is exercising a function similar to that of the poet when he refuses to confine his role to intermediary between the creative work and the general viewer in the mere transmission of the former's meaning. Eluard expressed this attitude when, in pursuing the trajectory of his friend Max Ernst, he observed that the artist made us enter full force into a world where "we consent to everything" and "nothing is incomprehensible." He perceived that when Miró responded to his set of poems *A toute épreuve,* on the eternal theme of love and death, he made "everything transmutable into everything."

The common meaning that demands consensus on the part of the critic is that art is a response to existence, to its web, to its dilemmas, not explicitly but implicitly presented with varying degrees of graphic ambiguity made effective through nonrepresentative channels such as the simulation of the vision of the child, of the first man, of the insane, of the dreamer when he can snatch the dream at its source. In pursuing this course the critic is substituting not a subtext but a subartifact as a juncture between the original artist's provocative object arrangement and the viewer's attempts to invent or envision in his own right and in his own way. Any other activity in response to a work of art turns the critic into a historian or philosopher.

In all fairness, let be it said that the semioticians and the philosophers have been sensitive and curious about the new dimensions needed in art/poetry criticism. Foucault in *Les Mots et les choses* and the Estonian Yuri Lotman in his book on the structure of the artistic text show themselves fully aware of the ongoing struggle between the artist and his critics. In both cases the apposition is perceived in terms of codes and perspectives. Both tackle the problem of differentiation and the need to change gears in the process of critical reception, but neither comes to any positive conclusion as to how the change can be effected. Foucault discerns a break in codes around the end of the eighteenth century, when analogy based on historical memory was, in his opinion, no longer sufficient to produce a smooth continuity of referentiality in explaining the artistic text. There resulted, he claims, the end of representative discourse. There ensued, according to him, disorder, fragmentation, and dispersion. Identity of elements has been replaced, he says, by identity of relationships, and what the critic has to note is the succession rather than the resemblance of processes to get insight into the functioning of the arts compared. He seems to be going in the right direction but offers little beyond the theoretical that might be applicable and testable for interartifactual research.

Yuri Lotman admits the need for what he calls transcodage. He observes that when the language of the text is familiar, the critic may be able to get by in treating the work as if it were a nonartistic discourse; but he recognizes that when the critic is dealing with works that have been created under the aegis of a different code, the critic must also fashion a new code for its reception, otherwise he will virtually distort the intentions of the work of art in his struggle to subject it to his inappropriate existing code. But he compares the process of finding a new code to a form of "cross-breeding" instead of requiring a drastic change of direction. There is awareness here but not originality.

To listen to an American voice now, the philosophy scholar Arthur C. Danto declared in a symposium that "only in relation to an interpretation is a material object an art work." If it be so, it does not follow that the mere fact of its having been interpreted guarantees that it is an artifact. Interpretation in its standard definition and limited to philosophical speculation does not necessarily mean that it can determine what is an art work. A tool perfected will not in itself make a machine function if it is not the right tool for the particular structure or for its operation. The key may fit into the keyhole but will not turn. The components of the comparison or relationship between a verbal and a painterly work have to be inherently compatible in terms of the theoretical principle that proposes to demonstrate through the chosen relationship a new form of co-perception. It will not succeed otherwise to do anything but graft on each two separate interpretations. In other words, the critic may be able to observe and report interdisciplinary collaboration of two artists working in separate media on the basis of their understanding of what the two arts have in common, but the mere use of a common language in dealing with them will not disclose an interdisciplinary factor in the arts themselves.

In my judgment the hypothetic art and literature critic who tries to understand the new bonds developed by the verbal and plastic forms of creativity needs a nonlinear level of comprehension, which is quite beyond anything that can be accommodated by a mongrel form of criticism resulting from *métissage*. The current critical languages, almost mathematically rational and resistant to affective communication, make them unreliable as a factor in the presentation of interrelations in the arts. In their collaboration, the poet and the artist have experienced more daringly than any philosopher the changing perception about the material world in the concrete structure of its widening and deepening process. The critic-philosophers have not demonstrated in these past decades the imaginative capacities essential for the development of a critical response to the interartifactuality that has developed. Their admission that the arts have learned to step outside of the process of representation is a step in the right direction, but the critical need to define what has taken the place of representation has to go further than makeshift adaptations of philosophic-semiotic language. The interartistic studies that are on the increase need to develop their own language of criticism as a radical transformation in the expression of multifaceted aesthetic receptions. Such critical activities should be developing not a language of deconstruction but one that becomes a factor and an assertion of integration.

A lot of elements need to be sorted out to appraise interartifactuality on the part of the artist and understanding of it on the part of the critic. Maybe a new set of answers will emerge to challenge the notion that the "literary" and the "artistic" have been absorbed into the functional and the documentary. The undeniable fact is that they have changed course, and in so doing they are learning to live together in a more intimate way than ever before. Their increasingly parallel techniques pit human creativity against the elusive meaning of the universe.

February 12, 1992

V

HERMENEUTICAL CRITICISM AND THE SURREALISTS

At a time when the theory of literature was not of predominant interest in literary circles as it is today, the surrealist group was unique in perceiving the duality of the function of the creative artist: his concern with the process of creating as well as with the resulting product. The surrealists were in fact not merely *curious* about their various ways of achieving a state of creativity but, more clearly, they made *process* a more important motivation than the quality of the work that was fashioned through it. Although the general impression they have left about surrealism relates to their cult of spontaneity and automatism, the surrealists demonstrated an acute theoretical sense that can certainly be compared to the epistemological efforts of today's critics.

The self-consciousness the surrealists displayed in the choice and development of their creative activity is a marked departure from the way other literary movements had behaved, even flamboyant ones such as the battle of Hernani, which launched Romanticism in France, and the multiple variations of the Symbolist theories that marked that movement's progress. Poetry was for the surrealists an activity of the mind rather than a form of expression, and their theory involved a philosophy of life just as it does with today's phenomenological and poststructuralist critics. The parallel is striking, and an intertextual reading could shed light on the intellectual history of the twentieth century. The irony lies in the fact that the surrealists are virtually excluded from the frame of reference of the hermeneutic critics, the deconstructionists, and other recent theoretical writers.

The orientations in modern criticism are similar to those of the surrealists. Both are grounded in German philosophy, linguistics, and psychiatry. In both cases there was a general reaction against vague, generalized commentary on literary texts. In the *Traité du style,* Louis Aragon launched a diatribe against the critics, telling them that instead of flaunting their Légion d'honneur ribbons they should go back to individual texts, read them carefully, and comment on them with precision—an admonition that was to be heeded by the practitioners of stylistic and structural analysis thirty to fifty years later. Yet the targets and illustrations of such methodology have barely touched the field of modern poetry. One looks in vain for such references, and if once in a while there is a mention of Baudelaire such as the highlighting of "Les Chats," an article of Todorov on Rimbaud, an essay of Derrida on Mallarmé, or a political reading of him by Kristeva, such poetry is used in a peripheral context as illustrative of linguistic structures, rhetorical devices, or social behavior, and not in its primary function as meditation, mediation, and forewarning of surrealism. The occasional focus on Bataille, Artaud, and Leiris is also remote from connections with the theories of surrealism. Most often the current critical references are to traditional English, French, and American authors, or German Romantic poets who have been part of the critic's university background: surrealism, as well as most avant-garde poetry, came late into the French university curriculum, only with the student revolution of 1968, and it is still largely absent elsewhere.

The deplorable gap in intertextuality between surrealism and modern criticism should not, however, obscure the fact that both their closeness to each other in some respects and their distance from each other in more serious ways are of general significance to current intellectual and literary concerns; and they imply a crisis of direction in twentieth-century literature.

André Breton and his collaborators regularly cited their readings of Hegel, von Kleist, Feuerbach, Achim von Arnim, and Novalis, just as recent theoretical critics have done. If Breton's first manifesto was written under the aegis of Freud, the second was written under the guiding light of Hegel, with the declaration that all of surrealism proceeded from the Hegelian system. Breton specifically refers to the *Phenomenology of Mind* and relates to Hegelian dialectics the surrealists' intent to conciliate contraries in their basic method of perception of existence and of image-making in the arts. In summing up his intellectual directions in *Entretiens,* Breton concluded that "Où la dialectique hégélienne ne fonctionne pas, il n'y a pour moi pas de pensée, pas d'espoir de vérité."[1] (Let us hasten to add that professional philosophers may have misgivings about the interpretation of dialectics by the surrealists; but then, they also have raised eyebrows about modern critics who appropriate Hegelian texts and whom literary readers view as philosophers. The comparison of concepts here must be taken in the context of literary criticism in either case and considered—and excused if necessary—on a nonprofessional level where philosophy is concerned.)

The interest of the surrealists in German philosophy and literature was so inappropriate in an era charged with political hostility toward Germany in the wake of World War I that Breton identified such works as "written in the German language." Of particular seminal interest for the surrealists were the *Notes* that Lenin had taken of his reading of Hegel's *Logic.* These comments had their first printing in the fifth volume of the surrealist magazine *Le Surréalisme au service de la révolution* (1933) as the lead piece, with an introductory commentary by André Thirion. What Lenin had underlined were the very concepts that the surrealists were to appropriate for their theory of the surrealist image and, beyond that, for their perception of freedom of thought; the dialectics of interrelationships in objective, exterior reality, and the mind's search for unity among perceived contradictions. If it is supposed that all events, objects, and words are linked with all others, then a connection can be established between any of them at the will of the perceiver, thereby unleashing and compounding interpretations.

Like Lenin, the surrealists discovered through their primary and secondary readings of Hegel the universal elasticity that in its dialectic scope creates a manifest identity in apparent contradictions. Now this elasticity can be a source of both exhilaration and devastation. It can, on the one hand, turn into a total distrust of any system, and it can lead to a disrespect for all institutions if the chain of thought proceeds from a supposition of unity to a discovery of the contradictions. This direction leads to a propensity for deconstruction: from suspicion to irreverence and parody, and from irreverence to revolution as the ultimate solution. In less active manifestations it will create a state of nihilism and a self-destructive attitude. In the case of the surrealists, the response to what they understood of Hegel had led on the political level to defamatory outbursts against stationary mores and institutions, and to threats of anarchy rather than to constructive social action. On the other hand it also led to the question raised in the first volume of the surrealist journal *Révolution surréaliste*: "Is Suicide a Solution?"[2] The general consensus was no, although some went to the brink of suicide and others to actual suicide, as the history of surrealism can attest.

There was another side to their comprehension of dialectics, however, from apparent contradictions to unity; and this direction had a closer significance for the destiny of the artist than of the ideologue. Elasticity expands the possibilities of meaning (or interpretation) and the potential connection of all with all can cause what Salvador Dali in his theoretical essay "L'âne pourri" was to call "a delirium of interpretations."[3] This type of elasticity enriched the field of both the creative artist and the reader or beholder.

The implications of dialectics as they affected the work of

the surrealists and are affecting the direction of modern criticism have to do with the meaning attached to "hermeneutics." To date, Mario Valdés appears to have made the clearest distinction between phenomenological critics, deconstructionists, and poststructuralists.[4] But the common denominator of what "hermeneutics" means to Valdés is contained in his statement that a choice is to be made of the interpretative meaning over any fixed meaning of a text. In his *Identity of the Literary Text* he writes: "A text . . . does not achieve meaning within its own formal boundaries but only when it passes the threshold of potentiality into the experience of the reader."[5] By adding alongside the word "text" the terms "image," "object," and "life-experience," we have a definition of "interpretation" as understood by the surrealists. Decades before the current popularization of phenomenology that would generate applications to literary criticism, the surrealists attempted to demonstrate and perhaps prove (to themselves at least) the same hypothesis, based on their understanding of Hegel on the concrete level of the arts through verbal alchemy, object manipulation, and ambiguous behavior. They pointed out that they could make meaning fluctuate in the arts as well as in ideologies by changing vantage points in space rather than in time, and using varying levels of perception bringing into play the unconscious interpretations or leading to what they called "the irrational knowledge of the object." They could thereby establish conciliations between entities which on the surface appeared contradictory. If in hermeneutical criticism the indeterminacies are caused by changing horizons of expectation depending primarily on the passage of time, in the case of the poet/artist they are determined by degrees of interiorization leading to self-knowledge, as is the case with the phenomenological critics. In *Le Surréalisme et la peinture*, Breton states clearly the power of subjectification that transforms a reality circumscribed in time and space into a virtiginous one:

> L'erreur commise fut de penser que le modèle ne pourrait être pris que dans le monde extérieur, ou même seulement qu'il y pouvait être pris. Certes la sensibilité humaine peut conférer à l'objet d'apparence la plus vulgaire une distinction tout à fait imprévue; il n'en est pas moins vrai que c'est faire un piètre usage du pouvoir magique de figuration dont certains possèdent l'agrément que de le faire servir à la conservation et au renforcement de ce qui existerait sans eux.[6] (The error committed was to think that the model could only be taken in the exterior world, or that it even could be taken there. Indeed human sensibility can confer on an object of the most vulgar appearance a totally unexpected distinction; it is nonetheless true that you cannot make a more pitiful use of the magic power of figuration with which some people are endowed than to put it to the service and reinforcement of what would be perfectly able to exist without them.)

Such observations lead to the surrealist adage: "Nothing that surrounds us is an object for us, but is for us a subject." No matter to what degree the hermeneutic critic pushes the open-ended nature of interpretations, his basic preoccupation, as Valdés suggests, is the "questioning of the subject-object relation"[7] in terms of the same dialectic elasticity of the perception of phenomena.

As an important factor in indeterminacy, there was also building up, both in philosophy and in literature, a challenge to the constancy of meaning in language, consequently a distrust of language that betrayed inconstancy rather than stability and that invited hermeneutic response. The complexity of the role of language in the interpretation of meaning is a basic feature of hermeneutic criticism; it was equally important to surrealist theory. In both cases there are ample references to advances made by linguists of the nineteenth and twentieth centuries in the understanding of language as a source for knowledge as well as an instrument to convey knowledge; i.e., reading *in* language as well as by means of language. Roman Jakobson, in particular, analyzed the double function of the study of language as a designator of objects and in the guise of a self-referential metalanguage. This theory of Jakobson's can be explained, as I have argued elsewhere, in the area of poetics as the difference between the language of poetry and the poetry of language.[8] In this regard, Jakobson revealed his sense of the superiority of the artist/poet over the philosopher when he declared, in his important essay "Linguistique et poétique" (1963): "Ambiguity is an intrinsic inalienable property of all message centered upon itself, in short it is an obligatory corollary to poetry."[9] Jakobson, however, missed a remarkable opportunity to reference his statement, considering the fact that he was a contemporary of the surrealists, and that elsewhere in his work he shows himself to be well acquainted with the directions taken by modern poets from Rimbaud on.

The surrealists recognized the central position of language in poetry's intrinsically hermeneutic function. Breton mentioned "l'aventure dans le langage" on an equal footing with the aleatory adventures he and his companions had in the streets of Paris.[10] For them the power of language was double-barreled. If language could be considered unreliable, it was also man's most unique treasure—a comfort, a strength, a replacement for the divine Logos. This devotion to language dated back in poetry to Rimbaud's "L'Alchimie du verbe," and in the early twentieth century was globally manifest in literary avant-gardes; Hugo Ball described language's effect as "evangelical";[11] Unamuno thought it had a world-building power. Huidobro thought its function was world-creating; and Pierre Reverdy, the "cubist" French poet, thought it a miracle-shaping resource. But the massacre of language became a "cause célèbre" with the dadaists, who expressed their disappointment with its ephemeral significance, when it did not measure up to their desires, by writing in sand or on an erasable board.

It was the surrealists, however, who made their concern with the manipulation of language the pivot of their theories on poetry. In the *First Manifesto* Breton proclaimed: "Le langage a été donné à l'homme pour qu'il en fasse un usage surréaliste."[12] In the *Second Manifesto* he declared: "Il ne faut pas s'étonner de voir le surréalisme se situer tout d'abord presque uniquement sur le plan du langage."[13] In fact the guiding principle of his work focused on the polysemic character of language as the base for poetic creativity. In an essay of 1922 entitled "Les Mots sans rides," he proposed the liberation of words from their bondage; he announced that "on détourna le mot de son devoir de signifier,"[14] and urged that words that could not be detached from their congealed meanings and stereotyped associations be dispatched. He further aspired to an extension of the language of poetry through the appropriation of words not previously considered "literary." Among the ones he was to use subsequently in his own poetry were botanical, biological, and geological terms, whose capabilities as sign and symbol had not yet been cultivated, and whose potential reference values were wide open.

Breton's attitude raises the question of literariness: what lexicon is of appropriate use in literature? The corollary in art is to ask: what objects are appropriate for painting and sculpture? The lexical permissiveness was paralleled by the equally permissive use of objects as artifacts breaking down the barrier between art and nonart, which is one of the pivotal questions art perception has raised in the entire twentieth century. In this regard it should be remembered that the apprentice years of several of the major surrealists-to-be were spent in the circle of the journal *Littérature*. At one point, as its chief editor, Breton had the title dismembered into the homonym *Lits et Ratures*. The appropriation of a pejorative meaning of "littérature" comes from the final line of Verlaine's "Art poétique": "Et tout le reste est littérature." The surrealists' declaration on January 27, 1925, was "Nous n'avons rien à voir avec la littérature."

Proceeding from that background, Surrealism was fundamentally a rupture from literariness in its attempt to stretch the canon of the arts into the broader realm of the art of living and to thereby enter disciplines such as sociology, psychology, philosophy, anthropology, and linguistics, as illustrated by Michel Leiris's phonemic glossary in several issues of *Le Surréalisme au service de la révolution*.

Breton explained that he wrote out of moral preoccupations. At one point he almost quit writing because those concerns seemed to exceed the boundaries of literary activities. Modern critics have implemented this principle by giving interdisciplinary interpretations to works previously classified as strictly literary or artistic, thereby setting aside purely aesthetic gauges. But in adopting this approach, paradoxically these critics have overlooked those literary and artistic works created under the aegis of surrealism—with the dubious exception of Foucault's *Ceci n'est pas une pipe*—which had *intentionally* moved toward the discovery of multiple sources of knowledge through literature and had turned the practice of the arts primarily into an epistemological quest—a far cry from the previous ideal of "art for art's sake."

In other words, if the modern critic has been trying to find an episteme in forms of expression traditionally designated as literature rather than philosophy, so were the surrealists, but they claimed this activity as their primary privilege in performing as artists and not something to be uncovered after the fact, at the pleasure of a reading agent. To find knowledge in language, particularly by those most sensitive to it, i.e., the poets/artists, was part of the poetic act, not a surrogate function to be relegated to the readers, however sophisticated. The poet's knowledge involves recognition of the multiplicity of meaning, the catalytic power of associations and intellectual movement toward the unity of seemingly contradictory meanings. His goal in relation to the reader is not simply to bring about reception or understanding of a message in interpretations foreign to the writer's intent, but to provoke the reader toward similar processes in the direction of a creative act.

Coming now to modern criticism, hermeneutics concerns itself with interpretation that uncovers the variability of meaning in a linguistically variable text. It appropriates a methodology originally used in the deciphering of ancient texts of unknown contexts and applies it to recent epochs whose contexts are known but may have become irrelevant to current readers. Time, however, is not the only factor in the change of significance. The character of the reader or mediator has something to do with it as well, according to what is highlighted. In the current era the critic encourages pure rationalism rather than the powers of imagination; intuitive knowledge is totally discredited.

Critical hermeneutic activity is perceived as both a privileged reader's pleasurable intellectual activity and as a demonstration of the relativity of truth, moral values, and reality itself—all of which the reader is persuaded to admit. Politically, the aim of modern hermeneutics is to break down long-established biases of ideology and taste inherent in the text. The hermeneutic approach, however, also enhances the latent creativity of the critic by allowing him to produce a subtext, or vehicle, for his own epistemological search. Unwittingly, perhaps, the critic is using language as a poetic act. Like the surrealist, the hermeneutic critic appealed to linguistics. Through this affiliation he has found a major source of support in his pursuit of variable interpretation. The basic assumption is that signifiers and signified do not stand in permanent relationship, nor do they create invariable significations. Rather, they are involved in temporary and temporal associations. Time and place, as well as the innate propensities of the interpreter, play havoc with meaning. All factors outside the intrinsic existence of the text are in collusion to create meanings and hide others, thus violating the innocence of language. The interpreter can cause these ruptures, indeed deconstruct the successive and presumed a priori meanings or "signifying chains," and thereby add to the relativity of reality and truth. A fundamentally apolitical liberalism could emerge from such a presumption; but in the case of most deconstructionist hermeneutic criticism, inconsistency of meaning, whether discovered or effected, causes an irremediable irresolution, an impasse that has come to be called aporia, which leads to disenchantment without the energizing factor of the revolutionary spirit. The dark philosopher-critics, who through reading well-known texts have conveyed the ambiguity of the values of Western civilization through paradox and parody, have succumbed to the arbitrary character not only of society but of the universe.

It is interesting to note, by contrast, that the very same ambiguity simulated through creative writing rather than creative reading made the surrealists exploit the passivity or the indifference of the cosmic canvas (how strikingly this indifference is conveyed by Magritte!) in order to open the way for greater activities by artists in revising the world around them in the cultivation of a luminous immediacy, while increasing their tolerance for image or object through displacements and transformations.

The surrealists' attack on meaning virtually became an inquiry into the meaning of meaning. They overcame aporia with euphoria as they created new uses for both objects and words.

In his *Second Manifesto* Breton evoked two emblems: the revolver and the key. The revolver stood for destruction, the key for love and for hermetic thought. In each case Breton was dealing with transformation of static into convulsive renewal, whether of the individual or of his resources of knowledge. Because the conciliation of opposites was a medieval alchemical process as well as the basis of Hegelian dialectics, and because the surrealists had referred to occult sources, their activities and works were associated with the supernatural in the general public's mind. Their references to the philosopher's stone were taken literally and connected them with the fantastic. But, even as in the case of today's critics, the surrealists' fascination with the hermetic was not centered on the substance of old hermetic writings but on the process of thought involved in both the creation of hermetic texts and their interpretation. The process was more than a gateway to the discovery of layered meanings or to a demonstration of the alteration of meaning as the message moves from one horizon to another; it was also a means of creating, in a modern work of art, a palimpsest of meanings as in the ancient oracles. The key difference between the surrealists of the thirties and the critics of the sixties lies in the fact that what Derrida calls "différance"—discovery of meaning lying previously inert in the text and that can be indefinitely deferred—is consciously maneuvered (we might even say connived) by the surrealist poet or artist. His very consciousness of the game he is playing with his readers, current or future, by arousing their imagination is perhaps the most important part of the creative act. Releasing meaning from time and place and subserving it to the character of the perpetrator becomes his act of sublimation. *Je, Sublime* is one of Benjamin Péret's titles.

Roland Barthes perceives the pleasure of the text as an activity of the reader who is placing himself vicariously in the privileged position of the original writer and going through the movements of the work in terms of his own time, place, and ideological persuasions. Paul Ricoeur, the phenomenologist philosopher and critic, confirms Barthes's position as he defines such movement in *Time and Narrative:* "making explicit the movement by which the text unfolds a world in front of itself and aims less at restoring the author's intention behind the text."[15] In surrealism's case the "différance" consists of the artist's a priori manipulation of vision and meaning as part of his creative process, rather than as the result of the critic's re-creative process alone. The famous surrealist phrase "donner à voir" is applicable in both cases. In the surrealist's case, however, it was a more direct reaching out from author to general reader, with a virtual spurning of any critical interference. The ambiguity calling for a hermeneutic response creates an intellectual dilemma and results in efforts to arrive at systems through mediation between critic and reader. In surrealism's case a plurality of meanings would presumably lead to the recognition of the futility of system in the face of individual differences in the production of ambiguity (no intellectual cages contemplated or tolerated), even among writers of the same time and place.

The fundamental difference in the application of common linguistic and philosophical knowledge deals with the assumed readership. "For whom are you writing?" is the key question, rather than "why do you write?" The surrealists were first aiming at each other's reception and were beckoning to other creative individuals to join them; their ultimate dream was that one day ("le jour viendra" being one of Breton's favorite expressions) a more general readership would become receptive to their kind of writing, which aimed to make creativity more widely available.

For insight on who reads Derrida, reference can be made to the critical journal *Arc*'s 1973 special issue on Derrida. Catherine Clément wrote discerningly:

> They are university scholars, or litterati who know the history of philosophy, of literature, who have some familiarity with languages and the habit of frequent reading of Freud. They are young on the whole; and in general have broken off from the university establishment but not on any significant issue. All, whether university people or not, are readers who write: who use the texts of Derrida in their turn and not just to read them. In their writing and eventually in their teaching, they assure with the least loss possible and the most transformation possible, the transmission of a certain operative movement of the texts. What is transmitted through this tributary to the reading of Derrida is not a message, it is not a philosophy. It is a protocol of textual work. It entails a sort of strategic calculation; so that these books may have certain effects, political, psychological, etc.; along all the stages of the edition and reading, he has to write for those who can propagate these effects: teachers and those who write.[16]

Whereas the hermeneutic activity of today's university critic is directed to an elite readership, the surrealists had democratized the function of the poet/artist as potentially attributable to everyman's rite of passage from surface reality to deeper levels where antinomies cease.

If the surrealists attempted to engender creative living and writing—first among artists and eventually among the entire population in order to restore imagination's rights in a society that was more and more entrapped in rationalism and regimentation—the immediate applications of their hermeneutic techniques were in the direct range of the artist and poet. In the juxtaposition of different realities and in "the one in the other image," i.e., the modernizing of the rebus, both manners of viewing reality could be applied to the graphic as well as the literary arts. The surrealists were questioning a universe already beyond deconstruction. Representation is the expression of what is already existing, including the confirmation of accepted associations. Re-presentation, as the expression is used by critics practicing hermeneutics, refers to rearrangements as well as to negation through the reader's changing historical perspectives and ideological revisions. For the surrealists, creation, rather than re-creation, deals with the revelation of the infinite range of possibilities of any given entity or even of the universe. Their concern is not for restatement of an idea or of a particular relocation of an exterior reality; rather, the surrealists speculate about the trajectory. They are not interested in taking an inventory of meanings acquired to date. The permissive quality of analogies created by signifiers freed of their enslavement to built-in meanings is what Breton was searching for not only in written texts but in the cosmos when he went in search of the savage eye, the "nondistinction of sensory function and intellectual functions."

Since the surrealists' theories are an integral part of the work of art, intentionalism, a concept so denigrated by modern criticism, cannot in their case be separated from the text. The surrealists made intentionality the primary substance, more important than the results of the intention because they put a higher value on life than on artistic performance: "Pour moi nulle oeuvre d'art ne vaut ce petit carré fait de l'herbe diaprée à perte de vue de la vie" (Breton, *Fata Morgana*).

The surrealists would not accept the idea that there is no referent outside the text because they thought reference itself had a double meaning. Free association meant, indeed, freedom from semantic and historical reference, but autobiographical references were ingrained in the work of art, sometimes with subtlety but more often explicitly. Their lives were references melded into the text, setting the voice, interfering with the linear sequences of thought, or breaking into the juxtaposition of images. If Mallarmé had given primacy to the work that would survive its creator, the surrealists took a chance on surviving with and in the work or not at all. Intention revealed an awareness of process, which for them was the pleasure of the creative act, the fun *in* the game, and more important than speculation on the work's chances of survival. Intention gave the work energy, a different pulse in each artist; that is why any critical commentary on surrealism needs to include discussion of the artist's intentions. An essay like Max Ernst's "Comment on force l'inspiration" is a creative piece about the creative process.[17] Inevitably the realization of intentions can never be complete in surrealist works, since intentionalism deals with absolutes and the surrealist's applications occur in a relative world. There lies the surrealist conjunction between sublimity and annihilation, between liberation from congealed meaning and total absence of meaning. The contradictions' cancellation of each other had dismal effects in the lives of some of its practitioners.

For Breton, however, "le signe ascendant" always seemed to triumph over the frustration of lost loves, lost friendships, the disruptions and immoralities of war, and disappointments in politics. The philosophical intentions of the poet acting on his environment remained constant in spite of all the uncertainties. Beyond the years of his position as the principal spokesman of the coterie, the works in which the intentions were expressed are inseparable from the creative act. Although he went to the same source books as the phenomenologically oriented critics of today, Breton's knowledge of humanity's failures, through his participation in both World War I and World War II, made him a rabid but not despairing critic. In defiance of official history he unearthed cases of historical triumphs of spirit over event; i.e., his poetry on World War II deals with the idiosyncratic choice of heroes and heroines such as the revolutionary journalist Delescluze, the Albigensian martyr Esclarmonde, or the social theoretician Charles Fourier. Although these poems, *Fata*

Morgana, Les Etats-Généraux, Ode à Charles Fourier, written under the impact of war, could easily have been circumstantial, he gave ahistorical interpretation to the historical events that were the real but rejected references. These poems constitute an alternating current of theory and praxis, intention and performance. The conscious avoidance of associations of images with expected historical referents gives Breton's texts an independence from history that can be attested as we read the poems many years after the historical event. It makes them available for nonhistorical interpretations. But the personal referent, the interior I and its intentions are virtually engraved in the texts. The dialectics involved in the search for unity in contradictions, at a time when fragmentation was the order of the day, is the pivotal theme of the poem reflected in the mythopoetic use of the haunting evocation of the "momie d'Ibis," in *Fata Morgana.* In *Les Etats-Généraux,* written in the darkest moments of World War II, a poem that could have been the reflection and description of the direct, devastating power of event demonstrates, instead, the slippage from *abattre* to *bâtir,* from deconstruction to reconstruction of historical fact.

In sharp contrast, the fact that European civilization was walking a tightrope over a political and philosophical void after World War II left a younger breed of critics disinherited and discontent, unable to respond in any other way save through keen analytical thinking about the state of being facing the nothingness. The ambivalent response, neither directly political nor totally apolitical, has sparked recognition all over the world. In the process there has developed an instrument of propaganda that can transform decontrol into recontrol, destroying one set of ideologies in order to impose a dogmatic refusal of recuperation.

Curiously enough, the surrealists' attacks on capitalism were overt, and they were instigated by political acts or abuses of the moment rather than by general ideologies. The occasional efforts made by the surrealists at conciliation with Marxism never quite made sense (except when Aragon attempted to put them on a personal level). In promoting any kind of ideology the surrealists had far less impact outside their rank than have had poststructural university critics. The surrealist critics have had no impact on university critics, whereas hermeneutically oriented criticism has made deep inroads into universities.

Surrealist theoretical writings have had modest success, in sharp contrast with the universal acclaim that their creative works, principally in painting and photography, have enjoyed. Surrealist art has become a lucrative enterprise for collectors and exhibitors. The most recent, posthumous work of John H. Matthews on surrealist photography reveals a whole and yet untapped area of examples of the staging of the dialectic character of objects, the exploration of simulacre in photographic form that would have been beyond the capacity to signify verbally. The response the artist gives to the uncontrollable constrictions of the human condition is in another register from that of the critic simulating the process of creative writing. The common background of the current schools of criticism and of surrealist works is that, using similar events and books to arrive at quite different conclusions, each group made its primary target the reexamination of human knowledge of the self and its environment rather than its manner of expression. At the same time it created an upheaval in previous classifications of discourse that had put a barrier between philosophy and the arts.

If the hermeneutics of today's criticism were to use surrealist texts as a critical foil, they might well throw light both on the critic and on poetry's inherent hermeneutic function.

NOTES

This essay first appeared in *Symposium*, vol. 42, no. 3 (Fall 1988), 173–187.

1. André Breton, *Entretiens* (Paris: Gallimard), 152 (this and all other translations are mine).

2. "Le Suicide est-il une solution?" *RS* (1er déc. 1924): 2 (first published in *Le Surréalisme au service de la révolution*).
3. Salvador Dali, "L'Âne pourri," *SSDLR* 3:10.
4. Mario Valdés, *Phenomenological Hermeneutics and the Study of Literature* (Toronto: University of Toronto Press, 1987).
5. Valdés, *Identity of the Literary Text* (Toronto: University of Toronto Press, 1985), 299.
6. A. Breton, *Le Surréalisme et la peinture*, *RS* 4 (5 juillet 1925): 17.
7. Valdés, ibid., 59.
8. Anna Balakian, "From Mallarmé to Breton," *Writing in Modern Temper*, ed. Mary Ann Caws (Stanford: Stanford University Press, 1984).
9. Roman Jakobson, *Essais de linguistique générale* (Paris: Editions de Minuit, 1963), 238.
10. Breton, *Entretiens*, 135.
11. Hugo Ball, *Flight out of Time* (New York: Viking, 1974), 68.
12. A. Breton, *Manifestes du Surréalisme* (Paris: Pauvert) 48.
13. Ibid., 183.
14. A. Breton, *Les Pas perdus* (Paris: Gallimard, 1924), 168.
15. Paul Ricoeur, *Time and Narrative*, vol. 1 (Chicago: University of Chicago Press), 81.
16. Catherine Clément, *L'Arc* 54:16.
17. Max Ernst, "Comment on force l'inspiration," *SSDLR* 5: 43.

VI

TOWARD A NEW AESTHETICS

In answering a question proposed by Jean Bessière in a colloquium at the University of Amiens in the summer of 1990, one has to take inventory first of the concerted efforts in multiple theoretical thought to see what actual advances have been made in the development of a new aesthetics. But to do that it becomes necessary to unravel the ideological strains encrusted in the language and literature of the past two centuries we call modern times.

What strikes blatently in the work of the prominent critics of the end of the twentieth century is the spectacularly negative accomplishments, namely, to unload prejudice from literary language, and to set aside intrinsic meaning from the mentality of the time when the work was written. But since language vis-à-vis a reader with a literate frame of reference cannot function in a vacuum, the negative stance has often turned into a positive one: supplying new meanings more pertinent to the contemporary world and more compatible with the ideological orientations of the critic's own time and own upbringing. Some have gone so far as to suggest that language would have no meaning at all unless it provided these occasions for refills of meaning.

But a curious phenomenon occurred on the way to closer analysis of literary language. These erudites who engaged in the process of linguistic, textual scrutiny were by formation and environment more inclined toward ideological perceptions than aesthetic ones. They grew up deeply entrenched in the existential philosophy, sociology, linguistics—those positivism disciplines containing what was then (no longer) associated with Marxism. If, for instance, in the humanistic world, the expression "beauty" is a differential in constructing a hierarchy of perfection recognized as such by artistic minds, the focus was moved to a hierarchy of social relevances.

The things that now mattered were social situations, psychological attitudes, the levels of sexual (rather than aesthetic) pleasure, and data was selectively drawn from the "text" to build up the testimony preexisting in the reader's mind as a motivation for the initial interest in the vacated linguistic meaning to give it new living matter to house. The most vivid metaphor I have been able to give this process is the metamorphosis the Rhone River undergoes as it dips into Lake Geneva, bringing in its torrent the brown and raucous baggage from the Alps, depositing its encumbrance in the lake's waters and then emerging blue and serene headed in another direction. Whether the new load it will then take on is of a "better" quality is another issue, but surely it is different.

So far the operation is clear and it has achieved its goal. The next step is to fill the vacancy. The "literary" criticism or critical theory reflected in the work of the last decades of the century is creative in the sense that it throws new light on the human condition and demonstrates the variability of confidence in historical "facts." But if one takes away the literary reference system already established for texts already written within that system, the new scale of comparison will be inoperative unless one substitutes another system. With awareness of this obvious fact, some theorists have applied to their chosen literary texts a sociopolitical frame of reference, but it is one that is even more antiquated than the existing aesthetic one. It is like reading Balzac, Zola, or John Steinbeck in terms of Marx, Durkheim, Claude Bernard or Ricardo instead of viewing them in the light of more recent efforts for the modification of the literary reference system. In using literary texts as vehicles to interpret or support social or phenomenological concepts, the critic has been using terminology that is more superannuated than the previously existing concepts they set out to destroy as a common currency of exchange, whereas ontological perceptions were shaken to a more radical degree at the turn of this century than at any other time since the discovery that the earth was round and turned around the sun. To make any modification of literary value beyond the classical one of harmonious beauty it becomes imperative to redefine "reality," "nature," and "communication." I have developed this proposition in my essays "Problems of Modernism" and "Interartifactuality." But the reason I bring it up again here is that the most recent activities of the deconstructionists are including a new look at the problem of aesthetics and in the reshaping of it and, therefore, these concepts need to be viewed in relation to writings which we must perhaps cease to call "secondary" to the "primaries" of the literary artists.

The major sea change that occurred in the arts as a result of a previous challenge had to do precisely with attempts to demolish those concepts of harmonious beauty, of a rationally understood natural world, and a dialogical communication on the part of the avant-garde artists of the twentieth century. They had a general awareness of a changed scientific system of references and intuitively turned in that direction. One of the first poets to sense that without a new ontological perspective there could not be new forms in the arts was the cosmopolitan-spirited, French-naturalized poet Guillaume Apollinaire, who characterized the "new" poets as "pèlerins de la perdition." That did not mean to say that he broke the ontological frontier or, like Jules Verne, wrote science fiction. Most of his poetry that I would call revolutionary consisted of statements of intention with rather clumsy examples of a new aesthetics. Elsewhere in this volume, in the essay on originality, I have tried to explain the difference between the originator quality and true originality. Apollinaire's own aesthetic successes were to be much more closely linked with the perfecting of the old aesthetics (Symbolism) than with the attempts on an experimental basis at a new aesthetics. In his poems "Les Collines," for instance, he had foreseen that any new aesthetics had to tackle the problem of "the depths of awareness."

> You see the prophets rising
> Like those blue hills far away
> They will have precise visions
> And will transport us everywhere

There is not in the translation of these lines of "verse," any more than in the original, anything "poetic," either linguistically or rhythmically; they are important because they reflect Apollinaire's awareness that the studies into the psyche and of the stratosphere will have an impact on future man's sense of aesthetics. That the prophecy is taking longer to realize than he expected can be ascertained by the fact that the most recent "literary" writers cannot define themselves beyond the self-indictment inherent in the label of "postmodern" they and their critics have accepted.

In terms of the failure to determine what can occur after the "modernism" of Apollinaire or James Joyce, the prevailing tone of negativism in literary theory or the rehash of the few illuminations of a sensed "difference" consists of a mentality of refusal and relapse, the legacy of the nonartist philosophers with whose frame of reference literature was not compatible and which did not lead to its replenishment.

In retrospect—again aesthetically speaking—the whole twentieth century may be regarded as one of transition, most proficient in finding processes of emptying out old standards of aesthetic response rather than for filling new ones. That may be why we are such experts in studying the avant-garde and wait endlessly like Godot for a "new garde" that has not come to pass. The observation applies to music as well, whereas art and the cinema give more indications of movement, and theater is beginning in spite of itself to stir in urban lofts and small-town walk-ups.

A new aesthetics has not emerged despite the very wise concerns of some of the central figures engaged in theoretical writing on the current scene such as Jean Bessière (Professor Bessière ran a symposium in Amiens called "Vers une nouvelle esthétique" in 1990 and has since become the major literary critic at Paris III) to activate a recuperation of the literarity of the text within the framework of deconstruction methodology. My view, after a lifetime spent unraveling the intricacies of nineteenth- and twentieth-century modernism, is that to establish a new aesthetics it would have to be built on a demolition that occurred earlier in modern times than has been manifested in post–World War II criticism, that of the demolitionists among men of science—Cournot, Einstein, Heisenberg, Pierre Janet (the originator of Freudian psychology and surrealist automatic writing)—and the grueling work of astrophysicists, all tied together in the perception of a *dynamic* materialism comprehended in its far-reaching dimensions and applicable to all the sectors of the arts with much surer and dazzling promises than anything attributable to *dialectic* materialism.

In terms of what our scientific findings have uncovered, about both our exterior and our interior worlds, a new aesthetics would have to take account of a certain number of these new developments in human knowledge and thought. But before making any attempt to itemize these factors there is one constant to be recognized and that necessitates deviation from recent philosophically inclined literary criticism. Let us not be ambiguous about this: a new aesthetics cannot be based on a methodology that reduces art to its abstract subject matter. Art in any era or under any aesthetic aegis is constituted of concrete entities; it is not a vehicle to be used to transport you elsewhere. It has an ontological dimension in itself, and the degree of its effectiveness is measurable by its ability to fulfill human needs in both its creator and its respondents.

In the scope of our current knowledge of ourselves and the universe, here are some of the essential concepts that have to be confronted in a new modernism: first of all, the meaning of reality, which has been totally galvanized in the current century. It has gone from absolute meaning to relative, extended with infinite variabilities in the exterior as well as the interior world. People in all walks of life, other than the literary critics, are groping for a revised definition of the real and its relation with the artificial, calling it sometimes "virtual" reality, and it is exciting if somewhat ironic that the word "transcendental" has moved from religious and literary language to that of astrophysicists. These shifts in meaning are much more complicated than the Derridean notion of "différance," which deals with changes in sociopolitical views. The primary revolution of our time is not political but ontological. A prerequisite to a new aesthetics coping with the extensions of reality and the paths of ascension and descent replacing heaven and hell, and consequently any new notion of the beautiful, has to adapt to the new comprehension of *turbulence* within the human body and without. In this respect, two forces have been at play in this century. On the one hand, we have avant-garde efforts to readjust the notion of the beautiful, such as André Breton's "Beauty must be convulsive or not at all," and the efforts of some novelists, not read nearly so much as Joyce or Proust, to lift to the surface of awareness the layers and degrees of inner human reality. On the other hand, we have the critics who have restricted themselves to the role of undertakers in the interment of the beautiful in the old sense of the word, demolishing also the *better* and *the worse* as aesthetic standards. Their substitute standards have to do with ideological and sociopolitical priorities of the time.

What has been neglected is that without apparent militancy involved, other guidelines to the appreciation of the arts have deteriorated: the duality of the material and the spiritual, the dichotomy between the real and the marvelous, and the psychological distinctions between the conscious and the unconscious in favor of determinations of levels of consciousness. There is a whole world within us, the biochemical one that operates in virtually an involuntary fashion, and the mind's continuous battle between remembering and forgetting, the penumbras of dream and drug vision, etc.

When, early in the century, artists in several fields became aware of these new inroads into the epistemology that art feeds on, experiments were attempted such as automatic writing, transcription of dreams, stream of consciousness, recognized as avant-garde. In this connection the cultural importance of a little book, not widely read, *Anicet* by Louis Aragon, warned that the efforts of the avant-garde were not likely to be followed by a new garde. They were only making modifications of old models. Under attack came even the not-yet-so-great Picasso, whose adventurous spirit, Aragon thought, ran the risk of being corrupted by American commercialism. He attacked a diverse array of modernists for becoming elderly Lautréamonts and Rimbauds, unworthy pretenders to the hand of Mirabelle *(mira belle)*. And Dada was among these preliminary demolitionists that in Aragon's eyes fell short of new goals. His own early work, *Le Paysan de Paris,* dealing with order/disorder, was in line with a new face for literature. But he dropped the dream for the immanent realities of the Communist party in France and spent the rest of his life writing reasonable novels and poetry.

What was missed except in the theoretical writings of a few creative artists such as Breton and later Robbe-Grillet, the Hungarian Arpad Mezei, the Dutch Huizinga, the Argentinian Julio Cortázar, and others whose work I ignore, was that simulation and presentation had to replace imitation and representation, consisting of an irrevocable break with the old mimesis. Those who followed surrealist notions of analogy, the new novel's simulation of timelessness, notions of game theory, the subtler probings of consciousness, illustrated such budding theories. Readings in the texts of Hegel, Heidegger, Husserl, and Freud did not provoke in artistic circles the same alienation and dispirited response as they have in more recent critic-philosophers driven to stages of impasse, paradox, aporia, reflective of a traumatized post–World War II Europe to which I have referred in my essay "The Snowflake on the Belfry." On the contrary, all new aesthetic ventures require a leap in spirit, an effervescence and recognition of disorder mysteriously compelling in its unpredictability, and where there may burgeoning signs of a new order leading indeed to a new grasp of the notion of the aesthetic, but also to a new understanding of the creative mind.

Since the power to revise the universe in terms of the arts is the supreme endowment artists can hope to attain and the crux of their liberty, they are apt to be first in giving us insights into deep changes. First of all, it must be noted that there is a gap in all our branches of knowledge between awareness of a new truth or factor and the need or desire to adjust the world of human existence or of the arts according to that new knowledge. For instance, it took astronauts fifty years to experiment with the weightlessness envisaged and simulated by artist René Magritte in his painting *Château en Espagne*.

In recognizing the decentralization of the human universe the artists have not stopped there and gone into a slump like some of our philosophers. They went beyond to an attempted recentering which consisted of radical modifications of the relationship between nature and man. Nature was no longer at the service of man, granted, but was part of a new alignment between autonomous forces creating a free and passionate union, a willing union where the role of aesthetics as well as ethics was to break the barriers between the birth of a concept and the life lived (better expressed in the French *le conçu et le vécu*), realizing that the concept of nature changed as did that of reality. This does not mean that a new aesthetics has to deviate from the old adage "hold the mirror up to nature," as long as the reconstructors of a new aesthetics realize that they are dealing with a new notion of nature. The enlarged notion of nature would command an adjustment of lens to relate order to disorder, to encompass the predictability of phenomena to the aleatory character of cataclysms, to take a new look at chance, an effort initiated by Stéphane Mallarmé at the close of the nineteenth century. At the risk of being redundant I must assert that to be modern is not to go into the unnatural or science fiction but to have a more sophisticated grasp of the natural. The mirror must also stay but must reveal the invisible as well as the visible, identify the prevailing mysteries, those inner tremors that struggle against obvious perception, the vision of the deer as poet Jules Supervielle once tried to give us, the vision of the unseeing eye that James Dickey tried valiantly to convey in *Alnilam* more recently. Paul Valéry, who is hardly ever proclaimed a "modern," made some attempts at the type of reflection we would expect of the modern mirror in his long and for most impatient readers incomprehensible poem *La Jeune Parque*. His semantic exploration of the new (that is what *jeune* means in the poem) discipline of the study of consciousness should take us via the ancient figure of Narcissus to contemplations of the self beyond the mirror image seen in water. He transformed the self-adoring Narcissus into a knowledge-seeking one groping for discovery of what emanates between himself and the shadow: "That trembling, frail, and pious distance between myself and the water." Surely a new aesthetics has to move in that direction in its application of the most recent notions about "nature" whose dynamism and previously presumed random character surpass the means we had acquired in the course of centuries to measure and probe its resources and incorporate them into our arts.

Although the surrealists made the most spectacular efforts to demonstrate that the dichotomy between the rational and the irrational had to go, the problem of *how* to show the infringement of the dream on conscious awareness can be identified only selectively in their ensuing works in literature or the other arts. There is a difference between proclamation of intent and tangible effect on a new aesthetics. I have found in the course of my innumerable readings one remarkable instance of the application of the hypothesis in an outwardly modest work of a self-taught Chilean poet, Rosamel del Valle. His posthumously published poetic prose work *Eva y la fuga*, which I translated into English as *Eva the Fugitive* (University of California Press, 1990), is in my opinion a remarkable example of the overlaps and degrees of consciousness making of it a rare specimen for critical curiosity, but so far one critic of poetry has found it "incoherent" and it has made no stir on anyone in the front line of the discipline of criticism. Readers, academic as well as general, still go mostly for the obsolete and inflexible separation between dream and reality that betrays the old aesthetics and its diligent preservation of the old dichotomies.

Finally, in revising or reshaping an aesthetics for our time the very function of aesthetics has to be reexamined. What is the creative artist to communicate and in what way? In this respect already in the nineteenth century the "how" of communication had been challenged. The Symbolist endeavor was aimed at the simulation of musical communication, just as in the early part of the twentieth century the surrealists made parallel attempts toward realignment of verbal communication with painting. What these efforts have in common is the rejection of direct communication whereby generator and receiver identify the same form of comprehension, i.e., understanding what is meant to be understood. To reach verbally the ambiguous levels or registers of communication about reality, about nature, about time, they created devices that invite the imagination of the reader to make contact with that of the writer and provoke it into its own creative stance. This new notion of "poetic" communication has been implemented by a trial-and-error method but has not yet found solidification or codification necessary for participation in a new aesthetics.

The application of such communication has been occurring repeatedly for the past fifty years between the writer and the painter, a communication so characteristic as to leave a permanent mark on this century even as the preceding one was marked by the amalgamation of the qualities of writing with the techniques of musical composition.

These probes into the epistemological aspect of the pleasure of literary writing and reading is what prompted Breton to proclaim—perhaps without full comprehension of what he meant—that the drive to write was a "moral" one implying the overlap of ethics with aesthetics in the need to conciliate through the intellect that dares go beyond the limits of reasoning relations between the individual unit of selfhood and the turbulent universe that envelops it.

To pursue, then, the channel of communication between writers and painters of this century the basic premise is that the altered conditions and rules of comprehension of communication make possible a contact between the verbal and the visual which is not essentially dependent or limited to the conceptual, i.e., understanding not based on significations held in common or on parallel deviations between their commonly noted deviations. They measure instead the extent of the figurations which have no representative relationship between them. And those writers who are aware of these changes can all be characterized as serving a "poetics," the dimensions of poetry having to be measured not by exterior rhetorical rules but by differences in the way the mind functions.

To a certain extent social and political events in the orbit of the old ontology have been so dramatic and cataclysmic in Western civilization in the twentieth century that they have it in their power to become the dominant "subject matter" of literary writing, blinding the writer to the more radical changes of our knowledge of the universe. But that transcendental universe of which we learn more and more each day will inevitably become the major operational factor of verbal expression.

Some of the sensitive scientists of our time are unwittingly realizing our current aesthetic need better than our literary writers perhaps because it is their need as well as ours. According to biologist James Shapiro, the most recent quest in all branches of science is "to identify the mysteries, to see the problems of science where there are no solutions." In the search for new principles (which would correspond to our search for a new aesthetics) he goes on to say that the aim is to pursue signals: "And when the microbiologists link up with physicists and mathematicians to understand pattern formation, we will see a totally new science." Translated into the terms of our own discipline, we must also join the pursuit of pattern formation; the reduction of a unit of text to its particles has prevailed too long. We must move from the positivist approach to the holistic one of relationships between works and their creators, making of the collage techniques a preliminary step to attempts at synthesis inherent in intercommunication and continuity in the creative arts.

In dialogues such as Miró's with Eluard, *A toute épreuve,* and with Breton, *Constellations,* the exchange of images which creates a juxtaposition of presumably distant realities, the creative genius seizing the availability of this indeterminism leaves just enough of a margin of approximation between the private universe of the artist who first acted upon it and the one who reacts to it to establish a current of communications between them. The artist in the broad sense of the word establishes as many antennas as possible to reach the widest range of receivers, a relationship that Eluard perceived as a base of "consentement." In this perspective the old principle of clarity (eye-to-eye communication) loses its prime value in a new aesthetics to the power of multilateral meaning, whether in regard to text or canvas, in fact at the point where a so-called verbal text and a passive canvas are transformed into works of art.

This is a far cry from the psychoclinical optic of Lacan, whose point of departure is a constant rooted within the range of the reasonable and anything outside that range is treated as an aberration, as revealed for instance in the case of his analysis of a writing of Rousseau which becomes part of a data base and a "diagnostic of typical paranoia." If the meaning of the work of art is interpreted from the point of view of "the lived paranoic experience and the notion of the world it generates," the role played currently by psychoanalysis in relation to aesthetics is voided. At most the artist's personal life may be able to be scrutinized in terms of the "typical," but if art were to reflect merely the norm it could not be part of a new aesthetics, or for that matter was never part of any aesthetics. The progress that has been made in the discipline of psychology has been focused on pathological states rather than on that of tactical mental disordering under the direction of the imagination, rather than on the recuperation of "the savage eye" which functions at the suture of the clear/obscure, of the uncanny encounter of innocence and sophistication. No appreciable attempts have been made to link the scientist's knowledge and the artist's intuitions since the early efforts of Breton and his group. Instead the applications of psychological data to the arts by the critical mind have consisted in associating mystery and ambiguity in writing or painting with clinical examples of psychosis. To take another example of the activity that one might call "explaining away," this time in painting, there is the prominent case of Foucault, which I singled out in my essay "Interartifactuality." Foucault attributes Magritte's refusal of referentiality in his canvas *Ceci n'est pas une pipe* with heterotopia, whereas in fact the open field of references, the negative of the obvious, opens up if anything the area of the utopian. Foucault recognized, as the ultimate end of representative discourse, disorder, fragmentation, and dispersion (see *Les Mots et les choses*) when indeed we should be looking for the sources of a new cohesion. What is a positive is taken for a negative, hardly a foundation for a new aesthetics.

The union of poets and painters in the first part of the century had, then, produced some of the basic elements in the surge toward a new aesthetics, in establishing the vessels capable of communicating the degrees of the probe into human consciousness in relation with the chthonian layers of the inner nature. In their techniques and applications of a new ontological perspective, the possibility of a link between all aspects of human forms and the living and inert entities in the universe might be grouped in two forms of affiliations: juxtaposition and interpenetration. Beyond these movements toward connection and intimacy, communication included also efforts to simulate order behind what we call chaos within us as in the cosmos, so that we can talk of human "insanity" in the same terms as of eruptions in the cosmos. And as we do not question nature's liberty to deal with the cosmos, the same kind of control of their arts could be appropriated by the artists in their rendition of the cataclysms, aleatory currents, and entropies within the human framework as nature allows itself within the framework of the cosmos.

In Europe at midcentury, movement in this direction stopped as the concern for a new aesthetics passed from the poet/painter coalition to the novelist to violate the structure of narrative in order to approximate that of poetry. When I say "novelist" I am not referring to the standard successful ones such as Camus after World War II, the prosperous New York group, the philosophical ones like Sartre, or the great number of disciples of Kafka, Dostoevsky, or Proust. From the point of view of aesthetics all these represented superbly in their emulation of their masters the desperate mental and physical state of the human being after the war. But their renewal of circumstantial subject matter does not turn the method of their communication any the less paleolithic. In the play *La Ville* of Claudel, the character of Besmes was already waiting for Godot in terms of a dialectic similar to the later Samuel Beckett's, and the anonymity of Sartre's Roquentin in *La Nausée* is actually less advanced than that of Jules Romains's *Mort de Quelqu'un* in its techniques to convey the dispersion of man in an indifferent universe. Likewise another great concern of our time, the preoccupation with the other, hailed as an innovation, had been in circulation for some time to the indulgent chagrin of poet Francis Ponges: "That the I may be Other is one of the insights of man on himself to make life more difficult for himself, more worrisome" (see *Joca Seria*).

Rather the glow came from the direction of the "new" novel as it developed in France and diffusely in other Western literatures, giving intimations of a new aesthetics. There was in Robbe-Grillet's work the invitation to develop a new analogical system obliterating the old one, in Claude Simon's the more subtle technique of interplay of time and memory though less humanly gripping than in Proust, vision control that coalesces segments of consciousness, simultaneity replacing the linear in narrative and description. Then there is the meandering course of expression which is no longer prompted by direct encounters in interpersonal discourse and yet is more entangled than the earlier stream of consciousness. These alerted the reader to a new aesthetics *in the making*. But the response has been meager and has not marked in a definitive form the development of the genre.

Passing from the experimental stage of the novel we have obviously entered, in the last third of the century, into the age of criticism. But in terms of a new aesthetics the critical minds regressed instead of advancing. They have worked on texts of the age of reason and reinterpreted others of Freudian vintage. *Mind against Reason,* that tantalizing title of an early surrealist, René Crevel, who died much too young to make a permanent impact and whose seminal assertion has borne fruit in the physical sciences, has not been a driving force for critical thought. Perhaps the most marked effect of the European critics has been on the American intellectuals in whom they have belatedly awakened the theoretical sense of dialectic materialism, which is having a greater impact on our universities than communism ever did. The disciples of Heidegger and Husserl and more recently of Foucault have persuaded our critics to take seriously the proclamation of the dispersion of man, particularly of Western man with his codes and consequently with his arts. The mimetic representation of mankind as an abstract thought is somewhat bitter but has become popular and hence profitable in such circles and the young minds they control. The critic's aporia, coupled with the impasse in which structural change has fallen, gives not a promise of a new aesthetics but recourse to minimalism, mutism, theoretical verbosity; it is conducive to artistic aphasia.

Its basic fallacy is its misconception of how Byzantiums

crumble. Even if we were to admit that we stand at the close of a cultural millennium, the history these demolitionists distrust will tell us that cultural debilitations never wind down to zero. Cultures overlap; they suck on the organism they are destroying and sometimes retrieve best what can survive decay because all cultures have renewal ingredients.

Are we, then, really going toward a new aesthetics or not? The deconstructionists would like now to proceed toward one because they hear the voices of disquietude. But if my contentions based on my close reading of their texts, of the writers they have used as vehicles and of those they have neglected, bear me out, they cannot have it both ways. Like Dada they are on "a long corridor leading nowhere." A renewal can occur only if it is energized instead of preserved as part of the archaeological baggage, bluntly speaking cleared out of the sphere of influence of archaeologist Foucault and his disciples. The analysis of modern man has to contain dimensions beyond the basic hypothesis of the nil and void, or of the reduction of the good and the bad to a state of paradox.

The ultimate question is what part the critical mind now in center stage can play in instigating the creative spirit beyond the revolved epoch over which it has itself passed sentence. First of all, it has to admit that the creative artist's refusal of referentiality does not call for a heterotopic diagnosis but is a positive high-gear signal, a normal rather than a pathological sign, that even what we call "random" in the universe and represent as "absurd" in literature may not be as irrelevant and fragmented as we thought but part of a larger design of which we have not yet reached a holistic perception.

There are vast areas of exploration of human consciousness of our two worlds, the inner and the outer, that are deserving of what in various definitions we have identified as Art and from which will emerge a new notion of the aesthetic. This can occur only if the human race can preserve against so many odds its sense and faith in the desirable illusion of a universe that matters.

October 12, 1992

VII

SCIENTIFIC RELATIVISM AND THE ARTS

It is incongruous for one as preoccupied as I have been for so many years with the pursuit of the "absolute" in poetry to write on relativism in the arts. In view of my approach to poetry in a consistently different direction, my response to relativist theories and praxis relating to the arts could well be flatly negative, in which case my work in poetry criticism would serve as the substantive basis of my argument. But I do not believe in deconstruction for its own sake as a purely dialectical exercise. This essay, therefore, will have two faces: one will involve the questioning of certain relativist attitudes, and the other an examination of positive alternatives which I have seen at work in modernism and which I believe to be viable within and despite the seemingly relativist climate of the era.

First, let me say candidly and without reservation that I do not believe in "creative criticism." Creativity in the arts propels the subjective consciousness on to a level of existence that can break away from the collective consensus about what is *real,* preferring to it what we consent to understand as *fiction.* Otherwise the subjectivity expressing itself in the field of the acceptable *real* would be not an artist but a reporter.

Ortega y Gasset made the distinction between levels of viewing the same phenomenon very clear in "A Few Drops of Phenomenology," the principal essay in his *Dehumanization of Art.* In showing distinctions between the human beings personally involved in a death—the reporter, the doctor, and the artist—he observes a certain creative detachment on the part of the artist. I would go further and suggest that there is a virtual severance on the part of the artist from the phenomenon under observation.

The critic,[1] on the other hand, if a good one, is a supremely efficient reporter who, as an intermediary between the artist and the nonartist, creates a bridge between two distinct aspects of human cognizance. To serve in that capacity of mediator, the critic must also be something of a moralist, i.e., must possess an a priori code of values against which he tests the *fiction* of the creative artist and recasts it in terms of identifiable and differentiable components in regard to pre-established norms shared by the nonartists. He must want to exercise *clarity* by showing relations with the common reality and to establish a new connection—where the link had been spliced—by focusing on the deviations from reality which constitute the heart of that creativity. He cannot accomplish these two different functions of his métier if he takes the point of view either of the nonartist or of the artist. The critic's role is in the middle, between the secular heaven of the artist and the earthly habitat of the nonartist. He is in what Rilke would call the *Zwischenraum* with a voice neither of a god nor of a man. He is, to use Wallace Stevens's terminology, "the necessary angel."

If the critic, in the fashion of recent creatively inclined literary analysts, competes in intelligence and vision with the creator of the work perused, either he will overwhelm the work (as in the case of Roland Barthes commenting on an inferior work of Balzac in *S/Z*) or his commentary will emerge as a duplicate of the initial work. In neither case will he have served the role of critic as I have defined it, i.e., as a mediator.

If, on the other hand, the critic places himself squarely in the crowd, becomes a nondifferentiable receiver of the work, he may simply be articulating the norm of receptions and become the dispensable reporter. It is in this second category of malfunctioning that the problems raised by the concept of relativism tend to miscarry the intentions and realizations of the created work.

In the late twentieth century there can be no questioning the fact that our world is relative to other worlds, our rainbow relative to other spectrums we know not of—to the light of "second suns," to use the imaginative language of the surrealist André Breton. We receive moonshine and give off earthshine to another globe. We are not a center of the universe, and, unlike Descartes or Kant, most of us no longer believe that whatever concepts we harbor about good, evil, justice, beauty, or truth were there somewhere in the heaven/sky before we came to discover and recognize them. By extension of this nonanthropocentric acceptance of relativism, the nonartist, without any assistance from the critic, could and does conclude more and more that he can thereby equally reject the condominium of artistic values and ignore the frontiers between art and nonart. Of course, this conclusion has a far-reaching effect on the democratization of the arts: everybody on his own terms can accept or reject anything as a work of art by giving his own interpretation of pleasure and meaning attributable to the object/work/image of contemplation. At that point the nonartist no longer needs a critic, and the critic who supports the premise of the critical autonomy of such readers/contemplators/beholders has ipso facto eliminated his own special function. Furthermore, the do-it-yourself concept of reception does away with classifications indicative of value judgments comparing one artist with another, but also determining the better or worse manifestations within the work of a single artist: *Sarrasine* is worth as much as *Le Père Goriot,* a letter written by Flaubert carries as much importance as a page from *Madame Bovary!* What has then disappeared along with the function of the critic is the concept of taste—which is an absolutist intrusion into the relativist world. Actually, today the value-laden word "avant-garde" has taken the place of taste as a director of aesthetic consciousness. If the theory of relativism were to go far enough to eliminate the inhibitions which prevent nonartists from rejecting what has been prerated as "avant-garde," these receivers of the work of art might well reject, in their general rebellion against taste, the noncritical acceptability of the "avant garde" as a value. They might thereupon conclude that, if they do not like the profiles of Picasso or his bovine women, they may be permitted to cause mayhem with them, as Duchamp did with the Mona Lisa.

On the one hand, the elimination of the critic's code of values gives wide potential freedom of assessment to the receiver of the artifact who identifies himself as a critic at large operating under the guidelines of relativism. On the other hand, what happens to the individual who identifies himself as an artist, rather than as a viewer or a beholder, and who also carries into the world of art the relativist concept of the world of material reality? It would appear to such a person that if the relativist comprehension of the real world is applied to the comprehension of the art world, then it must follow that to communicate with persons of such apperceptions, the artist can name anything an art object acceptable to receivers no longer guided by a priori tastes of the collective tradition or of the critic's judgment. If such is the case, the artist need no longer be sensitive to the distinction between the world of measurable reality and the *fiction* world created by artists, in the global sense of the word "artist." In that instance, the transformation of the critic into a reporter can be extended to the artist-person; for he has also become a reporter, identifying himself with the measurable entities of the universe. Having eliminated the differential of art, we have thereby eliminated the mediator who showed the difference, and we have also eliminated the artists, who constituted that distinct and separate category of persons. Anything can presumably be art if it can solicit interpretation, and anyone can thereby be an artist if he can persuade someone to interpret his work. In this pseudoutopia all persons are potentially artists, since anything can be called an artifact as long as someone can so "interpret" it.

The great fallacy is, of course, the presumption that interpretation of an artifact makes of it a work of art. The age of collage is the product of a substratum of belief that entities can be related at random since, in the total schema of the cosmos, all are condemned to remain ignorant of the whole. Just as the notion of providence gave meaning to every act, so centrality gave meaning to every entity. On the contrary, randomness permits arbitrary choices of combinations of entities. Donald Kuspit says: "Collage, for the first time in art, makes uncertainty a method of creation, apparent indeterminacy a procedure." According to Kuspit, then, we can find "the flotsam and jetsam of everyday life set adrift in the collage,"[2] for, with collage, art is nowhere and it is everywhere; it becomes a freewheeling way of dealing with a random material, emblematic of fragmented experience. Perhaps that is a working philosophy of living in the modern world. It is indeed the basis of the obsession with the absurd, according to which even acts of violence and assassinations have no connection to a central emotion or belief. If the acceptance of a gratuitous world destroys the design for living, that is the business of each individual to determine in relation to his private life. But such personal choices do not eliminate, by the same token, the premises upon which the distinction of art as a separate sphere of existence survives.

Art, whether teleological, mimetic, or symbolic, cannot be factored into the common denominator of the real world. Even the recycling of ancient myths in modern literature is obvious evidence that the diachronic connections point to a superorganization that functions independently and makes art immune to the caprices of natural reality. We could go so far as to say that the work of art is as different from the natural object as a fetus is from a cancerous growth: both organisms have cells developing inside the human structure, and those growing uncontrolled could presumably be called an aspect of human "creativity"; but one is an organized pattern, the other a random growth.

If uncertainty and indeterminacy are elements of the human condition highlighted in our modern world, they cannot filter into "modernism" without breaking essential rules of the art universe. In many statements made by writers working in the area of human consciousness rather than in literature and aesthetics, art is being equated with diverse practices of ambiguity. There is a marked difference between the open-ended interpretation of a piece of writing or an artifact according to relative values in an era no longer bound to an absolute code of aesthetics or ethics, and the diversity of interpretations caused by ambiguity of structure indicative of sloppy production. The defense of a "text" mysterious because of faulty, nonsustained design or execution on the basis of its compatibility with our random universe is a very weak defense.

There have been hermetic writings since the beginning of literature. The most eminent recent manifestation is the Symbolist aesthetics of the nineteenth century; its *art poétique* was precisely to construct an intentionally polysemantic network to provoke multiple interpretations and thus enrich the experience of the reader. Indeed I agree with Hayden White that works with the power of symbolization are of the highest level of artistic creativity. As he says, "The extent of its value as an artistic work is marked by the range of response that it induces as an object . . . of self-consciousness about the symbolizing process of which it is an instantiation, in its beholders."[3] But when a message is ambiguous because of inadequate composition, it becomes unacceptable as art, no matter how many interpretations are provoked by its amorphous structure.

Art, to be art, must have an organization, an intention. Even when tapping unconscious data it must at the same time attain support from the human powers of selectivity based on supremely conscious forces of concentration. It has become the fashion in recent criticism to frown upon studies of intentionalism. This attitude was a largely justified reaction, on the part of W. K. Wimsatt and Monroe C. Beardsley[4] and fellow critics of an earlier epoch, against the abuses of overemphasis on what an author was aiming to express, rather than what he did express. Such practices had led to an exaggerated stress on the study of peripheral documents in support of such intentions. But by now the pendulum has swung too far in the opposite direction. If it is indeed foolish to distract the reader from expressed meaning to intended meaning, it is on the other hand a flagrant injury to the artist to disregard, and even to go so far as to contradict, his intentions. In his article "Appreciation and Interpretation of Works of Art," Arthur Danto has the courage to argue that in interpreting a work of art we should not consider the intentions of the author extraneous to our understanding of the work: "I believe we cannot be deeply wrong if we suppose that the correct interpretation of object-as-artwork is the one which coincides most closely with the artist's own interpretation."[5]

When the sincere artist is expressing his intentions, he is not writing up a proposal for funding which may or may not be implemented! He is analyzing his creative process, which is an integral part of his art. He is measuring his potential, estimating his reach. He is making audible his inner struggle, staking the foundations of his edifice. I am convinced that we would not appreciate Rimbaud's *Illuminations* as we do if we did not also read the famous "letter of the seer" which he wrote to his teacher. In fact, his prose poems collected under the title of *Illuminations,* printed in random fashion in the Symbolist magazine *La Vogue* in 1886, and even subsequently collected in a volume, did not make a particular stir until the famous letter was published in 1912, putting the poems in perspective as part of an intended design.

The discussion of process and intentionality is part of the organization of the work of art, the building of an absolute world having its total autonomy under the control of its own god, the artist. He spells out its values, its hierarchy, the relative functions within an integrated whole, satisfying his own and his readers' holistic yearnings.

If the human receiver or beholder of the work of art can survive in a random cosmos (we wonder for how long!), it is because he has come out of the organized process of the fetus, which has given him an inherent model for the process of organization—and no one challenges or tries to deconstruct that natural process of organization. In fact, those scientists who emphasize the quantum theory, the mathematics of probabilities, and biological haphazardness, and those nonscientists who conclude from these assertions that the whole of existence is gratuitous and random are practicing the fallacy of partial truth. If there is an appreciable degree of unpredictability in nature, there are also strict, impeccable timetables of organization such as the development of the unit of life and the cycle of the seasons, not to mention the rotation of the earth around the sun. The organization of the artist deserves the same respect as do nature's organizations. Anyone tampering with the artist's network (such as quoting out of context or psychoanalyzing it according to norms established after and outside of its coded systems) is threatening that survival.

Art is an ontological alternative to religion. In fact, I noticed with some sense of déjà vu in rereading Jacques Maritain's *Frontiers of Poetry* that Maritain was apprehensive about the modern poet's extreme dedication to the creation of an absolute, fictitious existence. Of course, what he called "modern" was turn-of-the-century and early-twentieth-century French poetry. Scrutinizing a tendency toward what, as a theologian, he would call "mystic" objectives in artists who otherwise avowed no religious inclinations, he was uncomfortable with certain of their postulations. In their search for an absolute without God, he, as a man of religion, feared that they might become confused about the poetic absolute and the teleological one. Maritain warned such artists that they might be venturing upon dangerous territory unless they were willing to surrender the poetic for the mystic. But most modern artists who grope for the absolute are not worried about such transgressions; even when they evoke medieval mystics, they secularize them.[6]

That there is a distinct and universally recognized gap between natural reality and the absolute world of the artist can most easily be tested by the fact that receiver-persons least sensitive to art works can nonetheless distinguish without hesitation between what is life and what is a representative creation of life. In support of the theory that there is a more and more apparent trend toward the nondistinction between natural reality and art reality, critics point to that most notorious of examples, the urinal of Marcel Duchamp. Duchamp presumably made the daring leap, crossed the barrier, breached the gap. The essential point overlooked is the manner, the tone, in which the urinal was offered as an artifact. Duchamp's *Fountain*-urinal was a manifesto, as was the moustache put on the Mona Lisa. It was a protest, a deconstructive act, bringing attention to what, to him, was a need to change a superannuated code of art, the very definition of the beautiful,[7] which sent him in search of readymades. He never intended it to be mistaken for an art work in itself. It meant to him what the revolver shot meant to André Breton in his *Second Manifesto:* a call to arms, a provocation, a challenge not to disorder but to reorganization, to the creation of new designs.

In this connection the role of the so-called unconscious must be called into question. Since the turn of the century artists have been said to make efforts to incorporate the givens of the unconscious into art. Automatic writing is a case in point. The harvest of automatic writing was considered by Breton as a supreme gift that life bestowed on the artist from the depth of its mysterious natural resources, but neither he nor coartists such as Soupault, Eluard, Dali, or Miró equated the disorganized data of the unconscious with art. In Breton's vocabulary, automatism is a factor; but another word follows ever in its traces, and that word is "vigilance." The unconscious can only be funneled into art if it is monitored by vigilance, which controls its randomness. Even the earliest enthusiasts of modern psychology, such as James Joyce, were cautious of the uses of streams of consciousness. Molly Bloom's monologue is not a replay of a taped random discourse. And Proust's so-called involuntary remembrances are artistic subterfuges. Let us not for a moment be fooled into thinking that the madeleine dipped into the cup of tea acted like a magic wand to recapture a long-lost reality and give it a verbal reincarnation as a natural and spontaneous matter of consequence. Perhaps a luminous moment was sparked, but Proust's reconstruction of the absolute world of the artist from the relative world of his memory was not an instant handout. To equate the Proustian childhood with the synthetic one he names and creates in his aesthetic search[8] is as naive as a recent researcher's slide collection of Valéry's native town of Sète, offered as an aid in the effort to capture the reality of "Le Cimetière marin."

Currently, the critic is more often guilty of pursuing the nondistinction between life and art then are the nonprofessional readers or viewers of the arts. The deliberate confusion perpetrated between the relative world in which we live and the absolute world in which art is nurtured and functions leads to a methodology of criticism that may well accelerate the demise of the arts. Sociology, psychoanalysis, linguistics, and philosophy have all adjusted their optic to a revision whereby the rejection of the absolute has been expressed by a reedited terminology. It determines and evaluates phenomena which, emptied of previous assumptions of autonomous codes, can now be interpreted according to newer concepts (no longer definitive) of life, time, space, and human responses. Now the critic, following the line of these inquiries into life, freed of absolutism, attempts to apply the language of inquiry to a domain which, in order to prevail, must maintain its yearning for the absolute (even in its current form of immanence rather than transcendence) as its sine qua non. It has been said that the new critic deconstructs linguistic codes that are prejudicial to the meanings inherent in the basic structures of the text-artifact. I would suggest that most often he succeeds in deconstructing the organization of the work of art itself, rather than the supposed residue of prejudices. For instance, in defining "symbol" Paul Ricoeur talks of "surplus of signification," thereby failing to distinguish between the nature of art and the nature of life. In nature's wilderness there are surpluses of weeds, and these surpluses are only in our human perspective; in the good gardener's terrain there are no surpluses, because nature's surpluses have been weeded out. Even so, when a viewer measures the work of art on a relative scale of less, adequate, too much and feels a "surplus," he is blind to the basic substance of artistic value. There is no surplus in the absolute totality of the work of art.

But if relativism is the inevitable philosophy of the age, is it driving modern man in a direction where art cannot follow? Or must art follow at the risk of losing its intrinsic differential? Must it run that risk, rather than cease to be a need in human life? My position is that the situation calls for neither resistance nor capitulation to relativism. There are ways of accommodating to it without identifying relativism as a basis for a new concept of the arts. It is one thing to view the artifact from the adjusted vantage point of a relativist optic, and quite a different thing to transplant artificially the relativist optic *into* the work of art.

Esoteric writers such as Mallarmé, Rimbaud, and Yeats and reticent ones such as neoclassicists have been the victims of the kind of interpretation that substitutes for their absolute codes certain relativist, permissive ones culled from recent ideologies. Synchronic approaches to their works rob them of their pristine meanings by suggesting that arbitrary meanings may be read into them. The process turns the work of art into a "text" or document, bringing it out of the absolute realm of the artist into the relativist one of the critic who has retreated from his intermediary stance back into the world of those for whom he presumably interprets.

But, one might ask, what is the alternative? In reading Rimbaud or gazing upon an El Greco, must our objective be simply to become aware of the breach, of the distance between our comprehension of the universe and theirs? In ages when real life was controlled by absolute values, as was the world of artists, the correspondence between life and its representation in the arts was easier. Of course, there is the danger that, if we can kill art by imposing on it a relativity incompatible with its intrinsic nature, we can also destroy it by increasing the gap between life as we now understand it and art, thus producing a diminution and eventual absence of communication between the two. I must concede that the current use of tools inappropriate to the decoding of art is, in a sense, prompted by the desire to find a level of communication between the artist and his search for reception. But this objective can be accomplished without violating the intention or meaning of the work of art. We can engage in comparative approaches, rather than artificially impose a process of identification.

Take, for instance, the matter of point of view in narrative: it is a question that has become almost an obsession of literary analysts. By contrast, most novelists were not overtly concerned with the problem until recently, and even in the twentieth century it has not been a major preoccupation for many of the most renowned writers. Modern psychologists, on the other hand—and legally oriented detective-story writers—have made current readers very sensitive to the process of detection of point of view and the relative interpretations of behavior such variations can bring about, bearing directly on determinations of truth, sincerity, deceit. As a result of such interest, works of art are reexamined to point out the "fallacies" in the apperceptions of omniscient writers and viewers subjected to disparate points of view. Awareness of this mechanism of point of view encouraged by a relativist attitude causes the critic to impose heavy burdens on works whose authors made no issue of this element of novel structure. The classic example is Sartre's article on François Mauriac,[9] in which he accuses the novelist of playing God by knowing, contrary to the rule of plausibility, the workings of several minds at the same time. Mauriac is accused, consequently, of creating a predictability of behaviors that may be in the power of gods to effect but that would confound psychologists. What Sartre overlooks is the fact that Mauriac's fictitious world does not consist of casebook histories; rather, it is his own private property, controlled not by laws handed down by Moses but according to the options of the creator of the novel. If Sartre wants to enter Mauriac's universe as a reader, he must accept the rules of Mauriac's game—or, having acknowledged that those rules are different from those he practices in the world of reality, he has the choice of comparing his world with Mauriac's artistic one, and thus exercising his role as a mediator. What he is not called upon to do is to impose *his* reality upon Mauriac's, and then chastise him for breaking his own (Sartre's) set of rules.

There has been controversy over critical methodologies and attitudes to which the notion of creativity is central. Because the barriers between genres have been lowered and the separations between media have been bridged by what is known as multimedia artifacts, does this phenomenon justify the infringement of the critic upon the realm of creativity? Many are taking a free-trade attitude, admitting the permissive character of art by all and for everybody's sake. I have no quarrel with anyone who wants to call his shoe a work of art, but I dare any critic to redescribe René Magritte's *Le Modèle rouge* in such a way that it can fit his lower extremity and serve him in the act of walking. That he may create his own model is his own business, but that he may infringe on some other person's model simply means, in critical (as in political) terminology, that he is usurping the absolute authority of the proprietor over his own domain.

Of course, it is far easier to protest than to predicate, and the second part of this essay will prove that point by being much shorter. My focus so far has been on the behavior of the critic committed to relativism; my observation has been of the realm of the existing art works, most of which through the generations of Western culture are the product of an absolute universe. Now let us turn to the artist himself, as he stands on the shifting sands, passing from absolute codes to relative ones in the realm of human behavior. Let us observe how the change has affected the search for the absolute in the domain of the arts. How have artists coped with the situation and, further, how can we suggest that they cope with it? Are they ready to decontrol art and surrender it to life? Or can they proceed as if nothing has happened? Is there a third alternative in trying to represent the relativist attitude toward life within the context of a controlled artifact? Artists have been answering "yes" to all three questions. Some have indeed abandoned the distinction between life and art: the makers of found poetry, concrete art, happenings, autobiographies that are in fact a collage of taped automatic discourses interspersed with strips of fantasy. I would be loath to call the authors of such production "artists" unless I could find a conscious principle of composition consistently observed throughout their work. There are also those who, according to their own codes, reflect or represent the random universe. Samuel Beckett is a past master of the art of representing the absurd character of the cosmos, but in reading him we are not meant to attribute to Molloy or Moran anything but a fictitious existence. It has been a critical fallacy to identify the personal philosophy of artists such as Beckett or Camus or Sartre with the attitudes of characters they have created to fit into contrived social contexts in which the gratuitous is heavily stacked.

In this respect, it is interesting to examine J. Hillis Miller's article about Faulkner's *Absalom, Absalom!*[10] He examines evidence of what might be judged to be (but is not) faulty construction in Faulkner's narration techniques involving vacillations in point of view and repetitions of narrations, both of which suggest an ambiguity of design. Then he explains that these ambiguities correspond to the lack of design in the lives of real-life characters. Normally, he says, storytellers "go beyond mimesis, to create something which is one degree or another a fiction not wholly grounded in its exact correspondence to things as they are." In the case of Faulkner he finds that the author desists from "making something happen" out of noncohesive facts of the reality he has observed. In other words, he effects an "analogy between the failure of a design in life and the failure of narration." Miller proposes that "this failure of a narration is, for Faulkner, the evidence of its validity, since only the failed narration, which exposes its loose ends and inconsistencies, can be an adequate representation." He concludes that in its very failure "as coherent design," Faulkner's novel finds its ultimate design, "which is to give knowledge, however indirect and fleeting, not of the facts of history or of life, but of the enigmatic power behind these." In this extremely subtle analysis which ascertains the process of Faulkner's deliberate ambiguity, Miller is suggesting that the closer observation of life and the subordination of the natural instinct of the artist to put order in the disorder and coherence into the randomness of life have indeed brought Faulkner into closer correspondence with mimesis, not through reportage (as it would have been in the case of avowed naturalists) but by accommodation of the creative process to the natural storytelling process. He shows his confidence in Faulkner's techniques of composition when, step by step, he demonstrates the deliberate elements of ambiguity by which Faulkner suggests the ambivalence of life itself. The work of Faulkner is "ambiguous," then, only to the logical mind viewing the work of art according to rules applicable to a documentary. It is highly compatible with the artist's interpretation of the nature of human existence.

So far, the analysis of Faulkner's intentions and creative success in seeming failure holds together convincingly. But as a mediator between the reader and the artist, perhaps the critic can go one step further in the analysis of indeterminacy. We could suggest that documentary reportage can also convey the inconsistencies of human behavior. How do we differentiate between the documentary text communicating the inconsistencies of behavior and a work of art having the same objectives? I would argue that in assessing ambiguities in the work of art, three dimensions should be considered by the critic as I have earlier defined him in the role of mediator. We have to discover whether the ambiguities have occurred because of faulty organization and composition, or whether they have been prompted by a desire for a greater approximation of reality (approaching, indeed, the structure of a documentary). Miller's explanation in the case of *Absalom, Absalom!* leans toward this second form of ambiguity. But the communication of ambiguities can also become part and parcel of a new form of artistic construction rejecting the mimetic for the artificial; in this case the artist persuades us to accept the contrived defaults of narration as a system of correspondences with human indeterminacy. In the course of this process he raises our vision to a level of creative fiction where these indeterminacies become acceptable to us. This process is more frequent in poetry than in prose. For instance, in Yeats the golden bird of Byzantium is a permanent existence although not a real one, situated in a location lifted by the artist out of passing historicity. In questioning the degree and manner of the artifice and the artist's control of the relative factors, the mediator has a valid basis for evaluating the quality of the work of art—not in terms of its current relevance to the relativist optic, any more than in terms of a teleological preestablished code of values, but according to his ability to be consistent in the manipulation of inconsistencies intentionally implanted in the artifact.

The development of creative ambiguity as the artist's response to the compounding of indeterminacy in cosmic and human movement was indeed the basis of Symbolist aesthetics, of which Mallarmé was the most notable and conscious master. In his aesthetics of ambiguity Mallarmé was not accommodating to relativism (which, as a thoroughly avowed agnostic, he accepted) but competing with it. In techniques that are very consistent, very precise and unambiguous, he developed an art of ambiguity to suggest on the artist's own terms the questionable human condition among dead constellations and blind paths and unexpected collisions in unguided vessels and in undirected courses. Hermeneutic criticism that produces exegesis to solve unilaterally the riddle of these symbolist poetic structures is a reductive process which actually transforms the creative simulation of relativism into a form of absolute meaning. A critical approach that would be much more relevant to the spirit of Symbolist *écriture* is the study of the artistic process and the identification of the components which succeed (and in some cases fail) to suggest the uncertainty of phenomena and the plurality of meaning (not surplus).

But the response to relativism which I would predicate, in lieu of the abdication of the absolute or the simulation of the relative with the controlled tools of the artist, is the attitude of certain moderns who, in the face of relativity of values and randomness of phenomena, cling the more closely to that world of the arts where they can create their own code and maneuver as they please, according to their own creative systems. They do not, as of old, latch onto a supernal organization; rather, in their longing for an absolute, they reinterpret the sacred in human terms and through human form.

The revised definition of "sacred" means essentially immunization from interference, possession of its own sacrament, a system of symbolization of which the correspondences are strictly intramural or self-referential to start and become intermural only when other artists accept the signal-making character of the work, a sign of the seminal power and "greatness" in the recycled definition of the word. It is "influence" in its most creative, transformational sense, and it was the basis of the remarkable spread of Symbolist poetry. The symbols that Mallarmé generated related to each other, and he indicated the role of the reader as an interpreter. The mediation was to be an internal one barring infringement from the external world. In that sense *Hérodiade* is an achievement of process, whereas *The Afternoon of a Faun* is a meditation on process. *Hérodiade* is the self-contained universe of the artist as represented by the enclosure in which the princess lives; the commentary of the nurse could be likened to critical interpretation which, in its effort to associate Hérodiade with the outside world, has no relevance to the enclosure. When the nurse touches Hérodiade's hair, her repulsion is that of the artist attacked by forces outside itself. The myth of Salome itself had become so common in the era that it had lost its autonomy in relation to the ordinary world, and by substituting the name Hérodiade for Salome, Mallarmé was making a revision—an effort to reconstruct the fiction itself, which had deviated into the mire of ordinary reality and lost the distance from it which a true myth usually preserves.

It is often pointed out that the surrealists broke with the cloistered world of the nineteenth-century aesthetes to return to the world of daily existence and to utilize it in poetic communication. The conclusion drawn from such a general statement might well be that, more than any previous group, they had arrived at the nondistinction between the real and the artistic. Had not André Breton stated in *Surrealism and Painting* that the surreal resides in the real? But he did not thereby equate the one with the other. The surrealists took the trouble to explain more explicitly than any previous coterie the process of transformation from the real to the artifact, precisely because of their awareness that the problem of relativism and its connections with the poet ("poet" taken in the broad sense of the word, encompassing the painter as well) was of more direct and urgent concern than it had ever been considered before.

The primary objective in the case of the surrealists was to recuperate the random and the senseless, the automatic and the fortuitous, and to introduce these elements into a controlled universe through the monitoring of the activity of the imagination, which in Breton's definition becomes a powerhouse of creativity. The rebus-type of poetic/plastic imagery utilized by ancient Kabbalists to suggest the hermetic character of a meaningful universe was appropriated as a central form of cognition and communication in surrealist writing and art, to convert the ambiguity of the void-cosmos into a multiplicity of desires named/consummated by the creative power of the poet/painter. This form of creative writing or painting predicates that nature's indifferent chance-mechanism can be channeled to satisfy human intentions, that disparate existences found in natural reality can be aligned into coherent correspondences in a universe in which the artifacts produce interrelationships.

Pascal's accommodation to human frailty was grounded in the proposition that the intellect's power to recognize physical mortality in a universe whose purposes were hidden from man gave him a certain power over the forces of darkness. We find in surrealist doctrine a total philosophic reversal: man's power over his ephemeral existence resides in his ability to engender purpose *where there is none,* placing a value on human creativity higher than that of a blind nature which gains its visibility through the artifact. American intellectuals interested in problems of relativism as it affects modernism should study the works of Breton more closely than they have up to now. Breton tackled the fundamental problem of our era and, in large measure, learned to cope with it: how to preserve the power and dignity of the artist in a teleologically undermined cosmos. He provided a philosophical basis to the need to revise notions of beauty in order to preserve beauty from total extinction. He set new norms for the quest for the absolute without naive displays of adherence to superannuated structures. His was not the secular humanism of classic vintage that placed man at the center of the *existing* universe—against which much of modernism protests. Instead, he made a broad-based appeal to the artist to confirm his centrality in the universe of the artifact, in the face of an admittedly nonanthropocentric universe.

In an article called "The Death of the Author," included in a collection characteristically called *The Discontinuous Universe,* Roland Barthes attempts to wrench the work of art from the control of its author and to surrender it to the caprices of the reader. He tells us that "a text is not in its origin, it is in its destination, but this destination can no longer be personal: the reader is a man without history, without biography, without psychology; he is only that *someone* who holds gathered into a single field all the paths of which the text is constituted."[11] I find this statement not only fallacious but perverse, reflecting Barthes's warped, twisted notion of collectivism.

Unity is organization; without a directed construct there would be, as I have attempted to demonstrate, no act of creation. Such a "text" would be worthy only of biopsy, not of appreciation or inspiration or desire for comprehension. After dispossessing the creator of the "text," Barthes proceeds to disown the reader by declaring him anonymous, nonhistorical, apsychological, in fact a monster from outer space. What he is probably trying to say obliquely is that many influences form a writer, and that these influences are amalgamated into his writings, to be perceived by future readers of diverse formations; no particular message can be handed down from one author to all readers in this relative world of fluctuating meanings. We could argue that by the very negatively expressed manner of his statement, he transforms a truism into a demolition of the creative function, robbing it of individuality, stifling it in ambiguity, and making it the target of an impersonal, amorphous reception on the part of an equally ambiguous, featureless humanity. If the emphasis on the word "without" is meant to suggest, in its negation of the specific, a multiplicity and diversity of receptions, the meaning is colored by a language that attributes to the human creature a dismembered, disconnected character, the better to underline the discontinuity with which he, Barthes, is himself obsessed. It delivers art into the stream of spatial floating. Theories of relativity applied to the arts have given Barthes an excuse for the devalorization of Western culture without offering an alternative. Other post-Sartrian pessimists have taken the same line of dogmatic postulations; for example, Derrida's disquieting attacks on referentiality, perception, and valorization in any form. The didacticism of the critic is projected onto the work of art, as evidenced in a quotation from Jack Burnham's "Systems Esthetics": "The specific function of modern didactic art has been to show that art does not reside in material entities, but in relations between people and between people and the components of their environment."[12] Such a statement evokes cognitive disciplines, rather than the activities in the field of the arts.

It seems to me that, more than ever before, it is imperative to gear to full capacity the power of the artistic imagination to combat the increasingly amorphous appearance of the world in which the human species finds itself. As individual performance and affirmation become more and more difficult in a society where we are bunched together in a state which Beckett calls "namelessness," the dominion of the artist over the fictitious world of his creation needs to be guarded both against the tools of inquiry intended for the comprehension of the material universe and against assessments on a scale of relative values from which the classification as "art" excludes it categorically.

The demise of absolute values may make the universe collapse, as perceived by Beckett's character Molloy: "I listen and the voice is of a world collapsing endlessly." Beckett describes what man might become under an indifferent sky, like Moran "ready to go without knowing where he was going consulting neither map nor timetable." But when Beckett writes of "anguish of vagrancy and freedom" he is talking of ordinary *Homo* not so *sapiens,* not of the artist. In highly Christian periods the arts were known to reinforce the spiritual concepts of the absolute. We can no longer expect that, but in the current acentric era the survival of any semblance of the arts depends on the artist's assumption of a role of leadership in a domain abandoned by its previous proprietors. The undermining of the spiritual absolute under the weight of evidences of relativity as a controlling factor of the universe calls for retaliation. We have drifted too long in the interregnum which Mallarmé declared almost a hundred years ago. Survivors of the millennium cannot abide in the sites of deconstruction; they must forge ahead. They cannot be expected to respond to pretentious simulations of a gratuitous universe by splashes of paint on canvas and the juggling of words on paper in the name of "art." There has to come a point when "post" becomes "pre," when late night is recognized as predawn.

NOTES

This essay first appeared in *Relativism in the Arts*, edited by Betty Jean Craige (Athens: University of Georgia Press, 1983), pp. 75–98.

1. If I am to pronounce myself on relativism, I have to do it as a critic and first define that role as I see it in relation to the general reader and the creative writer.
2. Donald B. Kuspit, "Collage: The Organizing Principle of Art in the Age of the Relativity of Art," in *Relativism in the Arts*, ed. Betty Jean Craige (Athens: University of Georgia Press, 1983).
3. Hayden White, "The Limits of Relativism in the Arts," in ibid.
4. William K. Wimsatt, *The Verbal Icon: Studies in the Meaning of Poetry* (Lexington: University Press of Kentucky, 1954).
5. Arthur C. Danto, "The Appreciation and Interpretation of Works of Art," in *Relativism in the Arts*.
6. Such was the objective of André Breton in his search for process in the alchemical writers of the Middle Ages, among them Nicolas Flamel and Abraham the Jew; he shared no religious beliefs with them.
7. Cf. Aragon, *Anicet,* for the parody of the search for the new beauty.
8. Let us not overlook the fact that the word Proust used was *recherche* and not *souvenir*—an active, creative search, and not a passive reception. Why the translators continue to use the wrong word escapes my understanding!
9. Jean-Paul Sartre, *Situations,* vol. 1 (Paris: Gallimard, 1947).
10. J. Hillis Miller, "The Two Relativisms: Point of View and Indeterminacy in the Novel," in *Relativism in the Arts*.
11. Roland Barthes, "The Death of the Author," in *The Discontinuous Universe,* ed. Sallie Sears and Georgianna W. Lord (New York: Basic Books, 1972), p. 12.
12. Jack Burnham, *Great Western Salt Works* (New York: George Braziller, 1974), p. 16.

VIII

MULTICULTURALISM
THE CASE OF SURREALISM

In the case of every intellectual upheaval I have witnessed in the past half century, surrealism has served as a base and as a trampoline from which to project isolated ideas into a context and become part of a continuity. I have been sorry to observe that so many philosophical, psychological, sociological, even scientific writers, groping for solidarity and holistic perceptions, have failed to connect with one of the most remarkable revolutions of the intellect in our time, surrealism. The journalistic uses of the term "surrealist" are a blight on human understanding and an offense to the search for breakthroughs in the ever-renewed human pursuit of re-adjustment to the nonanthropocentric universe, which was, of course, previously suspected but has emerged as an undebatable factor in current episteme.

Surrealism is not the extremely absurd; it is not a game to shock, not a provocation to violence. The general ignorance of its many positive meanings is not the fault of those who use the word indiscriminately. It is the result of series of very unfortunate occurrences in the dissemination of literary and philosophical currents in the Western world. That such an immense body of writing and other artistic expression missed for so long to be included in the education canon is an extraordinary phenomenon. Prejudice kept it out of the universities of the country where it originated until 1968; that is to say, its out-of-print works did not reach the educated French readership until almost fifty years after the flowering of surrealism. As a result, two generations of French intellectuals have been deprived of all but superficial knowledge of surrealism and have unwittingly excluded it from their frame of reference, which became heavy with ideologies that preceded and succeeded surrealism. Thus it lost its rightful place as a potentially massive referent in the theoretical dialogue. Translation projects that might have given our largely monolingual American intellectuals access to surrealism were slow to occur, and when they emerged in the seventies they appeared in small editions and went out of print before university students and scholars had a chance to realize how pertinent these writings were to their social and moral concerns. So it is that structuralism, deconstruction, hermeneutics, and most recently what is being called multiculturalism, all of which fall within the agenda of the surrealists and can throw light on their theories, have failed to drink at this abundant source.

But there is a philosophical difference between current notions of multiculturalism and the multicultural vision that was an essential part of the doctrine of surrealism.

Following the historical course of the present century one can perceive two ideological countermovements: nationalism and internationalism. The nineteenth century had witnessed the development of national identities all over Europe and at the same time ethnic resistances in the non-European world against European imperialism. The surging nationalisms created, as we know, the polarization of national rivalries, leading to a global divisive war early in our century, and perpetuated psychological antagonisms and political unrest for the balance of the century. Counteracting these assertive and aggressive nationalisms there arose in the wake of World War I two great waves of internationalism, espousing a common goal, to overcome paternal nationalism through fraternal internationalism: namely, international communism, and surrealism. And for a while it seemed as if they could join forces and be contained as one. But neither together nor separately did they prevent a second world war, which did not eradicate ethnic politics.

Communism failed to sustain that brotherhood of little people fighting oppressive dominations at home and abroad; it barely held together by force rather than persuasion ethnically diverse national entities within their borders only to let the end of the century witness the disintegration of a dream of integration of all the working classes of the world who were supposed to put their common lot above nationalistic concerns. The other, whose premise of universal liberty was identifiable with the liberation of the creative spirit in all men and women of all levels and classes, aimed at bringing together those who could be linked globally in free union and set an example for the larger unification. The aspiration was a higher basis of human cohesion than the national one. It has not yet succeeded in its broadest goal, but on the other hand it has not failed. All the modern arts have been affected by surrealism, consciously or even unconsciously, as in the case of the so-called postmoderns. And when the former admirable president of the former Czechoslovakia, Vaclav Havel, declared the end of the modern era, he forgot that "modern" is a label of transitory character referring always to the present and although much of the twentieth century's visions are no longer "modern," modernism still prevails in surrealism with an ever-renewable mechanism on an issue which the current moderns are treating politically and which surrealists have been probing for almost a century: the real and deep meaning of multiculturalism.

In his last public interview in 1964, André Breton declared that "we are all surrealists." But the sense of collective destiny confronting a world of divisiveness was quite different from what we mean politically when we talk of multiculturalism and when the *clé de voûte* of intellectual dialogue is *difference* in all the spellings and fluctuations of the word.

Let us examine the history of the surrealist alliance the better to understand what its potential may still hold for us in the conundrum of current multiculturalism.

Breton took his cue from the Dada group that had met in Zurich on neutral ground, linked in a shared repudiation of both national politics and the arts. At first dazzled by Dada,

Breton launched his own movement on an international scale in Paris, which of course had long been both a national and an international center. Though he kept the Dada language of rejection, his revolution had its very positive side, rejection linked to a sense of cooperation without rivalry on issues of concern to all humans: to exercise the imagination, discover the power of the dream on creative behavior, find a link between human and natural forces in the universe, to preserve a lifelong exuberance of youth, to use the power of language in provoking celebration, to raise to the highest degree the power to love, and finally to be disturbed by that chameleon and ever-present factor in life, the sense of beauty and its variations.

Although Breton strongly disliked Cartesian rationalism, he borrowed a very important device from Descartes which gave a universal element to his quest. To place his readers on their common denominator of mental capacity, Descartes had asserted that what we all share is "common sense." He thus put his readers on an equal footing with himself and with each other. Something we already possess at birth is so much more tangible than "equal opportunity." In the case of Breton's proposition, the common treasures are *desire* and *dream*. He starts his *First Manifesto* with "Man that definitive dreamer," and with all due respect to gender monitors, "man" here refers to both genders. If we can hang on to common sense, thought Descartes, we can dispose of all else, do a tabula rasa or deconstruction, and come out ahead. Of course Descartes was too optimistic and also too timid to proceed beyond the verbal. He did not try to implement his objective by action or in his writings.

Breton was a bit bolder. He had the French Revolution behind him. The revolutionary tone he adopted called upon an international coalition to join him in his attacks against common enemies: standardization in education, in religion, and even in the newly emerging psychiatry, which, he thought, had not fulfilled its promises.

He formed in the heart of Paris a loosely bound fraternity as nationally diverse in its composition as the League of

Nations. All who joined him were more loyal to their artistic or creative resources than to the countries from which they arrived at the rue Fontaine. Breton confronted quite a problem: to sort out the impostors, charlatans, and fugitives from justice or the revolver-prone from the genuine artists. There was, for instance, an Indian who paced his studio floor in ecstatic praise of surrealism only to betray little by little ulterior motives for seeking entry into the conclave. Whereupon he was precipitately pushed down the three flights of stairs.

A comparison of the surrealists' form of multiculturalism with that of Romanticism illustrates fundamental differences. All through Europe and making later inroads into the rest of the world, Romanticism manifested itself as a nationally rooted literary and artistic flowering, intimately connected with the burgeoning nationalistic consciousness. The relationships between Romantic *cénacles* were sparse and nonsynchronic whereas in every case the national heritage was central. National events yielded their subjects to artistic expression and often gave the works their particular resonance.

To the contrary, when *cénacles* developed around surrealism in countries other than France the rapport was much more ecumenical; the adherents, regardless of their ethnic backgrounds, drank in the blended waters of that well that was not foreign to any one of them: that Paris of the 1920s. In fact the Paris of the artists had little to do with France except in the use of the French language, which was remodeled to serve as an international medium.

The soil of this unique Paris had already been prepared by the previous coterie of the Symbolists. They too, coming from everywhere, from as far away as China, had sowed the seeds of internationalism in the arts. There was a strong precedent there although their purposes for the arts were quite different. They wanted togetherness to hide from reality, whereas the togetherness of the surrealists proposed to proceed into reality and to change it.

Those who gathered under the banner of surrealism were

quite diverse in terms of ethnic characteristics. In fact, the paradox of the very ethnically different creating a uniquely nonethnocentric bonding is at the heart of the matter.

First of all is the case of Breton. There were very regional qualities in this Frenchman who recognized and even hailed the North in himself and his Celtic kinship with Chateaubriand. "I delight in the wetlands," echoed this child of Brittany and declared his affinity with the misty ocean. The Gaelic heritage of Great Britain and Ireland was linked with continental Brittany in medieval times by a common body of myths from which Breton always drew for his idiosyncratic purposes. This closeness of race and milieu prevailed throughout his life in a tug of war between the regional *soi* (ethos) and the international *moi* (conscious and personal desire to link with others from other places). Everyone has his dream house, the site he or she or we might call the final living space before the eventual resting place. Breton chose St. Cirq la Pôpie in the heart of France, enveloped in medieval structure and legend, a hidden, private France, remote from touristic itineraries, where the Lot River crosses over stones that bear the memory of millenniums and where vestiges of Cro-Magnon fossils are embedded. One would not be wrong to surmise that he was groping for cultural roots in the heart of the native land. Other signs of cultural conservation were apparent: the revolutionary black shirt could not conceal the inculcated grace of a bourgeois gentleman who used the pluperfect subjunctive frequently in his monolinguistic deployment of the French language which he had guarded pure through his global wanderings. But the culture that inhabited him did not have a tinge of xenophobia, nor for that matter any visible gender conflict. He possessed a certain old-fashioned gallantry, revealed in his poetry as well as in the way he kissed a woman's hand. There was here cultural preservation in matters of idiom, behavior, and geography, and there was awareness of the genetic heritage in terms of how you saw beauty, how you perceived the power of the sacred while you screamed diatribes against established religions. But these elements were reconciled with that even more dominant trait whereby he would seek out fellow artists of totally different cultural background and find with them a kinship far more firmly soldered than with the rank and file of his compatriots. It was of Breton that he was thinking when Malcolm de Chazal, a writer from the island of Mauritius in the Indian Ocean, said: "a true mind cannot belong to a physical nation; it leaves that kind of thing to regional minds." Indeed, whatever ethnicity he harbored all his life, Breton was to adopt a nonnational attitude in his values on art and politics.

Of a very different breed was Max Ernst, that frontier brand of German, a mixture of Prussian and Black Forest with regimented precision in his writing and painting but ever prone to the shattering caused by a hard-to-control puckish imagination. Then there was Salvador Dali, from another borderline culture: the Catalan whose image of the tranquil sea was quite different from Breton's turbulent Atlantic. His exterior vivacity and explosive humor had nothing in common with the subtlety and stately manner of Breton nor the meditative wryness of Ernst.

And then let the fan open wide: we see them enter into a spiritual climate by means of the great artery of the dream, the blending of ethnic mythologies, the concerted cult of the inwardly directed eye which among multiple variants of landscapes creates a conductor between things and consequently beings, the eye which becomes something other than a reflecting mirror. And so there is a bonding between very disparate humans: between the Romanian Victor Brauner and the English Leonora Carrington in the way they catch anomalies, between the Silesian Wolfgang Paalen and Ernesto Domingez of Tenerife in the Canary Islands in the way they liquidize landscapes; there is a dialogue of imagery in the manner in which the Mexican Octavio Paz associates Aztec images with surrealist ones; Malcolm Chazal's "volupté" has much to do with the African Léopold Senghor's blending of human and natural dynamics; that delicate Dorothea Tanning creates phantasms in the surrealist focus that joins her to Toyen, the earth-mother central European I once met as she was bathing in the Lot close to Breton's summer home. The rainbow coalition of the surrealists included Wilfredo Lam, that African-Indian-Chinese-European born in Cuba; the rabbinical Kurtz Seligmann, who taught Breton the mysteries of the Kabbala; the Czech Viteslav Nezval, who invited the surrealists to Prague; the Yugoslav Marco Ristich, who was to become ambassador to France; the Swede Max Walter Svanberg; the Japanese Takiguchi; the Californian Man Ray and the Connecticut-bred Kay Sage; the Armenian Archile Gorky, whom Breton discovered in New York—all shedding national labels to assimilate the surrealist one. In this respect surrealism electrified the island republics even more markedly. Beside the Mauritian and those of the Canary Islands, surrealism bound the whole sector of the Caribbean. On his way into temporary self-exile in America during World War II, Breton made a first stop in Martinique, where he was received by Aimé Césaire, the most prominent poet of the Antilles, whom Breton called "the fresh supply of oxygen" and in whom he noted to a dramatic degree the capacity for refusal, i.e., the language of rejection. In Haiti, on his way back from exile, Breton with the surrealist subversiveness of his voice catalyzed revolution against a dictatorship. He was hosted by Saint-Aude Magloire, whom Breton characterized as "the wheel of anguish geared for ecstasy." Jean-Louis Bedoin, who gives such conclusive details about the union of surrealists worldwide in his book *Vingt ans de surréalisme* (1939–59), observes the international dimensions of black surrealism: "the black poets expect to speak for all, and not only for themselves and their racial brotherhood."

Perhaps the most widespread area where surrealism is actively ingrained is in the culture of Latin America. I have had personal contact with some of the writers and painters of Argentina and Chile, tried to capture the surrealist dream spirit in my translation of a posthumously published work of the Chilean poet Rosamel del Valle, and followed closely the work of the ever-productive poet-painter Ludwig Zeller, now residing in Canada. In these and many others I have observed the most successful expressions of seamless multiculturalism. There is a total knowledge and respect of the European background of the movement, in terms of both theory and praxis, kneaded into the native dough: the dream verging on nightmare, a special use of language to sustain them and convey a deeper layer of the subconscious, of human beauty's baptism in natural flora and fauna, of the dynamics of sexual attraction in concordance with the structures of cosmic phenomena, the mingling of the *moi* with the *soi* on the level of consciousness where the singular subjectivity of the writer is absorbed into the plural "we" and the collective pristine experiences of human existence.

Finally, what drives surrealism most directly into aboriginal mythopoeic is the blending of the chthonian with the ethereal. This is particularly striking in surrealism's identification with the anthropophagy of Brazilian native fundamentalism and its battle rites in which prisoners foreign to the tribe, among them European captives, became subject to cannibalism. The devouring of Europeans in colonial times becomes in terms of surrealism the devouring of European culture, analogically speaking, thus abolishing it and at the same time assimilating it.

But this long chain of multicultural adhesions to surrealism must not be construed as links among idiosyncratic loners detaching themselves from their various nationalities. They were joined from the beginning by very typical, purebred Frenchmen from the heart of France such as Marcel Jean, Paul Eluard, André Masson, Jehan Mayoux, as well as by very standard-looking Belgians such as René Magritte and Paul Nougé.

What indeed was the power of cohesion that turned all into a dynamic amalgam that generated on this old Western culture such a rich harvest of genetically altered fruits? Was it the product of a melting pot treated to microwave-heat intensity? I don't think so. Was there heterotopia involved which causes, Foucault tells us, the confrontation of distant realities? No. While utilizing ethnic resources, the surrealist phenomenon was not confrontational within its own orbit; it was not a sterile aberration. Instead, it was a euphorically motivated attraction of differing forces and heritages raised to a superethnic level, or lowered to an infraethnic base.

Beneath the fervent desire to pursue the arts in fraternal collaboration there was tremendous respect for the autochthonous characteristics of each, these very traits that had been obliterated by the cultural neutralization caused by standardized perceptions of ethnicity.

The surrealists dusted off these superficial cultural stereotypes to find the features of the linkage through the primordial. It was as if they were saying to the whole world: go find your cultural treasure and bring it to us to satisfy our mutual needs for freedom and joy, the better to tolerate the ominous sameness of the human condition! Try to distinguish between the obvious diversities and the substrata of unity that lie hidden! And mainly these cultures of what we call incorrectly the Third World all recognized the power of "the savage eye" of which Breton had spoken as early as in his first edition of *Surrealism and Painting* (1928). Breton sought out "the so-called primitive vision" which could create "a synthesis of sensorial perception with mental representation" *(Entretiens),* and he recognized it most in black sculpture and in the plastic configurations of the works of what he called the red race.

When some years ago I confronted Claude Lévi-Strauss with the fact that Breton had used "savage" in that fertile sense (and not as the opposite of "civilized"), before Lévi-Strauss made it famous, he admitted that the same ship had brought them to America.

At the source of all these ethnicities there were common wonders, clothed in different ways of expression so that multiculturalism was not a vying process or a battle for supremacy or separation but an opportunity to enrich the human species as a whole and lay the groundwork for communion. Among surrealists there may have been rivalries in terms of leadership of the group, but they showed no rivalry as creative artists in terms of their art. They all shunned literary prizes. They aimed at a planet without a visa. In Breton's important series of interviews *Entretiens,* which serves as his biography and has never been translated into English, he states that he would not opt for the abolition of history but would aspire to the *re*writing of it as "a universal history more and more needed every day to oppose the national histories" (my own translation of p. 284). It would be written collectively and aimed at global reception.

When Breton had observed the growing amount of power play in the Communist party, he had withdrawn from it; nonetheless he retained some of the basic premises of Marxism, particularly that of the original notion of international linkage in common goals combined with the recognition of ethnic diversities. The only other politically oriented group he tried to work with after World War II was the Garry Davis "Citizen of the World" movement in 1948, which unfortunately did not measure up to Breton's expectations.

But if Breton failed as an activist in his promotion of multiculturalism in the particular perception he had of it, it became incorporated in some of the best and least studied poems of his last period. In two long poems that are epic in their breadth, Whitmanesque in their resonance, he wrote feelingly about racial abuse and the need for fraternity. In *Les Etats-Généraux,* written in New York in 1943, he highlighted the ethnic talents of the Native Americans and the imported Africans but did not stop there to pit them against each other or against their white conquerors. Instead he found kinship between them and the surrealists in the recognition of a common existential destiny which suggests to all of us the unpredictability of events (particularly crucial in wartime) and the overpowering laws of the cosmos. Let us evoke a passage in my own rendition in the absence of any official translation of the poem in English:

All it takes is for the people to think of itself as one and become one
To rise to the meaning of the universal dependence of each on all in harmony
And understand that the worldwide variation in skin color and features
Tells us that the secret of its power
Lies in the appeal to the autochthonous genius of each race
And to begin with the black race, and the red
Have they not suffered the most offense for the longest time
And let man and woman look each other in the face
She to refuse the yoke he to forget his loss
Drafting board that trembles that quivers under the new light
Are we deconstructing or constructing? There lies the enigma

(The linguistically contained imagery of the "one in the other" in *abbatre/bâtir*, powerful in its brevity, cannot be directly conveyed in English.)

Breton renewed his plea for fraternity on a more political level five years later in his *Ode to Charles Fourier*, in evocation of the utopian syndicalist whose key word was "harmony." This poem was also written in America. Here he pays particular tribute to the Jews, long maligned, in an invocation that was very relevant at a time when awareness of the holocaust was fresh, daily history. He curses the gun and the incense dispenser as twin weapons of divisiveness in human relationships that cling to the petrified character of civilization, taken in its derogatory sense. The image of the Petrified Forest had struck him in his travels in Arizona. It was on this trip to the Far West that he had also discovered inscriptions left by the Hopi Indians, and it amazed him to note that the ethnographers who had interpreted them gave them a ring familiar to surrealist ears: for they spoke of the intimate relationship between the physical and the sacred in Indian cults. Later in *Entretiens* Breton comes again to observations about peoples of color and surrealism's alliance with them, particularly because of their subversive, anti-imperialist language and what he calls "revelatory" emotion, all attributes of what he calls "the superiority of passionate people over reasonable ones." He tells of how he got attracted by the Hopi and the Zuni and their mythology. And then one of the never translated quotes: "I was able to penetrate their inalienable dignity and their genius in such deep and disturbing contrast with the miserable condition to which they have been subjected. I cannot understand how it is that the abounding sense of justice and reparation the white man has been applying toward the black and the yellow races currently, makes exception of the Indian who has given so much evidence of creative power and who has been by far the most exploited."

It is a paradoxical and in my opinion tragic fact that the resurgence of multiculturalism in the United States is antipodal to that which I have described in terms of the surrealist vision. It has become a fragmentation process whereby the unsung ethnic writings have been brought to light with no attempt to discover what in their contributions has helped the literature of the United States alter the stereotype of Western culture. Multiculturalism as an agent of "difference" serves instead the politics of division and confrontation; it generates abject chauvinism, with each subculture fighting for its day in the sun. This politically correct attitude is a far cry from the surrealist interaction and amalgamation of works not alienated from their particular subculture but moved toward a cohesive notion of literature and the understanding of the creative spirit in the context of a universal history.

April 24, 1992

Part II

IX

INFLUENCE AND LITERARY RECEPTION
THE EQUIVOCAL JUNCTION OF TWO METHODS

What interests and impresses does not necessarily influence. Frequent allusions to an author, casual entries in journals or literary "confessions," are often misleading and are not necessarily indicative of basic literary debts. A writer may acquire a great deal of fame in a foreign country without exercising the least literary influence. Another may be regarded with contempt by his compatriots, or be inadvertently ignored, and one fine day become in a foreign land the springboard of a literary movement revitalizing a tired literature. Or an author may have what might be called a "false" influence if he happens to fall into the hands of a so-called borrower who distorts what he is trying to imitate or emulate.

The concept of influence, the need for redefinition, the measurements of its scope, have been basic preoccupations of comparatists; and in the discussions of the subject by Henri Peyre, Haskell Block, Claudio Guillén, and several others there has been less disagreement than uneasiness over the cavalier use of the term and the frequently myopic results of the search for influences.[1]

The notion of influence has been from the start the bread and wine of comparatist research. It has been examined from a biological point of view; Guillén discerns in the early considerations of Joseph Texte the notion of "transmission," which he associates with the study of the genesis of the work of art ("The Aesthetics of Influence Studies in Comparative Literature," Proceedings of the ICLA Congress in Chapel Hill, vol. 1 [1959], 175–192). Others relate influence to the notion of tradition, and, as Haskell Block suggests, this concept of influence can contribute to the understanding of the literary genre over and above the personality of the particular author or authors in question ("The Concept of Influence in Comparative Literature," Yearbook, vol. 7 [1958], 30–37).

The gamut of influence and the many avenues into which it can be channeled were amply discussed and analyzed by Paul Van Tieghem (Littérature comparée, Paris: A. Colin, 1931) with all its nuances and classifications, from initial reception to the deep and lasting imprint that jars the writer from his ordinary path and reveals to him new vistas. Van Tieghem also made distinctions between influences of persons and those of technique, subject matter, and ideas. According to this definition, "we must reserve this name (influence) for the modifications to which the work of one writer is subjected when it comes in contact with the work of a foreign writer" whether the influence is of literary or psychological interest (ibid., p. 135). Van Tieghem also pointed out the dangers of submitting superficial analogy of detail as basic examples of influence when there is revealed in effect only a common source of ideas.[2]

Others have equally deplored the futile pursuit of parallel studies. René Wellek warns against these parallelisms that mark neither authentic influence nor originality of contrast, and where as a matter of fact "originality" is misused.[3] Peyre distinguishes between parallelisms that have no true basis and those which lead the searcher to a synthesis and the discernment of "familles d'esprits" ("A Glance at Comparative Literature," Yearbook, vol. 1 [1952], 7). But despite the many admonitions, studies continue to appear under the artificially contrived label of "influence" or the utilization of those defenseless little words "and" or "in" to protect precarious hypotheses of international literary debts: Dante *and* such and such an author, Shakespeare *in* such and such a country.

The basic ambiguity of the term "influence" as it applies to the discipline of comparative literature consists not merely in the misuse of the term but in the confusion of methods. One of the basic fallacies seems to stem from the casual interchange of the words "influence" and "literary fortune." According to Van Tieghem, these words are in fact practically synonymous: "the study of the influence of a writer abroad is so closely related to the appreciation of his work that it is generally impossible to separate one from the other" (*Littérature comparée*, p. 117). He called this study of reputation "doxologie"; others call it "reception." Guillén calls it the "career" of the work. But whatever name we use, if it is true that this literary reputation is closely related to influence, it is nonetheless a definite phenomenon, separate and distinct, neither synonymous nor simultaneous. It is difficult but not impossible to determine it.

Some phenomena of nineteenth- and twentieth-century French literature can serve as compelling evidence of the need for a sharpening of the distinctions between reception of an author or literary trend and the varieties of influence. When Madame de Staël seeks out German literature, signals its originalities and rich new veins to her compatriots, she promotes its prestige in France. To awaken dormant imaginations, she evokes Nordic mysticism and the cult of the marvelous, the grotesque. She takes to task native writers who cannot liberate themselves from classical conventions. Victor Hugo, Stendhal, and others of the "romantic" coterie follow, as we know, in her path, giving in theory their wholehearted assent. But is this an "influence" of German Romanticism on the French? The confidence and admiration shown, the adherence to concept and principle, constitute knowledge, understanding, and some degree of superficial imitation. There may even be an attraction of a particular personality, but the basic impact on literary vision and form comes later, when German mysticism is less categorically analyzed but better understood through the gradual process of translation, better permeated through the efforts of intermediaries, who will have assimilated rather than interpreted it. If a Madame de Staël serves as annotator, a Baudelaire serves as medium. Before this mysticism can thrive on French soil, it must survive transplantation. As we know, it became readily available to Baudelaire through Poe, who was exposed to it through Coleridge, who in turn had it from Schlegel. The Nordic transcendentalism which Madame de Staël longed to impart to French literature had to undergo a veritable alchemy before it could affect or color the national character or *convention,* as Harry Levin suggests we call these general literary traits pertaining to national or group tendencies ("Notes on Convention," *Perspectives of Criticism,* 55–83).

To become a basic influence, the literary reception had to cross several boundaries. It evolved into the transcendentalism of Emerson, which would not have suited French inclination any more than undiluted German Romanticism. Edgar Allan Poe, ostracized in his own land, was to express the American version of German Romanticism in such a way as to affect the future of French poetry.

The noninfluence of Poe on Baudelaire has been too often explored to need any further discussion. But those who have proved so meticulously that Poe did not influence Baudelaire throw no light, strangely enough, on the chain of influences set in motion not only in France but in the rest of Europe as a result of the literary chance encounter of Poe and Baudelaire, which Paul Valéry had called "the magic contact of two minds" ("Situation de Baudelaire," *Variété II, NRF,* 1930, 144). Poe transformed the mystic quality inherent in Romanticism into a unity of the material and spiritual spheres. He unwittingly sparked an empathy in Baudelaire, whose translations of Poe were to enhance the notion of the absolute inherent in Poe's work.

It has been proved that the essay on the life and work of Poe, which serves as an introduction to Baudelaire's translations, is a gross plagiarism of an American article on Poe. But once we concede that biographical data are to a certain degree public domain, we are concerned with two or three paragraphs that belong to Baudelaire, the only ones that really matter. For in them he crystallized the mystique which was to serve as a bridge between Nordic mysticism and the materialism of the age of enlightenment from which France had been emerging. The same document which may be used to demonstrate plagiarism can also serve to reveal Baudelaire's literary taste, which was to become a strong factor in shaping post-classical French poetry. In these few lines Baudelaire shows his preference for Poe over Goethe, his recognition of the gap that separated French romanticists such as Lamartine and Musset from Poe, and his discovery of Poe's emphasis upon the exceptional in nature. Through his support of Poe, Baudelaire gave a new direction to French lyricism. Perhaps the thirst for the infinite manifest in the *Maelstrom* of Poe has no direct bearing on Baudelaire's "plonger du fond au gouffre" *(Le Voyage)*, but thereafter whoever read Baudelaire in France read Poe. The abyss of Poe deepened the "gouffre" of Baudelaire. Together they inspired what has been called "the great modern tradition." Mallarmé, Valéry, and Breton have attested to the tremendous and multiple repercussions of what thus developed into an authentic influence, cutting across literary conventions and transcending personal affinities.

The same lack of distinction between reception and influence has occurred in the evaluation of the international impact of French Symbolism and surrealism. Were Viélé-Griffin, Stuart Merrill, Arthur Symons truly "influenced" by Symbolism? Were Charles Henri Ford, Eugene Jolas, Arthur Cravan, or Kenneth Rexroth "influenced" by surrealism? Was it not rather a case of coexistence and an enthusiasm for cooperation that gave a sense of belonging and rewarded with an immediate but short-lived fame? Is not such collaboration based on personal contact rather than on literary attraction? Was it not a cult of the hero which motivated a considerable number of those who surrounded Mallarmé in the 1880s or André Breton in the 1920s, the fame of an idol, the promotion of an idea, a literary crusade, like a sudden shower which inundates but does not permeate or irrigate the ground?[4] An ideological cloudburst may flood the heart of the disciple but does not always cultivate his talent. Gide observes that it is in the nature of literary coteries to produce one giant and many underlings ("De l'influence en littérature," *Prétextes,* Mercure de France, 1938). The abortive influence is induced primarily by the dynamism of a personality, to which lesser talents are drawn and with which greater ones clash, until temporal or geographical distance is established.

What are the dangerous aftereffects of such ambiguities? One danger is that they bring about classifications which are inaccurate because they are premature, as in the case of the blanket inclusion of all French postclassical poetry as "romantic" without acknowledgment of the abysmal distances which really separate those bunched together under this undiscriminating label. The all-inclusive grouping is even more faulty in the case of so-called Symbolism, and it is only recently that literary criticism has begun to discern something other than symbolism in those who are supposed to have been influenced by it. The other danger is the death sentence hastily imposed on an author or movement that after an initial success, too loudly attained, seems to vanish on the literary horizon but is actually in the process of rallying, catching a permanent foothold, while the arcana of influences are silently integrated.

Along with literary fortune and influence, there is a third literary phenomenon, equally significant to comparatists and closely connected with the other two, that of "false" influences. This is not what Gide called latent or unconscious influences without which no genius could be nurtured. Rather I refer to those cases where a writer voluntarily seeks out a trailblazer but, having discovered the model, distorts and transforms its basic character. Examples of this phenomenon are abundant in literature and can provide a rich hunting ground for doctoral dissertations if the student is willing to seek out the quality of originality as well as the nature of the imitation.

There is, for instance, the case of the English translations of Baudelaire's poetry which turn him into a true symbolist. In the process of this symbolistic translation, the Baudelairean alchemy of human experience is lost. Whereas by the use of verbal analogy Baudelaire produced a fusion between the physical object and the attributes of the object in the state of dream or subjective consideration, in the symbolist transliterations it is the correspondences, the parallelisms that stand out. Although of secondary importance in the original, this quality is strengthened by the alternating use of concrete and abstract words, conveying the antithesis inherent in a dualistic concept of the world rather than enhancing the vision of its unity, which is a basic element of Baudelaire's universe. Thus the quality which Swinburne called "supernatural realism" in reference to Victor Hugo's last collections of verse, and which could have been more happily applied to Baudelaire, is lost in the translations. However, it is the translation rather than the original which helps to establish an English and American symbolist school, perhaps of greater scope and resilience than the French.

On the other hand, William Blake, whose literary language is typically eighteenth-century, is transformed by Gide and his other French translators between 1922 and 1947, with the result that he is turned into a modern French poet. Separated from the linguistic structure which marks his work historically, it blossoms anew, reveals greater perspective, a modern acuity of the senses. Through this transformation Blake is dislodged from his rank among the precursors of Romanticism and placed in the lineage of Rimbaud, Mallarmé, Jarry, and modern French poetry. Whereas the original inspired merely vague inconsequential affinities, which it would be entirely inappropriate to designate by the name "influence," the translations transfigure the work, producing a "false" influence, but one which illuminates Blake, making of him a new writer, a leader in modern aesthetics on a level with Mallarmé and Picasso. This is the sort of influence which Robert Escarpit calls "creative treason" in his *Sociologie de la littérature* (Paris, 1960; see also *Yearbook,* vol. 10 [1961], 16–21).

The misunderstanding which produces a "false" influence is sometimes derived from reading a translation which does not transfigure as in the case of Blake but causes an outright contradiction of meaning. Literary genius is seldom multilingual and must be often at the mercy of translators. The influence of German Romanticism in the period of the surrealists is partially based on an ambiguity. Coming from the generation of Tieck, Arnim, and Novalis, rather than of Goethe, this influence is spurred by the reading of translations which distort the meaning and more particularly the intent of the original. Thus, what Breton quotes as proof of Arnim's surrealism is the effect of an imperfect translation of Théodore Gautier fils, which in fact contradicts the intention of Arnim.[5]

As for the so-called influence of Freud, it is more "reception" and "mutation" than true influence. The Freudian method of interpretation of dreams, of automatic writing, has supposedly been one of the most incontestable of influences, since it is openly admitted, minutely described and illustrated. However, the intentions of the surrealists were entirely different from those of Freud. The aberrations of the mind, deemed pathological by Freud, were sought out by the surrealists as manifestations of intellectual caliber and flexibility which could enrich the domain of art. When Breton sent *Les Vases communicants* to Freud, the latter was dazzled and perplexed by the strange application made of his method. Upon being "thanked" for the influence he had exerted, he replied to Breton: "And now a confession, which you must accept tolerantly. Although I have received so much proof of the interest you and your friends show in my research, I myself am not in a position to discern what Surrealism is after. Perhaps I am not made to understand it, I who am so far removed from the field of art" (Breton-Freud correspondence, *Le Surréalisme au service de la révolution*, vol. 5, no. 11). The study of such a deviation, which stemmed from a desire to be influenced, does not reveal anything new about Freud, as the mutation disclosed in the case of Blake, but it helps to understand the surrealist orientation and to locate more precisely the particular contribution which surrealism makes in the probing of the depths of the human mind.

Tracing a literary fortune, evaluating an influence, discovering a "false" influence and thereby revealing originality—these are all legitimate objectives of literary research and can produce very fruitful comparative studies. In the quest for precision of criteria one becomes, however, aware that, more than verbal ambiguity, it is the confusion of methods of research that often erases the distinction between influence and fortune, confounding the very principle of study and leaving the reader in a state of disappointment after having been promised useful discoveries.

Upon the determined objective depends the choice of method. The search for influences tends to be analytical: a study in depth, microscopic and precise, where at times intuition overrides the deliberations of reason in its pursuit of cause and effect. The detail sometimes looms larger and more dramatic than the whole, and the single work of art becomes more often the object of scrutiny than the author as a whole or the epoch. But if this meticulous type of study is to achieve something more than the separation of the work into its parts, the investigator must exercise value judgments in regard to the findings and appraise the originality of the work in relation to the degree of imitation. Influences must not be weighed by their multiplicity or sheer bulk but by their intensity. Studies of this nature bear a close relation to psychological analysis and involve questions of language and aesthetics. One has to distinguish the exterior evidence from the fundamental imprint. Even when the proof is at hand, it becomes essential to determine its importance relative to the whole work, and to classify the data in terms of plagiarism, pastiche, imitation, or influence. It may become at times necessary to admit that the pursuit has been a thankless job and the end result of the documentation a false or futile juxtaposition. In this kind of research all the critical powers of the investigator and his ability to judge wisely need to be brought into play. And when these qualities do not measure up to the perseverance and care with which the data have been compiled, the results are pathetically inadequate. One is sometimes led to wonder whether any study of influence is truly justified unless it succeeds in elucidating the particular qualities of the borrower, in revealing along with the influence, and almost in spite of it, what is infinitely more important: the turning point at which the writer frees himself of the influence and finds his originality. This is indeed a sharper gauge of originality, and a more effective one than the ordinary approximations and conjectures by which originality is generally defined.

It is interesting to note that very often the influences of authors of the same nationality and language upon each other are negative influences, the result of reactions, for generations often tend to be rivals of each other and in the name of individualism reject in the work of their elders what they consider to be the conventions of the past. On the contrary, the education of a writer can be dramatically shaped by foreign authors, first because there is no longer a question of rivalry, and particularly as the reading of foreign literature is done generally at a more mature age when one may be more aware of the need for models and direction. By studying such influences the literary historian can reveal the stages of the development of the creative gift and thus go beyond the barren limits of descriptive criticism. For what is the point of directing the reader to a source of influence if merely to conclude that the influenced author drowned in it!

On the other hand, the study of a literary fortune needs the qualities of a literary historian more than those of the literary critic. Its documentation must be quantitative and impartial. The researcher must possess the long view of things and be able to arrive at a synthesis. Because he has compiled numerous references indicating wide diffusion of a work or a name, he is not thereby obligated to prove an influence. It is an error to infer that such a literary fortune is of no consequence unless it has an impact on a particular author and leads to a direct appropriation. But there lies the crux of the matter and the need for the distinction. The history of a literary fortune need not have as its target the effect of the reception on an individual receiver. It can be directed toward at least two other objectives of much greater significance.

First, the tangible evidence of the approval or rejection of a particular author at a given time can be a keen index of the spiritual climate of an era: tell me whom they read and I can tell you what kind of people they were. This is closely related to a sociological approach to literature. The impact of an author on a certain country, on the collective conscience of a public remote in space or time from the atmosphere which has nurtured his own writings, can not only reveal literary taste but also help to decipher the philosophic tendencies of an epoch—as was the case with Paul Hazard's study of the main currents of ideas in the eighteenth century. In tracing the degree of infiltration of a literary master in one country or another, one can arrive at the genesis not merely of a work of art but of the conditions propitious to the flowering of such a work. One can note the modulations of an idea and reach a more scientific, less subjective, yet more intimate notion of the culture of a nation and the moral texture of an epoch.

Second, the literary fortune of a given author amidst a foreign public does more to illuminate his own particular physiognomy than to throw light on the works of any single receptive party. It is not a simple appraisal of popularity, for it does not matter so much how many people read him as *why* they read him and *how*. The genius of a Rimbaud, a Whitman, a Dostoevsky gains in perspective when projected against a foreign backdrop. Foreign criticism can be to a certain degree more purely aesthetic, free as it is of native conventions and prejudices, and thus bring the true nature of the author into clearer focus. By this type of study, practiced with vigor and formality, could we not hope to arrive at a truer definition of the notion of universality?

Under the heading of literary fortune there are other resources available. Why was such a writer neglected by his contemporaries, why is another one tolerated to a greater extent abroad than in his native land? And not only do the successes beckon the literary historian but also the declines, the failures, and the disappearances of certain writers. And there are other subjects, supposedly exhausted, which need new approaches: the cases where the gradual metempsychosis from reception to real influence has not been duly observed. They are worthy subjects of investigation if they appeal to our judgment, to our sense of perspective, and to our courage as critics; above all, if they liberate us from the descriptive and biographical methods which heretofore have tended to engulf a large part of our research activities[6] and thereby veered us away from direct communion with the work of art, from that presence of the work which defies chronological time; for as Sartre has pointed out, the work can enjoy an existence independent of the life of the author. We have too long insisted with Sainte-Beuve that the work of art is inseparable from its author. The time has perhaps come when the search for the literary fortune of a book presupposes the liberation of the work of art from the bondage of the personality quirks and guises of the author, even if they helped to promote the work in the author's lifetime.

To study an influence one is obliged to look closely without losing a sense of distance. He who studies the history of a literary fortune must envisage the broad lines of the diffusion and its repercussions, but in order to determine what is basic and what is to be rejected as irrelevant and superficial, he must possess beforehand an intimate knowledge of the writer whose scope he is going to scan. On the basis of results observed, it seems to me that when the scholar tries to establish at the same time literary fortune and influence, he gets lost in a Cartesian forest of many devious pathways and fails to reach any destination at all.

In untangling the two procedures we can lighten the overload of meaning and intent concentrated in the present concept of influence and, sustained by distinct methodology, we may be able to steer clear of two primary pitfalls: critical dissection of the work of art and impressionistic statement of its value.

If, as recent critics so convincingly suggest, the study of influence relating one work to another could bring about a more clearly aesthetic approach to scholarly research, the appraisal of a literary fortune can orient us toward a more objective, more universally acceptable criterion of literary values. Both categories of research are indubitably at the core of the discipline of the comparatist who as historian, critic, and translator can play the role of annotator, medium, and connecting agent, not only to reveal contacts but to facilitate them, and to effect unions if not unity in the republic of letters.

NOTES

This essay first appeared in *Yearbook of Comparative and General Literature*, vol. 2 (Bloomington: Indiana University Press, 1962), pp. 24–31. An earlier version was presented at the Third Congress of the International Association of Comparative Literature at Utrecht, August 1961.

1. The concept was eventually to fall into disrepute, which has led Harold Bloom to reexamine the issue in *The Anxiety of Influence*.
2. Such was the case, for instance, of the impact of Swedenborgism in the first part of the nineteenth century and that of Darwinism in the second part.
3. René Wellek and Austin Warren, *Theory of Literature* (New York, 1949), pp. 270–271. See also Harding Craig, "An Inquiry into the Criteria for Determining Sources," *SP* 28 (1931), 86–98.

4. Matthew Josephson's *Life among the Surrealists* (Holt, 1962), glaringly brings home the fact that one can witness the advent of a literary movement, participate in its physical motions, and be in no way influenced by it.
5. For specific data pertaining to this case, see my book *Literary Origins of Surrealism* (Columbia University Press, 1947), 32, 37–39.
6. Harry Levin suggests in *Perspectives of Criticism* (Harvard University Press, 1950), 77, that "our literary history is largely collective biography."

X

OF ORIGINS AND ORIGINALITY

The root of the word "originality" is "origin"; in French the same root provides, along with the noun "originality," two adjectives of considerably different meaning: *originel* and *original*. The latter is synonymous with the English word "original," while the former means "of origin," as in *péché originel*, indiscriminately translated as "original sin" but more correctly to be understood as "initial sin," or sin derived from the essential origin. In ordinary usage, context will determine what the user meant, but here we will use the adjectives as special qualifiers to characterize writers and, in the distinction between the two words, show differences important to literary criticism as they reveal nuances rather than linguistic details about the creative process. Scrutiny in the application of the two adjectives may untangle one of the many ambiguities of critical language that disable the interpreters of literature. To make the desired points, the French *originel* will be used in this essay in the absence of a valid equivalent in the English language.

As our knowledge of the literatures of the world expands, we realize with our enlarged vision that words like "original" and "perfection," when used to acclaim a work of art, become measures of our own ignorance rather than indicators of our ability to evaluate the literary harvest. Actually, one of the tests of truly comparatist critics is that they are less likely to use the word "originality" loosely than monoliterary critics because even if they do not know the exact number they are more apt to realize the potential number of as good and better books rivaling for comparison. But, unfortunately, our quarrels are more often over words rather than ideas, and if literary history treads over uncertain ground it is because critical terminology has lagged behind and lacks the rigorous nonoverlapping vocabulary of chemistry and biology.

In exploring, therefore, the organic nature of the notion of originality, let us first of all admit that if *originel* emphasizes the idea of "origin" and *original* of newness, then the orientation of literary adventurers is quite different from that of colonizers of new terrain. In terms of literature, the originator is one who seeks new subjects, new forms, new attitudes—the stress is on "seeks"—whereas the "originals" make of the gained terrain a springboard to jump to the consequences that such discoveries hold for themselves. The "originel" writes manifestos, displays high-voltage enthusiasm; the "original" capitalizes, seeks adherents, tries to establish conventions, and accumulates disciples. This phenomenon is true not only in literature but in all the arts and in philosophy and religion. As philosopher Jacques Maritain used the term in *Frontières de la poésie*, "As in the case of saintliness, literary creation cannot be achieved except in an abyss of solitude, and that is why as soon as a literary school is established, originality evaporates and imitations abound."

The "original," widely endowed with critical attributes, can achieve something unique because he or she knows how to exploit, to perfect what others have discovered. But precisely what does the "perfection" mean which we find at the summit of the hierarchy of values? On the one hand it contains the idea of transcending what is already known, but on the other it skirts the notion of monotony and sterility. It all depends on which side of the mountain we climb; originality exists according to the slope we choose. So it was that Madame de Staël saw in the perfecting of the language and taste of French Classicism "the sterility by which our literature is menaced" and judged the Germans and the more Nordic Chateaubriand as "scouts of the army of the human mind" in *De l'Allemagne*. According to my proposed definition it is precisely the quality of the "originel" that she was sensing and appreciating.

The originator is an illuminated being who unveils, a pilgrim destined to be identified as a precursor or "avant-garde." Before the question left unanswered, the problem perceived but left without a solution, the adventure undertaken but overcome with frustration and left unfinished, these creative artists furnish the subjects and drama of exciting biographies.

The French poet Guillaume Apollinaire was such a pioneer, but his life span was too short, his time further curtailed by his enlistment in World War I, to achieve his vision. But he projected it in several of his poems, particularly in "La Jolie Rousse," which he wrote shortly before his death at age thirty-eight.

> Pity for us who fight forever at the frontiers
> Of the unlimited and the future
> Pity for our errors pity for our sins
> But laugh, laugh at me
>
> Men from everywhere and especially from here
> For there are so many things I would not dare tell you
> So many things that you would not let me tell you

The amazing thing is that no one was preventing him from telling us! But the trouble was that it was not enough to *say*. Prophecy is not creation.

While proclaiming the "new mind" Apollinaire had not conceived the form needed for the new modernism to which he aspired although he experimented with several. At most, having no other straw to grasp, he thought the new art of the cinema might be the new wing of a modern poetics, but he was not to be the one to fashion the "bateau ivre" of cinematography. Except accidentally he did not measure up to his own thirst for the "new" by which he was obsessed all his life, which was so ironically interrupted. The same could be said of the German poet Jean-Paul, who had declared "I is another" and located the domain of the visionary long before Rimbaud. But Rimbaud's famous letter might not have carried the marks of originality if it had remained a declaration of intention without the accompanying *Les Illuminations* by the same author.

The "originels" are the patron saints of the scholar; they make great subjects of dissertations, and they owe to the researcher a considerable share of their glory and posthumous reputations.

In making a distinction between "originel" and "original" we realize that originality no longer seems a spark or illumination but rather a metamorphosis and an aesthetic alchemy. The original rarely announces its originality. The process of configuration is more subtle and complex. The original mind becomes rather choked up by a convention or the development of a tradition at whose source there was an originator whose many imitators produced the conventionalization. Greatness skirts the "original" who succeeds in smashing the convention while drawing from it. There are many ways in which this is done; in examining works with which I am most familiar I see four forms of rupture or disengagement from the conventional, which is the antithesis both of the "originel" and the "original":

1. detour from or deformation of the conventional
2. total reversal of the conventional
3. satire or ironic approach to the conventional
4. the refining of a technique that situates a known idea in a linguistically unexpected climate.

With these points in mind, let us consider a few examples. Literature of classical inspiration is the most prominent illustration of the transformation of borrowed materials through deviations which are the indices of its originality. We can even posit that the "greatest" masterpieces of European literature are not "originel" but have dipped into sources others before them had found, but in their viability; they have proved to be among the most successful of this type of modification.

Let us examine a case of "reversibility" closer to our time. The notion of correspondences between heaven and earth, a notion so intimately attached to Swedenborgian religion, had become the philosophical basis of the Romantic vision as in Blake, Wordsworth, Novalis, and the American transcendentalists, in the early novels of Balzac, and in the late philosophical poems of Victor Hugo, which nobody reads anymore. Swedenborgism had affected the *écriture* of poetry with the almost automatic coupling of the concrete and the abstract in the formation of metaphors.

But in the midst of the direct application of this popular form of Christianity to literary perspectives, Baudelaire writes a sonnet called "Correspondances" and had he completed his poem along the lines of his first quatrain or simply illustrated in the rest of the poem the philosophy he had declared in the first four lines, one could think that the sonnet was dictated under the influence of the treatise of Madame de Staël on the German Romantic vision, and because of the technical impeccability of his verse Baudelaire would have been deemed a perfecter of the initial model *and nothing more*. But the rest of the sonnet transforms the known precept by a subtle deformation which describes not the correspondence between heaven and earth but that of the purely corporal ones in the purely material world, thus bringing attention not to the duality of the universe but to the unity of the earth, and opening the way to a brand new poetic orientation more compatible with a still unconscious changing mentality which makes him a century later a "modern" poet, readable, whereas Hugo no longer seems so (see my book *The Symbolist Movement*, 1977, for a detailed explanation of the process). In the same sense, Baudelaire makes use of another convention of the period, that of Sappho. Under his pen, however, Sappho ceases to be the symbol of a perverted sensuality (which was the standard attitude of the time). She becomes, instead, the personification of the fear to live and love, a theme to be adopted later by the decadent/ symbolist writers, reappearing in other guises than Sappho in Mallarmé, Laforgue, Villiers, Hofmannsthal, and removes the remodeled classic figure from the voluptuous images of the Lesbian to be found in Théophile Gautier and in the aphrodisiacally inclined Romanticists. Such a detour, crystallizing a new aesthetic or psychological interpretation of a stale subject, transforms it and makes of it the point of departure of a new convention.

Sometimes the detour is produced by a mind tending to combat and contradiction; this attitude leads to a total reversal of the original theme. More anarchist, more conscious, this contradiction of the original sense is one of the surest signs of philosophical rebellion in the literature of our century. The most glaring examples of this process come from the use of classical archetypal names to say the opposite of the message encrusted in them. Such are Gide's *Oedipus,* Giraudoux's *Amphitryon,* Sartre's Orestes in *Les Mouches,* and the Sisyphus of Camus; the case of Sisyphus is particularly blatant as the image of sorrow and oppression is transformed into one of stoical happiness. The originality of Camus lies in the fact that he defies the "originel" and initiates a new convention. But the convention went into a dead end instead of opening a new door. Where are the descendants of these revamped archetypes? Reversibility is indeed a form of originality, but it seems less capable of developing a convention of its own, particularly as the "originel" archetypes it attempts to reverse become less and less familiar to the modern reader.

A third form of originality is, as pointed out, satire and the ironic mode; satire implies exaggeration, irony a distancing and the elimination of sincerity or in distrust of the sincerity of the earlier writer. Less radical than total reversal, satire dips more widely into the social climate of the moment than into personal rebellion. One of the most brilliant examples of this type of originality was Nabokov's take-off on the Marquis de Sade at a time when Sade was being rediscovered by the literati, although it succeeded in the marketplace because most of its readers took *Lolita* as seriously lascivious. The theme of youth and innocence perverted by the corruption of the rich, the high-placed and the hypocrites of society explains the misfortunes of Sade's Sophie who, still a child, is sexually abused by an elderly gentleman who subsequently gets rid of her as of a broken doll. Nabokov takes the same theme and makes of it the flagrant satire of American society as he had newly observed it at midcentury, replete with its sexual obsessions. He also satirizes the independence of the young and their voluntary decadence. This time what happens is not simply a thematic detour or an antithesis to convey with indignation but a gross exaggeration (at the time he was writing!) which sets the tone, the climate, of a new era and conveys the impression of profound originality. Since Nabokov, the ironic adaptation of the "originel" has accelerated as a form of originality in modern and postmodern works along with the critical tendency of finding "irony" virtually everywhere in the literature of the past with almost total distrust of sincerity.

Finally there is a form of originality that derives from technique. It was through technique that Mallarmé, a meek man, demonstrated originality and rebellion against convention and initiated Symbolism, a school and a host of imitators who never quite understood the extent of his originality. Mallarmé chose one of the most common characters of his time: the faun. There were almost as many fauns as lilies and swans in literary circulation. But the author of *L'Après-midi d'un faune* did not become original by creating a totally different kind of faun from the common variety or by making it an instrument of personal rebellion or even a vehicle of satire. He used the standard, conventional faun: sensual, pagan, half-god, half-animal, speaking in human language. From that point of view, his approach was to be totally banal and conventional.

What he did, however, was to make of the faun an opportunity to demonstrate the power of language in devising a new technique of composition that was later to turn into the symbolist *écriture:* language appropriately used to express the junction of dream and the wakeful state, and in his poem he initiated another and far more radical advance in form, the simulation of the musical structure not by imitation of musical sounds but as a conceptual communication beyond direct discourse, implicit, analogical rather than overtly ideological. Extraordinary originality at the very heart of the most banal of themes!

The moderns have been particularly active in the quest for originality. The surrealists, for instance, first looked for originality in source materials such as substitutions of Celtic legend for classical subjects. But it was mostly in the field of techniques of analogical writing that they became fertile and original. It is true—and André Breton was the first to admit it—that the surrealists took over the authentic revolt of their predecessors; but if the search for a language that conveys the irrational and an art that takes over the power of creation rather than representation is already detectable in Saint-Pol-Roux and Pierre Reverdy as well as in the European painters of the time, the intentional postulation in relation to poetry did not get consolidated until the linguistic modifications produced transfigurations of the poetic image in the writings of Breton, Eluard, and other poets of the thirties and in visual parallels in the plastic arts.

Redefining originality is integral to the understanding of influence. Influence studies have gone into disrepute because they stop midstream in the tracing of origins and demonstrate mainly imitation and adherence to convention. The better part of the study of influence should be the discovery of originality, the turning points from adoption of something previously originated and transforming it into something truly "original." Once the origins have been discovered or the so-called "intertextuality" established, too often the study is terminated when the interesting part of the study has only begun and when the particular similarity should be projected into the larger perspective of originality.

In "Influence and Literary Reception" I posited that the reception of a writer throws light on the writer received as well as on the nature of his or her receivers, and that consecutive and degrees of reception and the character of the reception are gauges of the writer that unfold with the progression of time. In a parallel way, studies of influence should be able to enrich our appreciation not only of the writer who radiates but of the one in the receiving line of the rays. Was the receiving party drowned by the influence? Or did he or she overcome it; did it produce an alchemical effect on the convention and did the influenced party thereby become an initiator of a new convention? It seems to me that such probes could uncover a whole system of interrelationships lifting the fear of imperialism linked in nationalistic resistances to the discovery of influences and this broader comprehension of both influence and originality leads toward a deeper comprehension of universality.

NOTE

This essay is a 1992 revision of a 1963 article, "L'originel et l'original: nuance linguistique, distance poétique," *Proceedings of the Fourth Congress of the International Comparative Literature Association,* Freibourg, 1964, vol. 2 (The Hague: Mouton, 1966), 1265–69.

11

MALLARMÉ AS SUBVERSIVE THEORIST

One of the shortest prefaces in French literature is Mallarmé's on René Ghil's *Traité du Verbe*. It has, however, a pivotal position; it emerges as the kernel of his poetics and at the same time places Mallarmé's views of poetry outside and beyond that of the members of the Symbolist *cénacle*, although in unexpected concordance with other aspects of the cultural history of France in the period between the 1860s and the 1880s.

Normally, prefaces are platforms of overtly direct communication between author and reader, sometimes almost militant presentations of a theory that is to be put in practice in the body of the work itself. Such is Victor Hugo's preface to his own *Cromwell* or Théophile Gautier's to his *Mademoiselle de Maupin,* two red flags proclaiming breaks with literary conventions, hostility to the set ideas of the very audience to whom they are addressed. Their message is clear and self-contained, and the test is in no need of any particular exegesis.

Elsewhere, prefaces are sponsorships that familiar authors accord less familiar ones, as discoverers: such were the early prefaces attached to *Les Fleurs du mal* and to *Les Chants de Maldoror*. The rise of the literary fortune of an author can be traced through such successive prefaces.

Sometimes prefaces present a more profound communication than the work which they presume to launch and which instead they use as a vehicle to carry them in their own particular direction. In that instance, the preface becomes a testing ground for an idea further developed in a more elaborate piece of writing. In the twentieth century such a one is the continuous "preface" of André Breton's *Anthologie de l'humour noir*, interspersed with excerpts that illustrate to a certain degree but none totally his definition not simply of "black humor" but of the ontological crisis he sees developing through the cultural maze of literary history. Breton's commentary, if put end to end, becomes a book in its own right on the subject of subversive writing through several centuries in the context of the history of ideas.

Mallarmé rather casually at first sight seems to have inserted the same type of intellectual statement into a single page which is quite unintelligible by itself without referencing with other texts of his. It also gains in meaning when viewed in the light of developments in linguistics at the time of the burgeoning of his ideas about poetry. The several pieces of writings which René Ghil had collected under the imposing title of *Traité du Verbe* did not become for Mallarmé a vehicle, not an excuse for a platform, not a testing ground, but the revelation of a paradox that goes to the heart of the Symbolist aesthetics and to the problematic position Mallarmé occupies in the collective effort to relate literature to music following the precepts of Wagner.

As I have tried to demonstrate elsewhere,[1] there are two approaches to the Symbolist aesthetics/mystique, that of the 1860s and that of the 1880s. Ghil's *Traité* is a document of the eighties. It was to have five editions, of which only two carry Mallarmé's *Avant-Dire*.[2] In those first two editions it is an echo of his enthusiasm for several of the avant-garde personalities of Symbolism, mostly Mallarmé, whose style he imitates almost to the extent of creating a pastiche. It is a piece of representative writing and a source of motivation to the French Symbolists of the eighties. Mallarmé's *Avant-Dire*, however, is symptomatic of the sixties. Ghil's effervescent salute to Mallarmé, Wagner, Huysmans, Verlaine is more relevant to his contemporaries who were frequenting Mallarmé's *mardis* than is the theory Mallarmé encoded in the *Avant-Dire,* in which his references to the powers of language have nothing to do with the musical instruments and color correspondences Ghil conjures to enhance poetry. Ghil is dealing with language as an instrument to crystallize meaning and express affective states; it is a medium of exchange leading to the illumination of an idea, rendered more vibrant through the appropriation of the *timbres* of various musical instruments, each of which he associates with one or another of the poets of his time. Mallarmé, instead, is speculating on the power of language to alter reality, to stir the imagination, to refine the process of poetic thinking; he is giving the first signals of what down the line poets of the twentieth century were better to understand. Paul Valéry was to suggest in *Variété,* in terms of his own linguistic priorities, that words can be both a means of conveying thought and an end in themselves. When they contain their own universe of realities they become poetry: "poetry is an art of language."[3] René Nelli characterizes the same perception as "l'imaginaire au niveau des mots," or "les idées les plus hautes ne sont que l'aventure du langage."[4]

Ghil's concern was to render the language of poetry less explicit by making it serve the type of conceptual ambiguity achieved through music: "Un Poème, ainsi devient un vrai morceau de musique, suggestive infiniment et 's'instrumentant' seule: musique de mots évocateurs d'Images-colorées, sans qu'en souffrent en rien, que l'on s'en souvienne! les Idées." Mallarmé looked to language for his spiritual needs. He would not think of himself as "un musicien de mots" or of ideas as conveyed by "mots-instruments" in Ghil's terminology. He was thinking of music on the level of musical composition, contrived to minimize chance and to overcome the constrictions of the physical world, to create beyond circumstances of time and place a universal reality in *virtual* terms, i.e., identify a potential, the very notion of which might requite his hunger for transcendence. Again in René Nelli's more overt terms: "la poésie qui invente l'imaginaire à partir des virtualités [Mallarmé's word] non pratiques des mots."

We know that Mallarmé's life as a schoolteacher in his formative years had given him little opportunity for dialectic exchange; where had he derived such a high confidence in language and found such prospects for its poetic use? Actually, the attitude tersely expressed in his *Avant-Dire* emerges in much earlier writings contemporary not to the Symbolists but to the findings of philologists who had not only created a stir in linguistic circles but contributed on a larger front to the recognition of what Emile Littré had characterized as a "period of crisis."[5] He had noted in his two-volume *History of the French Language* that whereas historians are inclined to attribute developments in literature to political and social factors, new linguistic perceptions of successive stabilities, ruptures, and mobilities in the development of language have impacts on the shaping of literature that are just as significant as the sociopolitical. His work was a response to the prodigious scholarship of the German linguist Friedrich Diez on the etymology of the Romance languages; Sainte-Beuve commented on the comments of Littré in a more accessible reading in his *Premiers Lundis* in a long essay, "Du point de départ et des origines de la langue et de la littérature française" (1858). In the meantime, in the light of these discoveries, Mistral was recreating the Provençal language in his poetry. In such context Rimbaud's cry "trouver une langue" becomes steeped in historicity. So was the life-long rumination of Mallarmé about the capacity of language to replace the icons of religious identification. The statements presented in compact scripture in the *Avant-Dire* cannot be fully understood without reference to previous texts of Mallarmé, closer to the linguistic crisis, and to repetition of the same precepts in later texts; in 1898, at the end of his life, Mallarmé was questioned by a journalist of *Figaro* on the question of "L'idéal à vingt ans." How had his ideal in youth been affected in the course of time? His response was that his life-experience had merely served to wipe off the dust from time to time from his original illumination which prevailed from his earliest years. Whereas the study of the life and work of a writer generally reveals a process of change, development, and even reversal of attitudes, the *Avant-Dire,* published in 1886, demonstrates that in its repetition of principles first expressed in 1869, it prevails as a consolidation of a theory that he had already tested in his major poetic works. Thereafter there were to be reiterations, minor editing, and very negligible modifications. His is a core vision, and his little note in the *Figaro* piece has a very significant postscript in which he disapproves of any isolation of ideas or any reading out of context: "les miennes [pensées] formant le trait, musicalement placées d'un ensemble et, à s'isoler, je les sens perdre jusqu'à leur vérité et sonner faux."[6] In view of this attitude, discussion of the single-page preface amounts to a consideration of the totality of his thoughts "musicalement placées," meaning in structured fashion.

By the third edition of the *Traité,* Ghil was to reverse himself totally and reject the Master to move toward what he deemed a scientific positivism as opposed to what he considered to be Mallarmé's idealism. Clearly Ghil's theories did not have the consistency of Mallarmé's and the validity of that negative appraisal is, upon close examination, as questionable as the basis of his earlier admission of influence.

Mallarmé divided his text into two parts; he began and ended with references to Ghil's work and kept the center for his own theory of the poetry of language. He calls Ghil's objective "instrumentation parlée" and then, referring to his own notion of music, contradicts the Ghil proposal, the while acknowledging that the theory of instrumentation reflects the general attitudes of Ghil's contemporaries. But the part of the page reserved for his own theory brings out the distinction between the practical analogies in music and poetry and the functional parallel of the composition of music and poetry. For him music is not a support system for poetry in its *effects* but a model for a similar use of the mind to create poetry. The application of method, like the rigorous rules for the composition of music, can eternalize the temporal image conveyed by words in casual practice, into a virtual one that is immutable: "retrouve chez le poète, par nécessité constitutive d'un art consacré aux fictions, sa virtualité." These two different uses of music were to be more explicitly expressed ten years later in his discursive writing *La Musique et les Lettres.* There he noted the difference between simulating in speech the sounds of instruments and creating auditory evocations that unite with the visual to attain an integrated comprehension of existence, "l'entendement."

The special lexicon of new meanings relating to Mallarmé's theory are: language, Verbe, Parole, and Dire, all at the service of Rêve, Chant, Fiction, the latter series being substitutions for art and poetry. To understand the arbitrary meanings he attributes entails reference to several texts before and after the *Avant-Dire:* the *Diptyque (I D'une Méthode),* which was an outline of a proposal for a dissertation, actually never to be written (1869), *Crise de Vers* (1886) into which he inserted the theoretical part of the *Avant-Dire,* and finally *La Musique et les Lettres* (1895), the whole forming a network or "ensemble" over a twenty-year period.

In *Diptyque* he had been on the one hand obsessed by the multiple meaning of words, and on the other hand by that other music which he calls "voix intérieure" and which had nothing to do with instrumentation. There he had defined the Verbe as pure essence which through Parole assumes a circumstantial relevance to time and place according to each era in which it is pronounced; it is in this context that in the *Avant-Dire* he adjudges "l'ensemble de feuillets" of Ghil to have arrived at the right time: "il s'ouvre à l'heure bonne," in the symbolist timetable.

To create "the fiction" of the physical reality, however, the poet had to detach the image/object from its particular Parole which had produced the analogies of things by the simulation of the analogies of sounds; Parole is a variable designating successive efforts at expression through successive eras of changing practices, whereas the Verbe is the constant source, the Absolute of the poet's aspiration toward essence; to attain knowledge of it does not entail a stripping process but a retrieval, a probe behind the physics and physiology of human language. Physics is associated with the given material dimensions, physiology with the temporal changes in the relationships between objects and the mind's perception of them subjected to the historical contexts which succeed each other. The linguistic principles that govern the poet lead to a revelation of a primordial principle that defies all the principles which have generated series of Paroles in series of time units. The "Science mystérieuse du Verbe" gives it the position of an all-inclusive oracle.

In other words, Ghil's work is expressing poetic Parole through instrumentation as the appropriate form for his time, while Mallarmé's Method is the recuperation of the Verbe from its current Parole, which becomes a fictionalization rather than remaining a representation.

In an elaboration in 1895 of his earlier *Diptyque* notes, Mallarmé confirms the double-talk I detect in his preface to the *Traité du Verbe* by contrasting the common pool of vocabulary accessible to historical selection, i.e., the resource of standard representative writers, with that of his own higher aspiration, the fictionalization process which from the temporal sound ("signification courante") traverses the silence, transforming itself into "musiques mentales" or, as he earlier called it, "voix intérieure." In the substitution technique so common in Mallarmé, the "musiques mentales" is the equivalent of the "pure" state, the matrix out of which will develop future exterior representations. The conclusion one could draw from his statements and special connotations of words is that Ghil's *Traité du Verbe* is really a *Traité de la Parole*.

This distinction is more closely grasped in the antithesis that occurs between standard Symbolism, as it developed at the end of the nineteenth century, and Mallarmé's *écriture*. Rarefaction is the process most frequently associated with the type of poetry in which the Symbolists simulated musical impressions and produced an indeterminacy of communication. The characteristic most distinct in Mallarmé's poetry and to be emulated by the postsymbolists rather than the Symbolists was a technique of substitutions of one signifier for another so that a system of signs developed, as in musical composition, comprehensible only through the development of patterns to which the reader is exposed; and through repetitions of these substitutions in the *total* work the poet promotes the learning of a code. The language of the poet then becomes something *un*representative of the world at large, but representative within his work, and that is why perhaps Mallarmé conceives of his work as le Livre in its singular oneness, a veritable *fiction*.

The role of the philologists played no small part in the development of his lexicon, not only in terms of the rediscovery of the mysteries of linguistic evolution but in two other areas, more precise: the discrete character of the French language in fraternal rather than filial relation to other languages coming from Latin, and the functioning of etymology. What the linguists of the nineteenth century had stressed was the simultaneity of development of the Romance languages as siblings carrying large resemblances already ascertained, but also certain genetic differentials not sufficiently taken into account, among them the derivational factor relating to the direct impact of Greek beyond the indirect one through Latin, the participation in the formation of the language of Ancient Greek through Pelasgic pre-Roman invasions. This kind of implication is double-edged. It views French as a palimpsestic language of multiple-layered significations and it releases French from a historic restriction to the Latin derivation. Although it is common knowledge, particularly through the work of Charles Chassé, *Les Clés de Mallarmé,* that Mallarmé developed an interest in etymological uses of language which affected some of his unusual uses of common words, and that he came to this knowledge through his association with Littré, it is less known that Littré's pursuits of the origin of signification had a corollary even more important to poets: that denotation at origin, and successive connotations could be concorded in polysemic meaning *synchronically* to grasp total signification; his analogy is with fossils and stratification, "geological formations" as Sainte-Beuve[7] reports it. Language becomes a geological comprehension, since geography cannot be separated from its history. As we examine Mallarmé's system of arbitrary substitutions, it becomes clear that the knowledge of etymology did not simply take him to earlier ascertained meanings of signifiers, nor even synchronization of meanings, but more fundamentally to the general permissibility of altered meanings. A resurgent nostalgia for the practice of polyvalence stirs him to the possibility of applying it to current language, creating a potential for a mystery that might replace that of the scriptures or oracles of old if that power were exercised with care; that exercise with care is his notion of fiction, and results from Method. The process aims at abolishing the brute chance of word encounters. Instead, a maneuver makes optimal use of the opportunities of chance on the part of the Adept who aims at a total range of significations simultaneously. Thus, he envisages three levels of language: Dire, Parole, Verbe. Dire is the plebeian instrument of the Verbe. Parole as practiced by the Symbolists confronts and purifies Dire to some extent but is circumscribed in time and place. Verbe is language as source: "Never confuse language with the Verbe," he admonishes. The Verbe generates a composite of sacred dimensions; Method is contrived to extract from reality only its essential, nonrestrictive character. Where in ordinary Dire remembering conjures material details of reality of a time and place, the fiction of poetry, through Method, superposes forgetting which strips the object of all but its virtual or potential image through which the Verbe operates. In other words, the power of the Verbe is impeded without Method. It is in this linguistic context that the famous sentence of Mallarmé, which is central to the page of the *Avant-Dire* and reiterated in *Crise de Vers,* renders its full meaning:

> Je dis une fleur: et, hors de l'oubli où ma voix relègue aucun contour, en tant que quelque chose d'autre que les calices sus, musicalement se lève, idée même et suave, l'absente de tous bouquets.

The important word here is "absente," which is not the same as "absence" because fiction is not the same as abstraction for Mallarmé. It is not a fine distinction but a serious one. The very use of the "absente" belies the accusations made by Ghil in withdrawing Mallarmé's *Avant-Dire* from his later editions of the *Traité:* that Mallarmé had veered toward abstractions. The absent flower is precisely that nonrestricted but concrete reality which is the basic character of Mallarmé's poetry as well as of his poetics; it creates the absent presence of the nymphs in *L'Après-midi d'un faune* and of the Master in the empty room of the Sonnet in yx, as well as in an infinite number of other instances. His perception of a concrete sense of language as well as of the practice of its polysemic character owes much to the linguistic discoveries that reached his awareness in the sixties and which made him create a poetry categorically opposed to those who two decades later presumably learned from him. Ghil and some of his generation of poets went on toward a materialistic monism; their positivistic strategies are explicitly demonstrated in the fifth edition of the *Traité* where the alliance between musical instruments and abstract human qualities is at the opposite pole from Mallarmé's definition of the fiction of poetry.

F, L, R, S, Z, les Trompettes, Clarinette et petites Flûtes	D, GH, L, P, Q, R, T, X les Violons par les pizzicati, Guitares et Harpe Instruments percutants	LL, R, S, V, Z les Basses, Alto-Voile et Violons
Ingénuités, tendresses, heurs, rire, —Instinct d'aimer égoïste. Vouloirs.	Sérénité, désistement, deuil, —Instinct de vénérer. Passivité. —Méditation Ordre.	Volupté, amour, passion, douleur. —Instinct de se vouer. Méditation. —Vouloir passionné.

As mentioned earlier, a later generation, that of Valéry, was to grasp the message of Mallarmé: that language as the instrument of the Verbe can create its own imagery. This comprehension also forewarned of the eventual destruction of the conventional character of linguistic representation and forecast the "one in the other image" of the rebus. Both the destruction of representation and the use of the rebus image were to become the essential trademarks of the surrealist *écriture*, although the philosophy of life beneath the surrealist mode was to be quite remote from the symbolist mystique.[8]

In the light of the double concept of music, an error can be noted in contemporary critical commentary. Very frequently Mallarmé is evoked in support of the theory of the disappearance of the author from his text. The basis of the association of Mallarmé to the authorless text is a sentence from *Crise de Vers* quoted out of context:

> L'œuvre pure implique la disparition élocutoire du poète, qui cède l'initiative aux mots, par le heurt de leur inégalité mobilisés; ils s'allument de reflets réciproques comme une virtuelle trainée de feux sur des pierreries, remplaçant la respiration perceptible en l'ancien souffle lyrique ou la direction personnelle enthousiaste de la phrase.

Reading it in the context of the distinctions Mallarmé made between two separate perceptions of the role of music in relation to poetry, we note that the detachment Mallarmé is talking about has to do with "elocution," or imitative musicality. He is not saying that the poet himself has disappeared from the poem, which indeed would give the deconstructionists a field day in shuffling signifiers and signifieds. Instead, Mallarmé has enumerated earlier in the article in no uncertain terms what he means by "elocutoire" in terms of the history of versification and its modulations in recent times. He desires the replacement of such elocution by a method which releases the words from sonorous music to their natural "heurts" (shocks) in unequal quality (hardly the character of music as conceived by nineteenth-century standards of harmony) and the image he gives to illustrate this thought is not a lyrical one but of visual analogies of fire on jewels and the qualifier is "virtuelle," a word we have come to associate in his vocabulary with "pure" as opposed to circumstantial or temporal reality. The new notion of music described here has little connection with the old lyrical versification. One remembers that the word "heurt" used twenty years earlier in *Igitur*—a work that was not to be published in the lifetime of his contemporaries—had the same signification of annulment of the experience of sound as the commonly accepted product of the auditory sense.

If, as Mallarmé believed, the aim of poetic language is the Beautiful, i.e., contained in the realm of aesthetics, the Verbe embodies a greater poetic function, a form of episteme, disengaged from successive concepts of the relativity of the Beautiful.

His brief preface, then, read in the light of his other pronouncements, revealing very idiosyncratic definitions of language, Parole, Verbe, is a subtle way of setting himself outside of the coterie of which he was ostensibly the leader, to search in solitude and with difficulty a form of poetry which would be impervious to reinterpretation, to the practice of "diffe*r*ance" because it would be beyond the reach of any specific interpretation, at the source of a mental process combining the affective and the intellectual to become that purity associable with the gold of the philosopher's stone.

An extraordinary parallel may be noted between the end of the nineteenth century and the end of the twentieth in the merging of scientism with rhetoric. Mallarmé fought the unholy alliance with all the subtlety of an old sage.

NOTES

This essay first appeared in *L'Esprit Créateur*, vol. 27, no. 3 (Fall 1987), 58–67.

1. See A. Balakian, *Symbolist Movement. A Critical Appraisal* (New York: NYU Press, 1977).

2. See *Traité du Verbe* (Paris: A. G. Nizet, 1978), which includes a comprehensive introduction on the five editions by Tiziana Goruppi.
3. Paul Valéry, *Œuvres complètes* (Paris: Gallimard [Pléiade], 1957), 1324.
4. René Nelli, *Les Cahiers du sud,* no. 362–363, 28.
5. Emile Littré, *Histoire de la langue française* (Paris, 1886), lv (conclusion of the introduction).
6. Stéphane Mallarmé, *Œuvres complètes* (Paris: Gallimard [Pléiade], 1953), 883.
7. Sainte-Beuve, *Premiers Lundis,* vol. 3 (Paris, 1858), 121.
8. See A. Balakian, "From Mallarmé to Breton: Continuity and Discontinuity in the Poetics of Ambiguity," in *Writing in a Modern Temper,* ed. M. A. Caws (Palo Alto: Stanford University Press, 1984).

XII

THE MONOLITH OF ROMANIA
MYTH OR REALITY?

Does Romania survive as a distinct and monolithic classification in European literature?

Romania is a reality still unchallenged as far as its linguistic history is concerned: the homogeneity of its origins and the course of its orderly national mutations highlight the relationships of parent to sibling and of sibling to first and second cousins. In the clarity and concreteness of this linguistic continuity it is natural to assume that equal proximity follows in what is written in languages that are cognates of each other. Consanguinity should lead to contiguity, but has it actually done so?

If it can be ascertained that there is a relationship between the developments of the separate but related languages, does the same contiguity occur among literatures of Romania in the manifestation of the various facets of literature such as myth identification, expression of emotions, creation of images, reflection of life philosophies, and the various degrees of involvement of these national literatures in major international literary movements? The inevitable corollary to the question is: if indeed a parallel evolution occurs in these cognate literatures in the orbit of Romania, is it an incestuous phenomenon or has there been intermarriage in the process with the literary developments in other linguistic families, causing the breakdown of the monolithic character of Romance literatures?

In pondering the two faces of the problem, I have paid

heed to two types of opinions or positions before attaining my own judgment. On the one hand, I have sampled literary criticism to ascertain to what degree those literary critics, who are also creative writers, have had a conscious awareness of this presumed cohesion of Romance literatures and of the consequential gap between this group and the rest of European literature. On the other hand, I have reexamined some of the more audible critics in the Romanic sector who have proposed for Romance literatures in particular, and for European literature in general, a conscious and voluntary departure from the common Greco-Roman heritage.

Only after recapitulating some of these authoritative references will I proceed to my own bias in examining fundamental qualities of what is Romanic and how and where it has been preserved, or lost to foreign invasion.

When one examines generalist essays such as those of Benedetto Croce, T. S. Eliot, Ortega y Gasset, Octavio Paz, and Ezra Pound, one notes that the literary relationships recognized by these writers are on a global basis. The comparatist optic inherent in these critics is not limited to Romance literatures. For instance, when Croce discusses the baroque his analysis applies to the German and English as well as to the Romanic literatures; and he objects to the dichotomy established between Germanic Romanticism and that of Latin character. On the other hand, Ortega y Gasset, comparing classic theaters, finds more distinctions than cohesions between the presumably related literatures of France and Spain. In their essays on Western culture, Eliot and Pound emphasize European rather than Romanic unity. For instance, in his essay "The Function of Criticism" Eliot takes Middleton Murry to task for forcing a distinction between French and English approaches to classicism and Romanticism. In his article on Dante, Eliot does not see Romanic frontiers when he associates Dante with Villon and Chaucer; their contiguity is one of time and historical event rather than of linguistic orientation. Eliot speaks of "a directness of speech which Dante shares with other great poets of pre-Reformation and pre-Renaissance times, notably Chaucer and Villon" (*Selected Essays,* Faber and Faber, 1934, p. 240). For Pound, much of poetic form of all Western European writing derives from the Provençal, whether written in cognate languages or not. The affinities erase these language barriers when Dante and Browning have their common sources in Mantuan legend, when Guido Cavalcanti's "In un boschetto provai pastorella" and Swinburne's "An Interlude" are linked through the common form of the pastorela. (Cf. "Troubadours—Their Sorts and Conditions," *Literary Essays,* New Directions, 1954.) In other articles demonstrating the derivative character of European verse forms of Provençal origin, Pound includes Chaucer and Spenser just as much as the French Pléiade. To refer to a much more recent work, Paz, in his discussion of literature from Romanticism to the avant-garde in *Children of the Mire,* is still using the gauge called "Western" rather than "Romanic." In fact, he makes a point of including the Anglo-Americans in the relationships he is trying to establish or sustain. He says: "I am not trying to deny the originality of the Anglo-American poets, but merely to indicate that the movement of poetry in English can be fully understood only in the context of Western poetry" (*Children of the Mire,* Harvard University Press, 1974, p. 120). The examples could be multiplied; the ones I spot-checked lead me to the conclusion that modern critics discuss literary works or trends without intentionally classifying the Romanic together, and when they are interested in group differences they tend to juxtapose individual national literatures rather than to oppose one group of cognate literatures to another.

On the other hand, writers who have attempted to make a conscious break with the notion of a permanent Romanic monolith have not aimed at a fragmentation or a totally national independence but at a realignment on a larger base, a base that includes the Anglo-Teutonic as well as the Romance literatures. Such was the position of Chateaubriand and Madame de Staël in the nineteenth century, and their stand is supported by Ortega y Gasset and Croce in the twentieth. The culture bed that Chateaubriand and Madame de Staël selected as a substitute to the Greco-Latin one was the Judeo-Christian, particularly as it was crystallized in the Middle Ages. The underlying objective of both *Le Génie du Christianisme* and *De L'Allemagne* was to bring about the separation of France from antiquity so that she might find her literary destiny in a broader European context.

In their intense enthusiasm for Christianity as a literary reference both Chateaubriand and Madame de Staël failed to realize that Christianity was still in its historic phase and could, therefore, not yet become a working mythology. Chateaubriand deplored the mythic ineptness of Dante's and Tasso's Satans. Milton's, in his eyes, fared a little better. But the best case Chateaubriand could make to prove his point that the Christian material was superior to the pagan was to draw his examples from Racine, where he found the pagan characters embodying a Christian morality. It is to be noted that, in drawing on examples, his references to English texts such as Milton's are on the same plane as French ones without discrimination as to their national heritage. The comparison is based on the assumption that they all suffer equally from the same reliance on antiquity; and all departures from this despotism of antiquity are equally heroic and mutually coherent. Consequently, he regarded Romanticism from an international rather than a national vantage point because of its collective effort to depart from antiquity. "La littérature romantique est la seule qui soit susceptible encore d'être perfectionnée, parce qu'ayant ses racines dans notre propre sol, elle est la seule qui puisse croître et se vivifier de nouveau; elle exprime notre religion; elle rappelle notre histoire; son origine est ancienne mais non antique" (*Le Génie du Christianisme*, Oeuvres complètes, vol. 2, Imprimerie J. Claye, p. 130). In other words, Chateaubriand's invitation to modern national literatures to abandon their allegiance to Greco-Latin sources succinctly confirms the fact that, regardless of their individual histories or linguistic derivations, the

Anglo-Teutonic as well as the Romanic have had repeated and overprolonged recourses to classical antiquity.

The intention of the theoreticians of Romanticism to undermine the mythological subsoil of the Romanic monolith did not, however, succeed despite occasional recourse to Teutonic myths and to localized cultural references. Although Romanticism is often characterized as a Nordic movement, its great themes and archetypes are derived from the fountainhead of the Romanic heritage.

How did the Symbolist movement fare in this respect? After those poets of diverse nationalities who were gathered in Paris, at the inception of the movement, returned to their respective countries to explore local myths and folklore as legitimate bases of symbolist communication, there resulted at a certain moment a diversity and dispersion of references in symbolist writings. Yeats captured the Celtic; Lorca the Andalusian; the Germans, local characters and phantom figures of the Rhine; the middle Europeans, the local ethos. But the separations that the search for ethnic sources created were national rather than grouped by linguistic families, and the eventual return to the stylized myths of antiquity was collective and global. The Greco-Roman myths served as the unifying factor in the universal code which symbolists fashioned across their separate linguistic divisions in their search for a universal language. Mallarmé's faun may not have been the orthodox Pan of antiquity but it was recognizable by a Romance as well as non-Romance readership; so was Yeats's Byzantium and Rilke's Orpheus; and no one tried to replace the myth of Leda and the swan with a Christian counterpart.

In more recent times, the surrealists renewed the cry for a new mythology to replace the ancient ones. Of these the loudest heretic was André Breton, who sought out the strains of subversive occultism as countercurrents to the heritage of Greco-Roman elements. But in avoiding both the standard Hellenic and the Christian symbolism, he chose myths from Provence and Languedoc which were those of alchemists and of Christian heretics of Cathar origin; these myths, when probed deeper, turned out to be of a Judeo-Christian blending, coming to the western part of the Mediterranean basin from Alexandria and tracking back to Pythagoras. If Breton was able to create a new frame of reference for himself and for some of his followers in the emblematic use of such figures as Osiris, Isis, Melusine, and Esclarmonde, they did not rise out of exceptional usage to overthrow the ones which were germane to Romania and had proved pervasive beyond the confines of the Romance literatures. Ironically, in a more pristine guise the tie with antiquity was reinforced rather than severed. The mythology of Romania was not only a resilient reality, resisting contenders, but an aggressive and imperial one impeding newer literary contexts from getting a foothold in European literature.

The fact is that it is Europe which in its literature has been a monolith from Britain to the Ural mountains, expending its common literary heritage in constant waves of renewal; and that heritage has not remained the unique and exclusive property of the countries whose languages derive from the Greco-Roman matrix.

The reality of Romanic cohesion must not be sought, then, in its mythological referential system, since it has become and still remains the common fountainhead of literatures written in noncognate languages. And yet, despite the homogeneity of a heritage that transcends linguistic groupings in Europe and, by extension, in other places where literature occurs in European languages, there are elements other than subject matter and the mytho-symbolic code that sustain the reality of Romania by separating it from the rest of European literature.

If the unity prevails in the parallel historical development of its cognate languages, so too there is a certain literary unity that derives from the unique connotative functions of those languages, conveying a philosophical outlook which is ingrained in the literary image-making process. Madame de Staël perceived this truth remarkably when she said: "On pourrait dire avec raison que les Français et les Allemands sont aux deux extrémités de la chaîne morale, puisque les uns considèrent les objets extérieurs comme le mobile de toutes les idées, et les autres les idées comme le mobile de toutes les impressions" (*De l'Allemagne,* p. 7).

There is an element of materio-spiritual reality inherent in the languages derived from the Greek fountainhead, which is a crucial factor in Romanic literatures to this day. Classicists such as Louis Ménard and A. J. Festugière have noted that the morphological ambivalence of Greek words gives the translator the option of sanctifying the material or materializing the spiritual; in other words there is a monistic philosophy sealed in the language itself. I think that the basis of what Madame de Staël observed was the carry-over of this linguistic code into the Romance languages and consequently into their view of existence. This organic connotative process, inherent in these cognate languages, is intertranslatable but does not bridge the language barrier as one tries to convey the ambivalence into Teutonic and Anglo-Saxon idioms in general. In the Romance literatures, particularly as I have noted in nineteenth- and twentieth-century writings, the spiritual corrects reality, and the concrete invades the ideal through the alchemistic character of these languages. In the Nordic languages the spiritual splits phenomena into separate and dichotomous entities, and the languages are conditioned to the expression of that duality.

Just as in the Christian paintings of Spain and Italy there is an inherent sensuality never totally submerged or banished from mystical representations, so too in the metaphoric structure even of such so-called abstract poets as Mallarmé there is a concrete dimension to the essence extracted. In "L'Après-midi d'un faune" the ideal is represented in the transparence of the grape skin emptied of its pulp. Only in a negative expression of the concrete can Mallarmé suggest the abstract. In fact, the suggestive vagueness in French symbolist poetry is most often achieved through ellipsis in syntax rather than through the choice of words, for the words themselves too often fail to surrender their sensory connotations to the poet's search for the ineffable. In typically English, American, and Germanic literatures, on the other hand, the image is either totally sensual or metaphysically abstract, except in those very poets to whom the Romanic writers are drawn, such as Poe, Swinburne, Whitman, Rilke. In the case of Eliot, he is attracted both ways at once, and he becomes an ambivalent technician caught between John Donne and Jules Laforgue, between Hopkins and Mallarmé.

It is in the language factor, then, as it applies to literary expression that we can find the surviving reality of the monolith. And I attribute to that reality the fact that a movement such as surrealism can be conveyed well in Hispanic idioms and not very well in the Anglo-American or German metaphoric mediums. What Paz calls "a religious atheism" in modern literature (so characteristic of surrealist writing) is naturally embodied in the Romanic metaphor but hard to capture in Anglo-Teutonic languages, which demand from the writer nonambiguous options between the mystical and the material. The melding of connotations, which the Romance languages have achieved within the severe rigidity of their syntax, has not yet been attained by the freer languages.

If, then, it can be said that there is a real survival of Romanic texture that creates a metaphoric homogeneity and with it a certain dynamic materialism in Romania within the broader collectivity of the European mythology, there is nonetheless a contemporary erosion of that reality. Early twentieth-century avant-gardes were perhaps the last stand of that Romanic unity. Picasso was a Mediterranean, so was Valéry, so were Reverdy, Saint-Pol-Roux, Apollinaire, and Marinetti. And so was the ultimate choice of that Celt, André Breton, who embraced the provençal emblems: surrealism and its antecedents created precisely that mode of expression that put spirituality in the material object and had the language to express it.

But since World War II there has been what one might call the alienation of French literature from Romania. If morphologically it is still a Romance language, semantically it seems to be wandering into foreign fields. With the infiltration of Eastern European philosophies, that integration of the spiritual with the material has virtually vanished, allowing for the domination of the abstract through the desensualization of literary language. Indeed, consider the recent reinterpretations of classical French literature. If Christian attitudes can lend themselves to the kind of explications of Racine we find in Roland Barthes's and Lucien Goldmann's writings, are we to conclude that Christian symbolization, which for so long resisted mutation by preserving its historicity, has finally succumbed to mythification and in that state takes its place in a totally new referential code in literature? With the waning of the anthropocentric universe, literature wavers between animism and nihilism. As the Eastern wind breathes down upon France, the animism still glowing in the autumnal light of Romania withdraws more and more from its Northern sister. The departure of such an essential member leaves us to witness the cracking of the monolith. Dare one suggest, with apprehension, that French is ceasing to be a Romance literature, and warn that the de-Latinization of the French language and its writers will inevitably turn the reality of Romania into a myth?

NOTE

This essay first appeared in *Comparative Literature Studies*, vol. 25, no. 1 (March 1978), 23–29.

XIII

AT THE FRONTIERS BETWEEN POETRY AND THEOLOGY ACCORDING TO JACQUES MARITAIN

There has been a general trend for critics to trespass on the discipline of philosophy and for philosophers to invade the domain of literary criticism. Philosophers apply their terminologies to a form of conceptual writing which is practically devoid of one of its own, and they test their criteria of intelligibility and logical consistencies on areas of cognizance whose interface is something called "imagination," which neither criticism nor creative writing has been able to define. They have used tools too cumbersome and too sophisticated to explore something delicate and evanescent, and the result has been a type of scanning which often picks up the unessential in the work of art, or that mechanical part of the process that is tedious to the creative artist and from which he tries to shield the reader in his effort to give him the *light* he has captured and to hide the wiring that conducts to it. By learning how the lamp functions we are not the more impressed by the luminosity of the lamp—unless, of course, the "we" identifies readers strictly science-oriented. But poetry has not yet been declared a high-priority need for the scientific mind.

As a literary critic and pursuer of the Poet, I have been rather shaken of late to see my favorite poets become pawns in the maneuvers of philosophers and ideologues who succeed better in telling me what is missing in the poets than what they possess to spark my own imagination and embrace the parabola of the factor we call "imagination."

It is in this state of diffidence that I returned to a philosopher-critic I had long neglected. A rereading of Jacques Maritain's *Frontiers of Poetry, Situation of Poetry,* articles on painters, aesthetic dialogues. "La Clef des chants"— erroneously retitled in English "Freedom of Song"—and *Art and Scholasticism* restored somewhat my spirits and coaxed me to revise some of my recent antiphilosophical prejuduces.

Maritain was first of all admirably qualified to write about the arts, not because he had a logical mind, which, of course, he had, but because he had a sensitive one as well. He considered poets as closely affiliated with saints and angels, although he worried all his life about the darker angels of poetry. He was nurtured in all the arts and came to put music on the level of sublimity: "Nowhere better than in music does there appear to the philosopher the very mysterious nature of the creative idea or factive idea, that plays a central role in the theory of art."[1]

As I look back on my own past, in the war years in the shadow of Columbia University where I was feverishly searching for a dissertation topic, Maritain was one of the two catalysts of my own enchantment with certain French poets. The other was Paul Hazard, an eighteenth-century scholar. I make a point of this fact not for the purpose of injecting an autobiographical tone into this essay but because it is very significant and curious that the two critics of literature who appeared to me most effective in understanding the most ineffable, the most intellectually tormented, emotionally wrenched poets of the modern age were Maritain, Thomist theologian, and Hazard, schoolman of the Age of Reason. Although Maritain emphasizes that Baudelaire looked askance on poetry criticism by nonpoets, those two men disciplined in rational thinking, the one riding on the road of Reason to divine truth, the other to secular light, practiced what one might call "the poetics of criticism." They estimated that the most important intellectual revolution occurring in the millennium was due to a group of French poets who had in full cognizance tried to cross the frontiers of philosophy and theology.

The lives of these two French scholars crossed mine in that era, never to be duplicated, when Paris lent its intellectual crown jewels to New York to keep safe from the barbarians. Imagine being a student and having access to Hazard, Maritain, Jules Romains, Claude Lévi-Strauss, St. Exupéry, Maeterlinck, Gustave Cohen, André Breton, Yves Tanguy, et al.! I remember Maritain's ascetic white head, the pale purity of his face; he was a displaced person but on target with his communications, and always accompanied by his beloved wife, Raïssa, who was a poet and collaborated in many of his poetic meditations.

Maritain's approach to the arts was from the center of the aesthetic cognizance outward rather than as an outsider-narrator or—to use the horrible new word—discussant. Paradoxical as it may seem, Maritain, a devout Christian closely conversant with God's Word, was close to the artists who were devout, like Léon Bloy, Max Jacob, and Paul Claudel, and at the same time he was impartially devoted to the "maudits" and rebels such as Baudelaire, Rimbaud, Lautréamont. He was also tolerantly trying to understand what new and troubling tremors were shaking tradition in the persons of Picasso, Pierre Reverdy, and André Breton.

Had he been a literary critic by profession, he could have been excused for turning a deaf ear to the avant-garde or for underestimating or deriding its members. As a theologian and philosopher, he did not even have to worry about them. That is why his insights into poetry and art are the more noteworthy and add to his total work a remarkable dimension. In the *Dehumanization of Art*, Ortega y Gasset, responding to the same avant-garde manifestations, gave a testy though subtle analysis of the *effects* of the creative artists' new orientation on the reader/viewer. Maritain, considering the effects as side issues, explored better than Ortega y Gasset what poetry was trying to become. He probed the innermost core of the poetic process instead of describing the outcome:

> It is perfectly true that art has the *effect* of inducing in us affective states, but this is not its *end* or its *object;* a fine distinction if you will, but still an extremely important one. Everything gets out of hand if one takes as the *end* that which is simply a *conjoined effect* or a *repercussion*.[2]

One of the most feared practices in modern criticism is "intentionalism." It is considered naive and futile to discuss aesthetics in terms of the expressed intentions of the creative artist. It is what the reader finds and takes rather than what the artists tried to offer that counts in the opinion of many prestigious critics of our time. The implication is that too often the artist's self-assigned commissions are arrogantly beyond his power to deliver, and of course the modern sophisticated reader is apprehensive of deceit and collusion. Suspecting themselves to be somewhat more intelligent than the writers of the "texts" they are reading, the professional readers set themselves up as advocates; facts, evidence, are what count, not what was meant to be experienced and conveyed.

Maritain's meditations on the poets he selected are based on the hypothesis that for the first time since the dawn of creative-intellectual process, the poet-artist has demonstrated self-awareness and has thereby not only expressed his intentions but also drawn his readers into the operation, inducing them to experience the magical and tantalizing adventure which produces the work of art. In probing the process, Maritain hails and at the same time fears two notions relating to the intentions of the poet. One is the concept of "purity" applied to the arts, the other metaphysics. "Pure poetry" had become a slogan initiated by Abbé Brémond, who had tried in the 1920s to carry the cult of visual eradication of the poetic object and the nonspecific referential naming of material things within the confines of the poem and in so doing exceeded the conjectures of Stéphane Mallarmé. Although one would have expected an ascetic to support such an attitude of self-negation and rejection of material dimensions from the poem, Maritain was apprehensive that such paths might lead the artist into a misconception of what true asceticism was, and in his inherent inability to espouse it, jeopardize at the same time his possession of his own domain. Fearing that this "purity" might be confused with that of the saints, Maritain deplored the general use of the word itself in its spiritual context by outsiders aspiring to the mystic's meaning of "purity." Such aspiration might lead the poet to suicide or at least to silence because of the unattainability of "purity" within the limits and expressive range of the human condition.

The other danger Maritain envisaged was the confusion of the poetic Angst with the spiritual one. Although he judged the source to be the same, Maritain thought that the poet would be deceiving himself if he substituted the one for the other. One could say that Maritain predicted Promethean failure for this form of attempted transcendence. One is reminded of Mallarmé's image of the bird with the broken wing. The danger can be avoided if the bird/poet can measure the range of his flight and not exceed it, and thus avoid human physical damage in aiming for spiritual goals which are off limits for him: "From poetry alone they expect, in the midst of a despair of whose sometime tragic reality they cannot be unaware, an improbable solution to the problem of their lives, a possible escape toward the superhuman" (*FP*, 32).

In this respect the readers of Maritain in English translation will be misled by the use of the word "spirit" in the English text as an equivalent to *esprit*. It is true that Maritain uses the ambivalent French word in both meanings, but he capitalizes when it means "Spirit." In this particular instance, where he is speaking of the poet's breakthrough, he is referring to the poetic mind: "The major role of Baudelaire and Rimbaud was to have made art push back the frontiers of the mind" (*FP*, 28). He would never admit that the poet could conceivably break into the supernatural sphere, closed even to the saint. It is already a remarkable breach, as he observed, to achieve the kind of mental metempsychosis that alters material realities touched by the imagination of the poet. Without understanding the particular connotation of the word *esprit* in French, the reader of the text in English would be hard put to understand how Maritain's fascination with the quasi-metaphysical process noted in poetics could be related to Thomism. Maritain can make this conciliation because he believes with Thomas Aquinas that "intelligence is the sister of mystery" (*FP*, 47). In other words, Maritain—like the poets he selected for study, beginning with Baudelaire and Rimbaud—believes in the intellect's capacity to deal with mystery, a broader sense of intelligence *beyond* what he calls "intelligence considered in its rational functioning" (*FP*, 72). If the Thomist envisages the activity of intelligence as a threshold to the spiritual, Rimbaud had uttered the same verity in a simple statement: "Par l'Esprit on va à Dieu." The frontiers of poetry are thence at the frontiers of the mind before the metaphysical leap reserved for saints, and "the frontiers of the spirit" makes absolutely no sense in terms of poetry or even in terms of human spirituality.

In following the poet on his perilous path Maritain noted three stages: first, recognition in one's self of a deep spiritual need; second, the revelation and desire to share the process of the distillation of the human experience, through which knowledge arises; and third, the crystallization of the work in a universe parallel to the one created by God, the poem in its own closed universe, controlled by its own code and laws, reminiscent of God's *but not of God's kingdom*. In such a perspective, the most important aspect of the study of the poet is indeed the cognizance of the poetic state and the intention of making use of it on a metaphysical level for purposes which in their prodigious aspirations cannot have an optimal chance of success. Would we appreciate *Les Illuminations* as much as we do if we had not read "La Lettre du voyant"?

That is the kind of question that could arise from Maritain's proposition. Because we know how high Rimbaud projected the poet's destiny, are we thereby able to fill in the empty spaces in the fragmental proses and call them a supreme form of poetry? According to Maritain, having this empathy with the becoming of the poet is a higher poetic experience than the pleasure of the texts that result from the process. What the poet has put down can hardly be a total achievement. A poem will give signals that go beyond what is ipso facto recorded, says Maritain.

> Art, as far as it is under the orders of Beauty does not stop, at least when its object allows it, at forms nor colors, nor at sounds nor at words taken for themselves and *as things,* but it takes them also as being able to make known something other than themselves, that is to say as *signs.* And the signified can become a signifier in its turn, and the more charged with meaning the object of art becomes . . . the more vast and more rich and more high will be the possibility of joy and beauty.[3]

Each work is blessed with the totality of the passion that transforms the material object into something ignited and empowered. And here Maritain uses the word "surreal" in its most spiritual connotation which in a later writing, "La Clef des chants," he accuses the surrealists of having aborted: "It [surrealism] occupied for a moment in this country the active peak of poetry; its revolt, its will to deliverance, the despair on which it was nourished, constituted its greatness. . . . it was its spiritual inconsistency that made it succumb so fast" ("La Clef," 173–174).

For Maritain poetry is more than simply a branch of literature. It is knowledge, it is an ontology but "it [knowledge] wants to be expressed and is expressible only in a work."[4] And he admits that this ultimate objective of the artist to surpass the limits of art puts him in a problematic situation. The poetic mind, to which Maritain pays profound respect, is deluding itself. In using methods similar to the saints' to delve into the mysteries of the material reality, poets are indulging in a pseudo-mysticism which deceives them into thinking that they have reached sacred ground: "And they not only confounded poetry with metaphysics; they confounded it with morality, and they confounded it with sanctity" ("CPK," 57).

Maritain's use of the words "poet" and "poetry" is global and conjoins the notion of poetics in the Aristotelian sense. It is quite similar to Apollinaire's declaration that one can be a poet in all domains. According to Maritain the term "poet" surpasses that of artist or rhyme maker. These are artisans more concerned with the aesthetic quality of the product than with the quality of the producer. In Maritain's sense, the poet's operations verge on self-immolation, and they may conceivably never reach the point of creating the purported object of his effort. Maritain would prefer him to the artisan who is overwhelmed by self-admiration in viewing his created work.

To be a poet is to attain the outposts of the inner being, what Maritain calls the "poetics of integrality," similar to the ascesis of the saint; yet there is significant difference because the poet must avoid the spheres of abstraction and, instead, direct the creative power toward concrete goals. The distinction between an artist and a craftsman is, according to Maritain, that state of grace which carries the poet into his work but without for a minute abandoning the integral totality of the vision to the unit of the work. It is by this virtue that the distinction between poet and painter ceases: "If a painter belongs, like the one in question here, to the family of the very great, it is by reason above all of his *poetics*."[5]

According to the situation in which Maritain sees the poet—between the world of pure abstraction and a state of captivity in the concrete—he faces two pitfalls. He may try to become a seeker of the absolute where his human dimension will make his entry impossible or become so involved in the thing he creates that he will exhaust himself, his generative force spent on what we could call in today's scientific terminology cloning his own creation. The example Maritain uses is Picasso, who was great for a while, then repeated himself. Or, on the other hand, the poet may go so far as to think that he is a savior of humanity.

The paradox in this analysis is that the analysis itself falls between two worlds. Maritain uses the language of theology to describe the poet in action while admonishing him not to aspire to theology. "In showing us where moral truth and the authentic supernatural lie, religion spares poetry the misconception of believing itself made to transform ethics and life itself" (*FP*, 46). The application then of religious qualifiers to describe poetic experience is not meant to absorb poetics into religion but to determine limitations of poetic mysticism. His position is compassionate and severe at the same time as he reveals almost in spite of himself how torn he is between his allegiance to the poet and to the saint.

Although Maritain conveys a pretty clear definition of the term "Poet" in its generic implications, his concept of Beauty is somewhat ambiguous. In categorically separating Beauty from Truth he tells us what Beauty is not rather than what it is. He assigns Truth to the domain of God and His scholars, and Beauty to man. But a clear definition of Beauty can be found nowhere in his writings on aesthetics, not in his contemplation of art, nor in his reconstruction of the edifice of music, nor in his description of the thorny path of the poet. It is conceived as a mysterious essence deep within the psyche of the poet, of which rays fall on the work; it comes closest to his notion of divine love, shared with all yet given totally to each.

Through illustrations which encompass the entire history of the arts, of which he is extraordinarily knowledgeable, he does not make a discriminate choice of one standard of the beautiful against another, that is to say that he does not delve into the forms that Beauty can take or has taken but rather discourses on the function of recognizing the beautiful. Here he adheres closely to the Thomist principle that the mind is an intermediary between the perception of the senses and the supernal. In this context the recognition of Beauty, as he keeps repeating, is an activity of the intellect, although the *delectation* of the object of beauty depends to a great degree on the senses. Far from denying the material character of the form of beauty, Maritain warns against attempts to rarefy the beautiful. The aesthetic experience/knowledge consists in the conjunction of the intellectual power with the material object, transformed through an element called in turn "radiance" and "splendor." What the artisan can achieve by constant perfecting of methodology or system is not as significant to Maritain as the intensity of the intellectual activity; and, therefore, he tends to favor the intentionality of the moderns over the accomplishments of the academicians, finding in the disorder of the avant-garde a more genuine comprehension of the relationship between the subjectivity of the human artist (in contrast with the divine artist) and the forms he shapes in the material world.

Beauty, then, is not a specific, tangible reality but "essentially an object of intelligence" (*A et S*, 31). He then concludes that "such is also the beautiful in art, which works upon a sensible matter in order to give joy to the mind" (*A et S*, 32). Here again the translators of Maritain are dismally misrepresenting the process of his reasoning when they substitute the word "spirit" for "mind" at precisely the moment when in terms of his cognition and creation of Beauty he is placing the artist and his process in the human context and accepting from the Divine only the "ray" or "radiance." The "ray" does not penetrate directly the material world itself as in the visions of the Romantics in keeping with their Swedenborgian philosophy but is absorbed into the human intelligence through which alone, according to Maritain, human art can overcome simple imitations of the natural. If he meant "spirit," then he would have allocated the artistic operation to the realm of the divine, which is precisely what Maritain was trying to combat in his effort to correct the misapprehensions of the artist who thinks he has become some kind of saint.

Although he emphasized the intellectual character of poetic creation and comprehension of Beauty, Maritain was not identifying the intellect with logical thinking. He tells us very categorically that "at the heart of logic itself poetry and poetic knowledge have no place" ("CPK," 47n.). For him, as for the surrealists, the chambers of the mind are many. But for him the depth to be explored to find "the formation point of the creative impulse" (*FP*, 202) is not the unconscious domain heralded by the Freudians of his generation. Maritain's ambivalence toward the work of Proust can be explained on the basis of his conviction that what arises out of the involuntary memory with the aid of the conscious exploration of the psyche lacks the grace and spiritual recognition of the found data. Maritain's distrust of Freudian methods extends to those poets, and particularly to the surrealists, who thought they could apply experimental methods in psychoanalysis to the work of art. "Nothing was more puerile . . . than to ask that methods used by a police inspector, a somnambulist, and a professor, mistaken for the arcana of Physical Science, be used to explore the so-called abysses of the soul and capture poetry" (*FP*, 174). He felt the surrealists wrecked their revolution of the human spirit by dragging it into two equally pestiferous mires: psychic automatism and dialectical materialism.

According to Maritain it would be ignoble for the poet to let his pen automatically set down the dictation of his unconscious and its frivolities. Instead he had to exercise extreme vigilance in monitoring the depths of being, "a vigilance of mind, so subtle and so prompt, prepared by the interior silence, that it will discern at the edge of darkness all the forms that pass under the starry vault of the heart" ("La Clef," 174). Strangely, Maritain did not seem to realize that his "vigilance" was not far afield from the "qui vive" of Breton in *Nadja* and the role of sentinel that Breton attributed to the monitor. By a remarkable coincidence in the same period when Maritain was suggesting an alternative to passive recording of the unconscious, Breton had written a poem called "Vigilance" in which he was monitoring precisely in the manner suggested by Maritain his dream on the edge of mortal oblivion and trying to pluck its *radiance* and *splendor* but without admitting an assist from the divine. The difference between the two was not in regard to apperceptions of creative process, and what Maritain named "radiance" was quite compatible with Breton's "iridescence."

The disparity lay in the purpose assigned to the arts. For Maritain the poet had to reveal not what was most humanly representative but best representative of the human. In rejecting the randomness of human data and its introduction into the work of art, Maritain brings us face to face with value judgment in the context of a recognizable a priori code. The independence of aesthetics from morality—which was the primary struggle of the artists of his time—vanishes into a moral judgment concerning poets and poetics in the broad definition that he set up for those terms. Had he not stated in *Art et Scholastique* (1920) that the work of art had its own rules and had to be free from any outside sanctions? (see *A et S*, 99–107). Yet by a rationalization that is Kantian while rejecting Kant, Maritain is committed to a predetermined code of morality which, imprinted in the real world, gives it its order. The artist cannot comprehend integral reality without a grasp of its moral interface, and if these premises are accepted, then it would follow that without a comprehension of morality, there is no comprehension of reality but a blurred and distorted universe reflected in the work of art through the malfunctioning of an optic that relays a defective vision. "If the artist is morally deformed, his very art . . . risks having to pay the wages of this moral deformity" (*FP,* 66). Taking this statement not from an ethical point of view but as a critical theory, we find Maritain pursuing a hypothesis of old French vintage, derivative of Sainte-Beuve, presuming the total dependence of the quality of the work of art upon the character and formation of the artist: such fruit from such a tree. It is diametrically opposed to current trends—supported by Mallarméan theories—which consider the autonomy of the work of art as the basis of its validity and viability, and any infiltration of the idiosyncrasies of the artist are worth noting only if deductibly apparent in the work itself.

Modern criticism is categorically opposed to generic analysis of the qualities of the work of art. Moreover in casting off moral evaluations, it renders itself innocent of aesthetic evaluations as well. The modern critic's complacency before the aesthetic elements of the work of art seems to give credence to Maritain's contention that without the recognition of good and evil the survival of the notion of beauty is as precarious as its physical flowering "on a dead branch" (*FP*, 66). Thus, if we in the latter decades of the twentieth century are embarrassed by the moral dogmatism of Maritain, we have to concede that what we admire is his passionate embrace of artistic beauty irrevocably conjoined with the ethics of his judgment. Maritain cannot easily ignore the Christian that he is when dealing with the problematics of the arts. Apostle of freedom elsewhere in his writings, Maritain seems to ignore the century-old struggle of the artist to free himself from moral standards extraneous to his own artistic universe. He reprimands André Gide, the iconoclast, not for his rejection of God but for his flaunting of "the gratuitous act" in defiance of the moral code. On the other hand, he approaches the works of Dostoevsky and Mauriac principally to find in them the faces of Christianity and to highlight these as dominant traits of the works rather than to concern himself with the novelists' efforts to discover psychological truth.

Maritain seems to say: if the artist cannot be a good Christian let him at least be a tormented one like Rimbaud. At times he equates the moral struggle with the poetic struggle, and the spiritual vigilance which he demands of the artist with a form of practical watchdog ethics not particularly relevant to his deeper comprehension of the struggle between immanence and transcendence which he himself has highlighted as the plight of the modern poet.

It is interesting to note that whereas Maritain is so cautious lest the artist confuse asceticism with aestheticism and the search for beauty with the yearning for the absolute, he throws caution to the winds when he himself as critic confuses moral vigilance with artistic vigilance: "I say that in actual fact a work is Christian to the extent to which—in whatever manner and with whatever deficiency it may be—there courses through the soul of the artist something of the life that makes saints and contemplatives" (*A and S*, 211n.). He seems to imply that although all Christians are not great poets, only good Christians can be great poets. The poet must have some of the very characteristics of the saint, without thinking of himself as a substitute saint.

There would appear to be almost a naive dogmatism here were we to take these pronouncements at face value and out of context of his thought and out of the climate of his time. What gives understanding if indeed not credence to these declarations is the basic attitude Maritain demonstrates toward the age in which he lived which he called "the cadaver of the Christian world" as he faced with fear and dismay "the dissolution of civilization." It is as if he were trying to catch at any straw that might save the arts from the general turpitude he discerned. He would have liked to believe with his contemporary, Guillaume Apollinaire, that the future of aesthetics would be in step with truth and "bonté" as Apollinaire had proclaimed in one of his last manifesto-poems, "Les Collines," which Maritain quoted. The poet's statement seemed to sustain his own feeling that ethics and aesthetics could not be separated and that the only chance for a renaissance of the arts was through that alliance.

Yet, even if today we may be uncomfortable with the dogmatism which asserts itself when the moral issues interfere with his aesthetics, his track record of critical judgment after the fact is noteworthy. Although Maritain did not consider himself a literary critic except by avocation, he emerges fifty years later in retrospect in a much better position as a prophet of literary resilience than many a professional critic. We know how badly Sainte-Beuve in the previous century fared in his judgment of his contemporaries although he was a masterful scholar in reconstructing the achievements of the Classical Age. He was condescending to Baudelaire, lukewarm about Flaubert, and he extolled a great many contemporaries whom time has proved unworthy of being remembered. In the era between the two world wars it would have been much more fashionable for Maritain to discuss favored, traditionally acceptable novelists and dozens of swarming poets considered great by their happy publishers.

Maritain, a conservative in terms of ethics, demonstrated a weakness for avant-garde aesthetics, not for the results achieved but because he saw in such manifestations a spiritual motivation: he was drawn almost in spite of himself to the tormented, the audacious, the rebellious. In spite of his adherence to the notion that a moral code is the gauge of aesthetic purity, he was seduced by the very poets he was reprimanding. Few respectable critics would have bothered to get angry with Breton and his manifestos. It was easier to dismiss him as a troublemaker. The cult of Rimbaud had not picked up any momentum in the 1920s and the saintly Abbé Brémond was a more popular director of poetic consciences. After his premature death Apollinaire had entered the literary purgatory of provisional oblivion. No one ever mentioned Pierre Reverdy except in a historical footnote as the director of some avant-garde magazines.

Maritain thought these poets important not as technicians but as figures in a spiritual drama. There was a certain trepidation that the epistemological drive of the poet might in some future time exceed the pace of the theologian. He had said, perhaps in jest, perhaps in wishful thinking, that to do the job right Proust really needed the assistance of a Saint Augustine: "To write the work of a Proust as it asked to be written, would have required the inner light of a Saint Augustine" (*FP*, 118). He discovered perhaps that the only hope for the world of the future was the closing of the ranks of the poets and the saints, perhaps finding the poets to be the only species worth saving. He discovered greatness according to his understanding of the greatness of the poet, yet he made the astute judgment that there might not be future perfectors or developers of the models left by those he considered pathblazers. He estimated that the disciples would be lesser luminaries than the series of isolated poetic constellations with whom he found himself privileged to share a moment in eternity.

Maritain's writings reveal almost in spite of himself his own inner struggle between the artist's version of metaphysical anguish and the theologian's understanding of the absolute. But every time he was tempted to cede ground, he drew back in fearful realization of the implications of too intimate a relationship between the emissaries of the arts and those of religion.

Maritain had realized that Mallarmé in his pursuit of purity had usurped sacerdotal functions; this poet's aesthetic ascesis had put the life of the poet at the altar of the art. Maritain had not read the surrealist Breton too closely, and indeed at that time who knew much more about Breton than his manifestos and his political utterances? Had he probed further, he would have found that the number one surrealist, and the only sustained and "pure" one, was offering poetry as a substitute religion—precisely in the way Maritain had feared that some poet might dare to do, whereby Man would take back from God what he had accorded Him: the power to create and control not simply the universe of the work of art (which had been the limit of Mallarmé's goal) but the common habitat of the living, for art would then be not a substitute to life but the very channel through which alone life might be tolerable.

The purposes of the poet are not the purposes of the philosopher, although they may be using the same language and the same metaphysical distress signals of the color of the time to propel them. The poet, within the definition of Maritain himself but beyond the limited expectations Maritain set to his jurisdiction, seeks no tangential relationship with theology. Maritain tried to use his natural sympathy for the poet's condition in the present world to encourage him, then, to indicate to him where his power would stop, and ultimately to lead him beyond poetry into religion. As he admitted, "mysticism is in fashion; asceticism less." He imagined that by showing the poet his limitations, not as an antagonist but as an accomplice, he would accomplish the evangelical act of leading him *beyond* poetry into ascesis, his critical function having an ultimate religious motivation. Little did he seem to realize that mysticism would follow asceticism into the category of the unfashionable.

Maritain's projections of the ideals of the poetry of the future predicted the odds to be against the poet:

> To recuperate man and the truth of his nature, resume contact with earthly reality (and perhaps also with divine reality), and to cure himself also of an avarice and of a spiritual sensuality too often considered a form of purity in itself, all this without betraying its own destiny and autonomy, this is for the poetry of tomorrow a frightening task, rendered harder, yet more difficult, it would seem, by circumstances of a moral and social order where the world is placed today. (*FP*, 73)

The breach between the world in which Maritain was nurtured and in which he postulated, and the second half of the twentieth century, with its more and more pronounced acceptance of a nonanthropocentric and indifferent universe, is so deep that the position he allocates to the arts in relation to philosophical speculation and human communication may seem of no current consequence.

Admittedly there are no incidences of great religious conversions among men and women in the arts today to bring up considerations of the relationship between artistry and sanctity. And works of Maritain are not apt to inspire whatever readership may come upon them toward either ascesis or poietic.

But there is one fundamental element of Maritain's writings on aesthetics which if heeded might well give pause for thought in respect to the direction that literary criticism has taken in alarming acceleration in the last three decades. We may or may not agree with Maritain's contention that the arts are the dialogues of humans within the confines of the material world in preparation for the sublime dialogue with God; but his admonition about the nature of poetic knowledge is not contingent on religious faith, and it is of serious import to critics of any or no spiritual persuasion. "Poetry is knowledge," says Maritain, "but to make of it a *means* of knowledge . . . is to pervert it" ("CPK," 68–69). He adds that if it were knowledge it would be "furiously inferior to geometry." It is a statement well worth pondering as we observe to what extent in modern criticism the study of a poetic "text" has become an exercise in logic. Minds attuned to logical cognition have tried to apply their methodologies to the analysis of poetry in direct contrast to Maritain's assertion that as the subject of dialectic discourse, poetry and poetic knowledge have no meaning and no place.

After repeated exposures to recent critical commentaries that treat poetic communication as if it were a language of inquiry, one realizes that the very poets Maritain selected as best illustrative of the situation of poetry between the throes of the poet and his deeds are now favored for study for totally different reasons: to prove either their character weakness or their linguistic strength. The arts, perceived by Maritain as indices of "spiritual superabundance," are subjected to inquiries intended to drain them of the very mysteries which according to Maritain were the signets of Beauty. For were the significations terminably decipherable, the art would become an activity of knowledge and lose its creative quality. In focusing on the "text," critics tend to eliminate the creator, whereas Maritain would say, "if there is no man, there is no artist" (see *A and S*, 90).

It is because criticism today is confusing the "text" as a source of knowledge with the poem as an example or evidence of a constant and continuous creative activity that the notion of Beauty has virtually disappeared from commentaries on literature; and the tendency is not confined to the study of poetry, but this so-called hermeneutics has spread to music and art criticism as well.

Whereas in the case of Maritain the powers of philosophical conceptualization were directed toward the recognition of the discrete identity of the arts as opposed to speculative knowledge, today procedures of analytic philosophy applied to the study of literary/poetic "texts" obliterate the aesthetic factor, and it becomes indeed a very grave question whether in so doing they do not at the same time pulverize that quality which is the differential between "text" and poetry. Jacques Maritain unwittingly touched on what has become one of the burning issues of modern criticism.

NOTES

This essay first appeared in *Renascence*, vol. 34, no. 4 (Summer 1982), 245–259.

1. "La Clef des chants," in *Frontières de la poésie* (Paris: L. Rouart et fils, 1935), p. 179; hereafter cited parenthetically in the text as "La Clef." *Frontières* is cited parenthetically as *FP;* all translations from this edition are mine.
2. *Art and Scholasticism,* trans. Joseph W. Evans (New York: Charles Scribner's Sons, 1962), p. 204, Notes; hereafter cited parenthetically in the text as *A and S.*
3. *Art et Scholastique* (Paris: L'Art Catholique, 1920), p. 79; hereafter cited parenthetically in the text as *A et S* (translations mine).
4. "Concerning Poetic Knowledge," in *The Situation of Poetry,* trans. Marshall Suther (1955; rpt. New York: Kraus, 1968), p. 51; hereafter cited parenthetically in the text as "CPK."
5. "Three Painters," in *Art and Poetry,* trans. E. de P. Matthews (New York: Philosophical Library, 1943), p. 28.

XIV

ANICET, OR THE SEARCH FOR BEAUTY

Among the astonishing areas of neglect in the criticism of twentieth-century literature is the substantial work of Louis Aragon. The oversight is the more surprising in the light of resurgent interest in Dada and surrealism, extending to collateral references such as Jarry, Roussel, and Artaud. André Breton has fared better, although the scholarly attention to narrative has overstressed the importance of *Nadja* and underestimated Breton's poetry.

In perspective, Aragon may well loom as the Victor Hugo of this century. Like his predecessor he has had an active role in forming a literary movement; he has had his politically and patriotically inspired phases, his colossal narratives; and if he was not exiled at a certain period in his life like Victor Hugo, he has known what it is to be a stranger in his own land, evidenced in the poignant poetry of *En Etrange Pays dans mon pays lui-même*.

The current preoccupation with structural analysis puts Aragon at a great disadvantage. He writes plain, vigorous French; he is not neurotically subtle; he takes his structures where he finds them—in the satirical novel, the sotie, the historical romance, and a poetry largely conveyed in romantic lyricism except for a brief early period in which he indulged in Dada *écriture*. In *Le Paysan de Paris* and in *Le Traité du style* Aragon crystallized and intellectualized the precepts of surrealism better than most of his colleagues who practiced the surrealist metaphor.

But in his earliest prose work, *Anicet,* he accomplished something even more significant: he gave the "materialization of a moral symbol in violent opposition to the morality of the world in which it emerged."[1] These are the words with which he was to characterize some years later the sense of the marvelous which he shared with Breton and a few others in their search for a concept of the Beautiful to replace the standard and tired ones. If the symbolism in *Anicet* is overt in its personifications, its negation of the ethics of the avant-garde of the historical moment makes it an unusual monument in the history of literature, not only in French literature but in its global and epistemological context. *Anicet* tells us how the spirit of surrealism was ignited; but beyond that, its satire of contemporary figures of the artistic world, lightly shaded, is a pretense and a screen for something much more fundamental that troubled Aragon in 1918 as he began his emblematic tale, something that remains one of the essential problematics of twentieth-century literature on an international level: the perilous struggle of the Beautiful in art and writing.

The central magnet of the "Panorama," as Aragon calls his narrative, is a woman named Mirabelle. If "belle" obviously stands for beauty, "mira" may well imply a reflection—which indeed makes her the center of a multifaceted courtship. But it also suggests the mirror vision, the false appearance, the semblance, implying the mistake that the generation of 1918 may have made in its definition of Beauty. Presumably, an old lover, Guillaume, characterized her as "Mire aux yeux d'argent"[2] (untranslatable because the double connotation of silver/money does not come across in modern English, whereas in its French ambiguity lies an element of satire). As the *récit* progresses it becomes obvious that Guillaume was none other than Apollinaire, and that he was not referring to the color of her eyes but to their venal concerns. "That explains this court of masks around her, and its recruitment, and this symbol of beauty in the hands of the merchants" (x). Her gravitation toward wealth results in the choice she eventually makes of a husband: an American multimillionaire businessman wins her hand in a courtship in which his rivals are among the most talented artists of the time.

In identifying Mirabelle as the symbol of modern beauty, Aragon is stating a hypothesis, to be verified or demolished in the analogical progression of the work. At first, the most prestigious artists credited with having remodeled the concept of beauty at the dawn of the century are seen under veiled names and in Guignol exaggerations, arguing about her function:

>   —I tell you that she is a solar myth
>   —A conception of the mind
>   —An obsessive idea
>   —An image
>   —A symbol
>   —Shut up, said Anicet, she is a woman of flesh and bones, else we would not have found her so beautiful. (185)

Mirabelle's background is examined, and it will not take much deciphering to realize that Aragon is giving the reader his version of the history of the concept of Beauty from its beginnings. She first emerges in the Western world through the constraining realism of a Mediterranean maturation. She assumes a fatal power of seduction that destroys men; she becomes an object of fear and persecution: "mothers threw stones after her as they chased her from a village in Asturias where she had gone to hide a painful secret" (189). She eventually attracted the attention of the bizarre—or shall we say "avant-garde"?—Harry James (a suicidal character whom we subsequently are led to identify with a veiled embodiment of Jacques Vaché).[3] The attraction produced instant results: "suddenly he leaned toward Mirabelle, drew her to himself and made her a mother" (190). Retrospectively, Mirabelle passed judgment: "Nobody in the world has ever done so much good and so much harm at the same time" (193). In fact, the Mediterranean Beauty's illicit alliance with the Absurd produced an offspring which, according to Mirabelle's account, was sold as trash.

In Paris, the mecca for the worship of Beauty, the adulterated and modernized version embodied by Mirabelle was wooed by seven identifiable archetypes: a titled crook, an actor, an artist, two poets, a dandy, and a metaphysician. Bringing her their gifts as masked scavengers, they offer her a wide range of alternatives, all resulting from "three preliminary conditions" without which modern Beauty cannot be courted: "theft, lie, mystery" (63).

The glass ball presented by the first suitor is a kaleidoscope that presumably has powers of transcendence. But modern Beauty is capable of using it only to contemplate her own image as the center of all the universe, limiting thus the infinite potential of vision to a confined and narcissistic perspective. The agility of word and movement, the flair for creating illusion, the prestidigitator's aplomb constitute pointedly the stylized stereotype of Jean Cocteau.

The second gift is a polygon of iridescent taffeta containing a beautiful face in its design. In ripping off a piece of the cloth the thief has cut into the face. The iridescence is an illumination of reality; yet there is an element of clumsiness that destroys the beauty inherent in the ever-changing colors. Despite its damaged appearance it is more powerful than the kaleidoscopic luminosity of the first character's ball, which, placed upon the magic though mutilated cloth, loses all its transfigurative quality. The speech of this second masked figure with the lofty lip contains the lexical characteristics which were to become associated with the future leader of surrealism: iridescence, enchantment, the marvelous, the personal spectrum that extends from grey to rose.

The third suitor is a clown, the Charlie Chaplin archetype, the first great star of the new medium for the representation of Beauty on celluloid. Under the name of Pol, he roams through Aragon's novel, giving it the ragtime version of Beauty, the mechanical, accelerated sense of reality. His contribution to modern Beauty is an elixir in the form of a tangerine: "this bizarre little fragrant sun" (60). He procures it at great and comic risk to himself and disrupts the systematized structure of a theater audience as he snatches the precious golden apple from a vendor. All he can do to remunerate her is to give her a spectacular acrobatic performance of his flight. Much valor is displayed, and stunningly succulent is the fruit, but rapidly consumed. Aragon gives a succinct indictment of the value of the cinema to aesthetics: brilliant, gilded, savory but ephemeral—so much effort for so short a satisfaction. We are here very far from the high hopes that Apollinaire had entertained for film as an eventual replacement for the word in the making of poetry, i.e., the Beautiful.

The accent of the fourth suitor suggests that he is either a high-class Italian or a low-class Slav; he brings a diplomatic document, which, if leaked, could cause catastrophic wars. It seems not too far-fetched to conclude that the allegory of the gift and the ambiguity of the place of origin of the giver suggest the involvement of a foreign conspiracy in the shaping of the so-called modern version of the Beautiful. There are elsewhere direct references to Futurism and overt ones to Dada. It is interesting to note that Aragon gives neither of these in any guise an important role in the shaping of the new aesthetics; but the foreign suitor in whom they seem to be amalgamated is among the most shady of the whole secret society seeking to espouse Mirabelle.

The fifth bearer of a gift is Omme, which is a homonym for Man and for the unit of electrical resistance. Although some critics have identified Omme as Jarry, Aragon's own 1931 preface names Valéry, who indeed fits more logically here as the suitor who brings a resistor and an element of measure, stolen from the Institut des Arts et Métiers. His concern for philosophic truth and rule-oriented humanism, pronounced in what Aragon calls a "white" voice, sums up the self-serving hyperbole of Omme: "the most useful present, the most urgent, and the most worthy of your character and mine" (63).

The next, a painter, whose manifest and later confirmed model is Picasso, has lifted the signal which railroad stations use to prevent collisions of trains. He compares the gadget to a red flower and reminds Mirabelle of the cataclysmic consequences of his theft: the possible collision of two rapid trains originating from distant points. Here the conquest of modern Beauty demands the sacrifice of order and risks terrible destruction. Had not Picasso caused, indeed, the collision and explosion of long-established and orderly systems, the breakdown of standardization and of accepted relationships?

The last donor brings the faded photograph of a Beauty of a past generation, of the time of the Blue Danube and of *Pêcheur d'Islande.* One thinks of Rimbaud's *Letter,* in which he chastised those whose search for novelty only led them back to "the spirit of things dead." Aragon is here passing a devastating judgment on Chipre, under whose mask is Max Jacob, generally presumed to have been an avant-garde figure.

If there are seven suitors in this scene, the secret society assures the new aspirant, Anicet, that the number of those seeking modern Beauty's hand is not fixed; it is flexible and ever-fluctuating, and she is indeed an equal-opportunity employer, which makes it possible for Anicet to join the ranks immediately. His gift is a stanza of verse, which is received with derision. He will have to do much better than that to prove a worthy contender for the favors of Beauty: "Don't be surprised by anything," said the fourth masked figure, "and act according to the dictates of your desire for beauty; thus by your actions we shall judge of your aesthetics better than we can by the six mediocre lines of verse you have produced" (73).

A composite methodology for the conquest of modern Beauty emerges out of this allegorical ritual: it is solipsistic, clumsily enchanting, ephemerally glittering, deliberately orderly, perilous, intriguing, superannuated, and amateurishly versified. As narrator, Aragon has not favored any one of the suitors, not even the one with whom he identifies. There is a definite distancing between the two roles he plays: that of participant, in the guise of Anicet, and that of third-person narrator.

Of his identification with Anicet he makes no secret. What is the meaning of his name? Since he mentions at one point "the fresh fragrance of anise," it can be surmised that he is a fresh, young, somewhat hallucinated being—a small pinch of anise. Anicet/anisette, the drink that he and his companions took when they were not drinking grenadine! The white and the red liquors of their youth were symbolic of that unusual combination of the pure and the sanguine which was to mark the special quality of surrealism among a host of avant-garde movements: the sensual reality of red, the power of dreams and the search for absolute beauty that the white hallucinatory potion provoked.

Anicet's story could have consisted simply of a solipsistic adventure in which he might have imagined himself as the champion of Beauty, delivering her from the beasts that surrounded her. He could have cast himself as the white knight in shining armor triumphant over a series of unappetizing Minotaurs. The cloak-and-dagger imagery of *Anicet* is reminiscent of Breton's poetry of the same vintage, but in Aragon's story it contains a measure of realistic irony, which eventually leads his not quite heroic protagonist to prison, to face the indignation and rancor of public opinion; the accusations against him are so grievous that they may well drag him to the guillotine. His achievements in the defense of Beauty have had a destructive rather than constructive character. He succeeded in eliminating two of the unworthy suitors: the metaphysician of "white" poetry and the American multimillionaire. In the course of a tumultuous presence in the arena, he also managed to burn a number of classified museum possessions representing the Beauty of the past: paintings by Boucher, Meissonier, Millet, Greuze, and Pissarro were destroyed by his libertarian vandalism. He burned his personal bridges as well: "the chains fall: I cease to be the slave of my past" (78). He even pretended to burn the money that his bourgeois family had sent him for his sustenance. It is a pretense recognized as such by Anicet himself, for even as he assumes the role of disinterested rebel, he calls his own bluff and replaces the thousand-franc bill he had destroyed by another one he had kept in reserve.

True, he may have cut himself off from his family, but he dragged his ancestors behind him in the figures of an aged Rimbaud in the first chapter and an aged Lautréamont in the last. Both are presented as superannuated factors, suggesting that even the most powerful firebrands of aesthetics wane in time and that the position of avant-garde is as short-lived as youth itself. As Rimbaud tells of his disillusionment, in a lengthy monologue, the reader realizes how rejectable he is becoming in the eyes of Anicet. At the end of his encounter with Rimbaud, Anicet discovers that he has slept with the same Hortense whom Rimbaud loved and then abandoned— in other words, the young rebel had pursued an aging concept of Beauty at the very moment when he was thinking of himself as avant-garde. "I noticed what old-fashioned potions I was using, I did not want to persist in my error, and I went off in search of the modern idea of life, of the line that marked the horizon of our contemporaries" (43).

But at the end of the scene with the seven suitors, just as he is declaring his dedication to Beauty and to love, the lights go out. He is left in the figurative dark, for if Hortense was secondhand, Mirabelle is fake; the sense of adventure generated in her pursuit is vain and futile. What she had really done is to open Anicet's eyes to the inauthenticity of what is called the new art. Anicet's function is to single out every one of the false pretenders to avant-garde beauty and to bring out their ineptness.

The methodologists also come under attack: "they looked within themselves with a system of mirrors. They did not care about their objectives. All they enjoyed was the method to be used to attain a goal. The world was governed by minds which reasoned about themselves" (141).

The most compelling scenes are those with Chipre and Bleu. Max Jacob's mating of poverty with poetry comes off as an artificial stance. Bleu's most recent triumphs are revealed as academic disgraces. The chapter in which Aragon describes Bleu's rise and fall is called, tellingly, "Decease." His *natures mortes* gave the viewer a wonderful sense of living forms, says Anicet, whereas his latest so-called masterpiece in praise of living form, called "Praise of the Body," is lifeless and stilted. "Anicet suddenly understood that Bleu had passed from the domain of love to that of death and glory" (118). The self-appraisal which Aragon puts candidly into the mouth of Bleu is even more devastating: "What a nonentity it is just the same!" (183). The last glimpse of Bleu in this ignoble gallery of false gods is in a newspaper account of his deposition at the trial of Anicet. He shows himself disloyal and unfriendly toward the young defendant. He speeds off to America to become the subject of much adulation and the recipient of much financial reward under the sponsorship of art critics such as Mr. Bolonais (undoubtedly a variation of the ambivalent sausage) whose function will be to establish and dictate tastes in art not only for the current generation but for posterity. Aragon is here not only challenging the validity of the new art of his immediate predecessors but questioning the operations whereby art is promoted and prestige is artificially generated. His satire casts the artist and the critic not in the intellectual battle against each other, which has for so long been the accepted dichotomy, but in an astonishing and shady conspiracy against a gullible public.

Was there anyone who could still salvage Beauty from false creators and promoters? There is the poet with the haughty lip and the clumsy hand who mutilated iridescently beautiful patterns of a face on cloth in the scene of the suitors. His name, we later learn, is Baptiste Ajamais. "He must have been born at the end of a great river in some port on the ocean for his eyes to have caught the grey glow and his voice to have acquired a certain sonority of shells when he said 'the sea.' Somewhere in his childhood, low docks slumbered in the heavy summer evening, and on their still waters there were sailboats that would not leave before the rising of the breeze" (114).

An extraordinary change of style occurs when Aragon is speaking of his friend Breton; the banal and pedestrian tenor of the conversation of the art establishment fades, and the poetic longing that was to characterize and distinguish surrealism from all the other avant-gardes is for a moment fixed on the strange young man coming from the funeral of Harry James, who, having buried the prototype of the absurd, floats in a state of transit, in search of something new.

Whereas Aragon's self-portrait is without glamour, and indeed full of candor and auto-criticism, he adorns his portrait of Breton with an aura of mystery, catches and isolates the rhythm of his speech. Whereas he is Anicet, the subject of transitory excitation, the name Baptiste Ajamais suggests prophecy and permanence, the infinite character of the search. Baptiste is the only one not impressed by the charms of Mirabelle. He tells Anicet: "The conquest of Mirabelle is but an episode, don't forget it, it is the first step in life toward a mysterious end, that I can perhaps discern" (132). When Mirabelle tries to seduce him by undressing before him, Baptiste, unmoved, stares at her coldly. By using Baptiste as his alter ego Aragon demonstrates the ambivalence of his own stand at that moment of youthful incertitude when he might have jumped on the bandwagon of his elders' definition of modernism but didn't. The trouble with the world, according to Baptiste, is that nothing has happened since the world began (cf. 237).

Yet where does this purity of posture lead? Baptiste's saintliness is by no means total. He is seen playing with fire, but is cautious not to get burned. Anicet, on the other hand, is shown holding a lamp in one hand and a revolver in the other. The atmosphere that was charged with adventure and vertigo turns into a climate of confusion. All three principals of the narrative are condemned as inept. Mirabelle's beauty was a fraud, and she failed even as a fortune hunter. Anicet was in prison for having pursued false gods and false goods: did he not try to steal Bleu's latest paintings, only to find out that they were worthless? As for Baptiste, he beat a quick retreat to the country and was content to share the fate of Anicet vicariously through newspaper accounts of the trial. He was in the company of two old habitués of a café, one a certain M. Prudence who bore a strange resemblance to Harry James, and the other an old gentleman by the name of Lautréamont. Was Aragon making prophecies about all the graveyards of the avant-garde?

Anicet is indeed the portrait of the author as a young man, but the viewing of the young man is distanced—just as Candide is and is not Voltaire. Candide was the mocking of an attitude of optimism espoused and then corrected by the creator of the persona; in the same manner Aragon was Anicet before he created Anicet, and Anicet's illusion and subsequent disillusionment are crystallized in a self-critical portrayal. When commentators of Aragon quote from Anicet to illustrate permanent attitudes of its author, and when they equate Mirabelle with Aragon's notion of modern beauty, they forget that *Anicet* is but the record of an historical moment, and as Aragon has said: "I don't think people can understand anything about me if they overlook the dates of my thoughts and my writings."[4]

Historically *Anicet* makes an assessment of the avant-garde of the first two decades of the twentieth century. His rejection of the reigning champions of so-called modern Beauty makes this early work a significant document in the history of the modern arts. Whereas at a half-century distance the attitude of most literary and art critics has been to unite the avant-gardes in a continuous flow from Cubism to Futurism, to Dada and then on to surrealism, a scrutiny of *Anicet* opens a different perspective. Aragon viewed the early years of the century as apocalyptic rather than as avant-garde. He saw his elders in the pursuit of a false aesthetics and found his own contemporaries floundering even though they may have been rejecting the false prophets of a new Beauty. Despite his confusion, the young hero of *Anicet* conveys a deep sense of jeopardy in his handling of the symbolism of Art and Beauty to suggest the perilous state of what he calls "the last divinities of men" (162).

From the narrator's point of view the triumph of Bleu is as great a threat to the discovery of a new concept of beauty as the imprisonment of Anicet and the immobilization of Baptiste. Moreover, Aragon makes it clear at the end of the book that the spirit of absurdism, made incarnate in Jacques Vaché/Harry James, is not in his view the true spirit of modernism either. When Baptiste finds under the guise of M. Prudence his old friend whom he had thought dead, his devastating remark to the red-haired character is: "Harry James, I did not really believe you could have died, but now can no longer believe that you are living" (255).

In *Anicet* Aragon shows the threats to the cult of beauty in the twentieth century, but he offers no solutions. He leaves his young characters in a quandary and suggests that they had better not look to their elders for guidance or inspiration. Indeed, if we remember, this was the very time when Breton had lost confidence in Valéry and when his fondness for Apollinaire had lapsed from a professional to a personal level. The situation at the end of *Anicet* has a significant historical validity; it makes it clear that whatever future aesthetics was to emerge, the composition of a new *cénacle* would not be that of master and younger disciples, but a fellowship of peers, shedding the past and looking forward together but without a concerted platform. This phenomenon also explains why as a *cénacle* surrealism would be subject to constant disruptions as each participant found his own direction.

In the pursuit of a new sense of beauty (beyond the desire to prevent the demolition of the aesthetic principle), the next step in the strategy to save Beauty for our time was to come from Breton in his declaration at the end of *Nadja* that Beauty must be convulsive or not be at all. The championship of Beauty from *Anicet* to *Nadja* suggests a continuity that the Dada episode did not succeed in breaking up. The effort to dislodge Beauty from the passive center of an arena toward which the opportunists gravitated, observed in *Anicet,* was not an anti-art reaction: Beauty was thought to be a catalytic force shooting off lightning and producing upheaval. The desire for an aesthetics of dynamic power over minds is inherent in *Anicet* and was to be overtly expressed in the theoretical writing of Breton. In fact, surrealism was to distinguish itself from all other avant-garde movements of the century precisely in its efforts to prolong some semblance of the notion of the Beautiful in a world where the Harry Jameses appear to have triumphed, demolishing both ancient and convulsive Beauty.

In 1929 Valéry, who survived Aragon's verbal annihilation of him along with the other perpetuators of what he considered a false notion of Beauty, reactivated the question, and his prognosis for the survival of the Beautiful was pessimistic and prophetic:

> A science of the Beautiful? . . . But do the moderns still use that word? It seems to me that they no longer pronounce it except in jest. Or else . . . they are thinking of the past. Beauty is a kind of corpse. It has been supplanted by novelty, intensity, strangeness, in a word by all the values of shock. Base excitement dominates the soul these days; and the current function of literary works is to tear us away from the contemplative state, from the passive happiness whose image was previously connected in intimate fashion with the general idea of the Beautiful. . . . In our time, a "definition of the Beautiful" can, therefore, be considered only as an historical or philosophical document. Taken in the ancient fullness of its meaning, this illustrious word is about to join, in the drawers of the numismatists of language, many other verbal coins that have gone out of circulation.[5]

In reiterating the alarm of the young Anicet, an aging Valéry was confirming Aragon's worst fears.

The truth of the matter is that the image of a precarious "pulchérie" has been with us for over a hundred years. In the midst of the Symbolist movement, which was presumably centered on the cult of the Beautiful, Mallarmé was foreseeing in cryptic terms the litigation of Beauty in "Prose (pour des Esseintes)" in 1882.

He was telling us that beyond the blatant hyperbole, the sorcery, the futility of imaginary landscapes ("de vues et non de visions"), the artifices of faded or exaggerated flowers ("Pulchérie/Caché par le trop grand glaïeul"), the resurrection of Beauty by the Symbolists had been only a survival on paper ("Anastase: Né pour d'éternels parchemins"). Mallarmé's fatal oracle unfolds as a testament of silence:

> Oh! sache l'Esprit de litige,
> A cette heure où nous nous taisons
> Que de lis multiples la tige
> Grandissait trop pour nos raisons.

In his last poem, *Un Coup de dés jamais n'abolira le hasard*, he had already given up aesthetics to pass on to his epistemology.

Were they right, these masters of Symbolism, like Mallarmé and Valéry, to be so faint-hearted toward the future of the cult of Beauty? As we notice how seldom the concept emerges in current literature except in coarse perversion, Aragon's innocent prescience is noteworthy. Unimpressed by the dazzling promises of all the avant-gardes that surrounded him, he had been able to identify Beauty as the major casualty in modern literature.

NOTES

This essay first appeared in *Symbolism and Modern Literature*, edited by Marcel Tetel (Durham, N.C.: Duke University Press, 1978), pp. 237–247.

1. Aragon, "La Peinture au défi," in *Les Collages* (Paris: Hermann, 1965), 37.
2. Aragon, *Anicet*, 214; I use the Livre de Poche edition from the Gallimard 1921 text. All subsequent quotations will be from the same edition. The translations are all mine. The work has not been translated into English to my knowledge.

3. Jacques Vaché was the young wounded soldier Breton had befriended in a hospital in Nantes, where he had been on medical service during World War I. Vaché was to symbolize for him, and through him for the surrealists in general, the antiestablishment spirit of cold defiance and grim humor which Breton amalgamated into the surrealist archetype.
4. Epigraph to *Aragon, une vie à changer,* by Pierre Daix (Paris: Seuil, 1975), The translation is mine.
5. Paul Valéry, *Léonard et les philosphes,* in *Œuvres complètes,* Pléïade ed., vol. 2, 1240.

XV

A TRIPTYCH OF MODERNISM
REVERDY, HUIDOBRO, AND BALL

Three poets of the early decades of this century shed light on the major paradoxes of modernism. I am not trying to establish this triptych to exercise random intertextuality nor as a basis for a study of influences. Geography separated these poets; the age connected them. From Paris to Zurich, to Santiago and Buenos Aires, the clocks were synchronized. Their affiliation resulted from a common cultural source that nurtured them and that they recognized: the revolution that had occurred in poetics in the previous century and that was to bifurcate modernism in our time.

In the context of modernism these poets have made the following permanent contributions, evidenced both in their poetics and in their poetry: they have relied on the power of the image to generate rather than reflect sense or sensation, they have attempted to redefine the apperception of reality, and they have focused their efforts on returning language to what Hugo Ball called its logos-function: "You may laugh, language will one day reward us for our zeal, even if it does not achieve any directly visible results. We have loaded the word with strengths and energies that helped us to rediscover the evangelical concept of the 'word' (logos) as a magical complex image."[1]

The other road of modernism leads of course to rebellion, deconstruction, relativism, nonanthropocentrism, collage, dehumanization, and the cult of the abstract. This bifurcation, which becomes more and more clear as the century nears its end, justifies references to the avant-gardes in the plural rather than in the singular, for indeed modernism has pulled in two directions in the twentieth century.

The deterioration of culture and its reflection in the arts is comprehensively described by Ball in his article on Kandinsky in 1917:

> A thousand-year-old culture disintegrates. There are no columns and supports, no foundations any more . . . churches have become castles . . . convictions have become prejudices. . . . There are no more perspectives in the moral world. . . . Above is below, below is above. The meaning of the world disappeared. . . . The world showed itself to be a blind juxtaposition and opposing of uncontrolled forces. Man lost his divine countenance, became matter, chance, an aggregate. . . . He became a particle of nature . . . no more interesting than a stone; he vanished into nature. . . . A world of abstract demons swallowed the individual utterance, . . . robbed single things of their names . . . psychology became chatter.[2]

If one believes that in the total scheme of the cosmos all are condemned to remain ignorant of the whole and are driven by unconscious forces, why should not art display these same forces of automatism and insufficiency of structure? The processes involved in these forms of the modern arts, then, are in a sense imitations of nature. When Boileau and Pope advised the artist to hold the mirror up to nature, the Cartesian or Newtonian assumption was that nature was orderly in its operations—and even in its aberrations—meaningful even in its destructive forces, intentioned by a superior will. Now holding the mirror up to nature reveals a nature that is random, purposeless, uncontrolled by any unifying consciousness. Thus the modern artist who sees this change in our perception of the universe is aiming at the same target as his predecessors; what has changed is his understanding of the character of nature.

But in the case of Ball's verbal painting of the disintegration of a world, the intention was not to hold the mirror up to this desolation. In fact, Ball's notion of the modern was neither to reflect the chaos nor to identify with it, but rather to react to it and offer an alternative—an optional universe. In the second part of the same article on Kandinsky he tells us that the artists are dissociating themselves from "this empirical world. . . . They become creators of new natural entities that have no counterpart in the known world. They create images that are no longer imitations of nature but augmentations of nature by new, hitherto unknown appearances and mysteries. That is the victorious joy of these artists—to create existences, which one calls images but which have a consistency of their own that is equivalent to that of a rose, a person, a sunset or a crystal."[3]

In an equally prophetic stance, Vicente Huidobro was saying, "The epoch just beginning will be eminently creative." His attitude toward nature was summarized in his famous cry "We will not serve." A bit more jaded than his two contemporaries, Pierre Reverdy hoped that the abject human plight might push the imitative faculties of the artist to the limit at which even if he was not capable of pure creation he might become convinced that he had acquired such a faculty.[4] Resistance to chaos in the search for creative powers was the alternate direction of modernism, strongly visible in the works of this triptych. *The inherent motivation of their writings was anchored in the belief that modern society's major forces of aggression would be directed against the physical universe rather than remain engaged in fratricide; there was a vision of man fighting blind forces rather than man fighting man.* This spirit is indicated in the very titles of their major works. Written in wartime, none of them refers directly to the war. Huidobro's *Altazor,* the supereagle, born at the age of thirty-three, the day of the death of Christ; Reverdy's *Les Epaves du ciel,* a viewing of earth as a sky fall-out; Ball's *Das Flug auf der Zeit,* flight out of time? Perhaps, but also flight out of the age. In all three the fate of humanity drives the poet to a defiance of the process of representation itself, whether of humanity, of society, or of the universe, rather than to an expression of disgust, to a visionary reality contiguous or adjacent to the natural universe but independent in its purposes.

Mallarmé's theory of creative communication had pointed in two directions: one from the interior, nonverbalized state of consciousness to verbalized exterior configuration, the other from the discovery of an arresting exterior object to interior distillation. The implementation of this dual optic is the basis of the dialectics of modernism, expressed on the one hand as the figurative and on the other as the abstract in the arts. The triptych here discussed opted for figuration. These poets expressed in almost identical language their faith in the image as the central edifice of the work of art, whether in poetry or in painting. Analogical communication produces a confluence of objects whose associations with each other are totally dependent on the author's will and his capacity to reshuffle word associations. These are *achieved* associations, not random ones. As Reverdy said in *Le Livre de mon bord,* "Art begins where chance ends."[5] Chance simply flirts with the artist but as an opportunist the artist exploits chance for his own designs. Huidobro calls this facility "superconsciousness."[6] In other words, as André Breton was to find out, automatism is nothing without *vigilance.*

The tolerance of object associations translated into image associations is well known as a gauge of modernism. From Lautréamont's spectacular metaphors to the much-quoted definition of image by Reverdy, repeated by Breton and Max Ernst, the technique had actually been expressed some ten years earlier by Huidobro, who had traced it back to Voltaire's *Philosophical Dictionary* in its definition of the imagination. Regardless of who said it first or best, the fact remains that in the early part of the twentieth century the theory of the image received recognition as the cradle of a hermetic process of creation. The association of disparate realities in the image was practiced for different reasons by different people. It was random game activity for many collage artists. It was divination of oracular ones; it was a process of gestation for still others. This last-proposed function is most significant in the case of Ball because he is generally known for his Dada interlude, and for the dadaists collage was a derisive activity. Ball, participating in Dada performance and talking about Rimbaud's powers of language at the same time, strikingly demonstrates as a simultaneously deconstructive and constructive artist the dichotomy of modernism. But his deeper adherence to the constructive is evident in his theoretical statements about language and its function in the creative process: "The new art is sympathetic because in an age of disruption it has conserved the will-to-image." He goes further to proclaim: "In principle the abstract age is over."[7] Although much was to happen thereafter to disprove Ball's contention, as late as the 1930s Reverdy was of the same conviction as Ball: "Thought can only recognize itself and judge its limits in the concrete."[8]

But before going further, we have to overcome a taboo of modern criticism: the so-called intentional fallacy, i.e., the relevance of the artist's intentions to the actual work accomplished. Those who object to the serious consideration of intentions argue that whatever intentions there may be should be inherent in the work itself and that outside of the work they have no validity. In the case of poetry, however, particularly modern poetry, the expression of intentions is in fact part of the poetics. Some, of course, include their awareness of process in the poem itself, turning such poems into poem-manifestos; Apollinaire and Wallace Stevens are two important practitioners of this genre. Others manifest their awareness of the process of the poetic act in their prose, considering poetic intention almost as significant as, and more consistent with their innermost being than, the individual sparks of the generative process that we call "poems." Reverdy said: "No creation is perfect except in its hypothesis."[9] The implication is that too often the artist's self-assigned commissions in this world are beyond his power, however brave—or arrogant—to deliver. The poetic process is itself the experience; the single poem gives signals that go beyond what is recorded.

Intentions and their less comprehensive implementations are virtually inseparable in considerations of the features of the modernism of the triptych here in question: problems of reality, image, and language, in both their poetics and their poetry.

The demolition of the concept of reality was not something new in the twentieth century. In the midst of a loudly declared school of realism in the arts, Baudelaire, Maxime du Camp, Champfleury, and Courbet connived to distort the definition of the obvious and static connotation of the word. Realists are dreamers, said Champfleury, and he called Gérard de Nerval a "realist" in his revised definition of the word. Had Baudelaire developed his fragment, "Puisque réalisme il y a," he might have been the theoretician of surrealism. The desire to redefine reality was for Baudelaire an epistemological need and search. "Every good poet is a *realist*,"[10] he said, thus dislodging that well-determined signifier from the commonly signified. Many years later Reverdy was to say: "The true poet . . . is he who has as his primary force, the sense of reality."[11] In his vision the poet is equipped with a dragnet to harvest his realities out of the miscellany of nature.

While Baudelaire was dislodging that particular signifier, "reality," from common usage, he was in fact opening the way for the poetic manipulation of all signifiers, making of language, rather than of nature, the matrix of poetic reality. And this reality, according to Reverdy, holds its own independent space "among the things that exist in nature."[12] As already observed of the title *Les Epaves du ciel,* each part of the composite is easy to envisage but together the unambiguous signifiers create an ambiguity, the cause of which is neither a complicated syntax nor a far-fetched lexicon, nor even some secret mythopoetic reference—practices which were prevalent in the leading poets of the postsymbolist persuasion, contemporaries of Reverdy in his early period.

The "oval" of *La Lucarne ovale,* which had no connection with the content of the poems, illustrates the geometrical preoccupations of both the new artists and the new poets.

Reverdy, like Huidobro, who entitled one of his collections *Horizon carré,* paid tribute to Saint-Pol-Roux; this unclassifiable poet had defined the "poet" as a geometrician of the absolute. Elsewhere Reverdy characterizes his eye as lozengical—another reference to geometrical form.

The next title, *Les Ardoises du toit,* seems innocuous on the surface. There appears no tension between *slate*—an earthy substance—and *roof,* equally tangible—and what is more ordinary than a slate roof? Even separating *ardoise* from *toit,* one can conceivably have a blackboard on which to write an ephemeral poem. But, wait, *ardoise* also means a credit account—on which the poet is free to draw for sustenance (elsewhere he has called the dream an exploitable mine), and with this extended connotation not only is the function of *slate* modified but it in turn alters the simple connotation of roof and assumes dimensions beyond that of housetops. Another seemingly innocuous title is *Cravates de chanvre. Cravate* (necktie), however, assumes an ominous change of function when coupled with *chanvre,* a weed used to make rope. The two words considered as individual and separate images are semantically innocent, but their rapprochement creates a lethal composite, for a *cravate de chanvre* is in effect a *noose.* But there is still another meaning lurking behind *chanvre,* for it is also a plant from which hashish and marijuana are extracted; so again we have the combination of the real and the illusion, of man gravitating toward hallucination and yet encompassed in a concrete reality of danger. The logos-character of words creates images that use natural data to mean something more. Curiously, the obvious reality of the moment, World War I, is obliterated from the poetry of this vintage, as it was to be from that of World War II. The same absence of the obvious conditions of life can be noted in the poetry of Huidobro and Ball from the same period.

In a poem called "La Réalité immobile," Reverdy compares the poem to a photo without a frame, thus extending the absence of referentiality from the temporal to the spatial. In a poem called "Minuit," this total lack of referentiality is striking in the presence of specific, concrete signifiers of elementary meaning and comprehensibility. "Minuit / La pendule sans fin sonne à coup de marteau / Sur mon coeur / En entrant dans la maison sinistre et désolée dont j'ai perdu le numéro" (Midnight / The clock endlessly hammers the hours / On my heart / Entering the bleak and desolate house whose number I have lost).[13] Passage from the limited to the limitless is often expressed through negatives and the adjective "last," or through an impossible comparison manipulating the signifiers of limit to cancel out their respective meanings. Such is the case in a poem called "Abîme," where we find a line such as "La chambre s'étendait bien plus loin que les murs" (The room extended far beyond the walls)[14] syntactically obvious, yet semantically unacceptable except as a poetic reality.

Reverdy is also capable of expressing flexibility of time without resorting to linguistic occultism. In "Ronde nocturne" the distant realities brought together are a cloud and a bell. The cloud's passage makes the bell ring. The poem ends with a vision of someone (persons are never named or otherwise identified in his poems) climbing to heaven or sky. The ladder cracks. It is artificial, adds Reverdy: "C'est une parabole ou une passerelle" (a gangplank or a parabola).[15] The phonetic word play cannot, unfortunately, be communicated in English. The final line: "L'heure qui s'échappait ne bat plus que d'une aile" (Now the escaping hour beats with only one wing) is neither linguistically nor referentially subject to interpretation—and no psychocriticism will help! *S'échapper* is a verb simple both in its literal and figurative meanings. Time and bird escape in different images, the hour and the bird beat time also in separate configurations. In association with "wing" both verbs carry simultaneously both levels of meaning. This communication is both existential and aesthetic, and if one were to examine reader reception, one would have to do so qualitatively rather than quantitatively.

If there are such associations, there are also total annulments of established relationships between objects and their meanings. A startling revision of perception is achieved by the dislocation of meaning in simple words and uncomplicated syntax. "Regarde / Les étoiles ont cessé de briller / La terre ne tourne plus / Une tête s'est inclinée / . . . / le dernier clocher resté debout / Sonne minuit." (Look / The stars have stopped shining / The earth stops turning / A head is leaning / . . . / the last bell tower upright / Strikes midnight), as we find in "Son de cloche" for instance,[16] or in "Minute": "La pendule les bras en croix / s'est arrêtée."[17] Do these seemingly apocalyptic pauses in human activities, according with the cessation of nature's movements, proclaim a world of absurdity, associable with Jean-Paul Sartre's gratuitous world? Some critics have suggested as much, but I would reject such a conclusion. Reverdy's poetry creates existential states of consciousness, but Reverdy is not an existentialist in the French sense of the word. If he sees emptiness around him, he is not seized with nausea by the indifference of nature and the universe. He populates it with a network of activities controlled by his own awareness of the dynamics of existence. Such is the case in a small poem called "Feu": "L'espace s'agrandit / Et là devant? quelqu'un qui n'a rien dit / Deux yeux / Une double lumière / Qui vient de franchir la barrière / En s'abattant." (Space grows big / And there up front? someone who said nothing / Two eyes / A double light / Which has breached the barrier / And is collapsing.)[18] If some twentieth-century writers have sought to compensate for the random character of the universe by appropriating social purpose in their writing, this is not the case for Reverdy any more than it was for Mallarmé; self-fulfillment occurs strictly on aesthetic terms.

The bridges or "passerelles" that Reverdy creates through verbal strategies between his inner state and the objects his eye absorbs are in keeping with one of the two modes proposed by Mallarmé, i.e., from the indescribable, spiritual state sensed in the abstract to objectification without psychological elaboration or intellectual analysis of the condition that gave impetus to the creative act. A line from Mallarmé's *Crise de vers* is often quoted to demonstrate that the voice of the poet must disappear into his work; but that need not be taken to imply that subjectivity is lost and detached from the poem. No poet worth his salt would make such a concession. On the contrary, subjectivity penetrates the language so thoroughly that it no longer needs the identity of the poet to do its work. It is a fermented entity that cannot return to its inert and flat form. The objects the poem designates have assumed the imprint of the writer.

If in studies of poetics Reverdy has remained somewhat marginal, Huidobro is hardly better known among readers of Latin American literature, let alone among those of general literature. The first major collection of his poems to appear in English came out only in 1981. As of 1986 the best references to him and his development are to be found in the comprehensive introduction to his complete works by a compatriot and sometime avant-garde writer, Braulio Arenas; the other solid source is a book devoted to the study of his poetic language by George Yudice.[19] These are in Spanish; in addition there are a few comparative studies in dissertations in French and English. The basic biographical data that interest us here are that Huidobro's voice was heard for the first time outside of his native Chile in Buenos Aires, then during World War I in Madrid, and then in Paris, where he arrived in 1916 and where he stayed for the next ten years, contributing to the same avant-garde journals as did Pierre Reverdy. The poetry of Rimbaud and Mallarmé was his literary matrix. There was also a strong philosophical factor in his development, namely the impact of Hegel and Heidegger. This double affiliation is evident in all of Huidobro's poetry. Like a Hispanic Victor Hugo, he provides such a prolific body of poetry as well as prose that the choice of references here becomes strictly eclectic, as one selects significant pieces in what is, not surprisingly, an uneven work.

I am particularly drawn to his *El Espejo de agua*, which marks a distinct break with his earlier symbolist-oriented poetry. Like the titles of Reverdy, those of Huidobro have intricate connotations in their apparent simplicity. The objective realities do not seem too distant here: mirror, of course, has had from time immemorial metaphoric affiliations with water. So here we see two reflecting agents juxtaposed. But is reflection a *state* or a visionary agent? Are we involved with a new kind of mirror? The very first poem, entitled "Arte poetica," initiates the animistic intimacy of the indeterminate "algo," like the "quelqu'un" of Reverdy. The referential discontinuity is accompanied even more than in the case of Reverdy by clear delineation of objects, be they man-made or natural: "Que el verso sea como una llave / Que abra mil puertas" (Let poetry be like a key / Opening a thousand doors).[20] But *llave* also means *faucet*, which brings us back to water, although on the rational level suggesting that poetry may be a key to open many doors is more acceptable. But in the wider circumference of double connotation the poem touches the broad notion of unlocking restrained energies, thus manifesting the process of poetic creativity. "Inventa mundos nuevos y cuida tu palabra" (Invent new worlds and watch your word). Obviously this is not to be a subconscious or intuitive pouring out of words if the poet is to mind Reverdy's "Art begins where chance ends." This advice is reinforced later in the poem by the simple statement that true vigor resides in the *head*. And when he concludes that everything under the sun lives for us, this is not to be taken for a spiritual anthropocentrism. To live for us really means to him: to be at our disposal. He had heard an indigenous poet say: "Don't sing of the rain, poet, make it rain." Rain is a result; *making it rain* is a creative process. In line with this image, Huidobro says in his "Arte poética": "Por qué cantais la rosa, ¡oh Poetas! / Hacedla florecer en el poema": Why sing of the rose, make it flower! Everything is there, in other words, not to be admired but to be manipulated because the poet, that agent of manipulation, is, as the final line of the poem tells us, "a small god."

In the second poem, having the same title as the collective work, "El Espejo de agua," the transformational capacity we guessed in the title, "the mirror," makes of it a river, then a watery globe, a fishbowl where all the swans drown, and as we go from one image to the next we notice that the orb, which also means globe, becomes more than a reflecting object; it causes an active assault on the swan-poetics of symbolism.

Mi espejo, corriente por las noches,	(My mirror, flowing through the night,
Se hace arroyo y se aleja de mi cuarto.	Has become a brook streaming out of my room.
Mi espejo, más profundo que el orbe	My mirror, deeper than the globe
Donde todos los cisnes se ahogaron.	Where all the swans drown.)[21]

In *Poemas articos*, where the contamination of Cubism becomes evident, we can find two kinds of poems, those featuring the passive juxtaposition of objects (what painters call nature-morte) and others more relevant to the pattern here described: images in movement, displaying the process of creation rather than the crystallization of the art process. This effect is produced, for instance, in a poem called "Marino," where the sailor demonstrates godlike activities in concordance with the image of a bird about to soar in initial flight. The creations are a series of displacements not of vision but of human and cosmic phenomena; it is indeed a broader extension of the "making roses" proposed in his "Arte poética." An ancient mariner (Huidobro was familiar with English Romanticism) intrudes upon the cosmography and disturbs the temporal structure of the earth as well:

Hice correr ríos que nunca han existido	(I made rivers run Where none had been before
De un grito elevé una montaña	With a shout I made a mountain rise
Y en torno bailamos una neuva danza	And now we do a new dance around it . . .
Y enseñé a cantar un pájaro de nieve	And I taught a snowbird how to sing
Marchemos sobre los meses desatados	Let us depart upon the floating months
Soy el viejo marino que cose los horizontes cortados	I am the old sailor Who mends torn horizons.)[22]

Like Victor Hugo's *La Légende des siècles,* Huidobro's *Adán* and *Altazor* encompass the first and last man. Although in *Altazor* there are many references to God and to Satan, these are not personal identifications of divinity; rather, they embody the powers of generation and destruction. The sense of apocalypse that has been associated in this poem with modern tendencies toward deconstruction can only result from a partial reading of the poem. The devastation is described only to give the god-poet an opportunity to rethink the universe. The seismograph has taken note of his birth. The sun is born in his right eye and sets in his left eye,[23] meditates Altazor, and he suggests that if God exists at all it is thanks to the poet. This echoes what he had earlier questioned in *Adán:* whether the poem exists because of the water perceived, or the water exists because the poet has perceived it. He wonders: "Si tu agua forma el canto / O si tu canto forma el agua."[24]

Independent in his breathing and in his nourishment, the new god-poet knows it is late: "there is no time to lose," "no hay tiempo que perder" becomes a refrain in canto 4 of *Altazor*.[25] His last image is that of a mill, but a mill reaching out eventually to constellations; distant realities again combined, the earth-power creating energy and by extension nourishment, and the cosmic power providing another form of energy, i.e., luminosity.

The epic poems of Huidobro rise to an ecstatic pitch at

which the aesthetic experience of creativity becomes a substitute for religious communion. The line between the messiah and the antichrist of magic, as he describes himself in *Altazor,* grows very faint.

But if the struggle between spiritual communication and aesthetic expression is evident in Huidobro, the artist's confusion between aesthetic ascesis and religious ecstasy was in the case of Ball to lead actually into religious conversion. In the interval, however, between Ball's Dada activities and the religious identity he eventually assumed, there is a body of writing consisting of two plays, two novels, articles, and what has been termed "a handful of poems." It just happens that the handful of poems consists of a hundred and twenty-three poems. One might say that Baudelaire and Mallarmé are also guilty of having written a handful of poems! Ball's commentators associate him with Dada and Expressionism, just as Reverdy and Huidobro get swallowed up in Cubism and Creationism. Ball's poetry is passed over simply as "obscure" and his spiritual experience passed off as a "bad trip."

I have examined these poems closely and see no overt rebellion of the social type that would associate him with the Expressionists. These are not ideological poems that might illustrate Ball's previously quoted fresco of social devastation. Basically, they can be divided into two parts, those addressed to love in general and to Emmy, his wife, in particular, and those in which he struggles with a universe in shackles and tries to apprehend those shackles for his own purposes. When the task becomes too difficult he calls upon a sort of divinity, using the names of God, Maria, Seraphin, and so on, much as Rimbaud used the word "genie" or "force" and Rilke "the angel." It is an appropriation of name and concept rather than an evocation of creed, baffling to the general reader just as the word "God" in *Le Gant de crin* has made many attribute a deep Catholicism to Reverdy. It is also a suggestion of the godly quality toward which Huidobro aimed in *Adán* and *Altazor.* One of Ball's poems actually appropriates the structure of the Twenty-third Psalm: he tries to define the presence that operates transformation upon this world and concludes with "Willst du die neue Welt erbauen." It could be considered a religious poem except that we are not at all sure that the *du,* written with a small "d," is not self-reflexive. Ball had not yet reached the moment of his religious crisis.

Clearly, the poems of Ball, like those of the other two here observed, implement the second process posited by Mallarmé: he goes from awareness of unease outward to its objectification. There is no verbal ambiguity or abstraction in Ball's poetry. These concise poems, studded with meaning, are chiseled in concrete. No mystification is created by syntax or lexicon. But in Ball's case the encounter of distant realities is achieved with the word itself. Through the miracle the German language permits him to perform, he produces what I would like to call a "bildungsgedicht." The permitted, legitimate practice of coining new words by tying together substantives into single words is here stretched to comply with the dictum of the whole new era that new words are necessary to create a new state of existence, and new objects to occupy legitimate spaces in the cosmos. The words Ball coins by combining those in the standard lexicon come as close to a new built-in figurative discourse as I have ever seen. Ball ties substantives together that annul each other's power to signify or that create a tension among multiple significations. The fact that he wrote sound-poems in his short Dada period has been overstressed as his only distinction in the annals of the avant-garde. Incidentally, these tone poems are often attributed to primal cries of fury or expressions of the absurd. This in itself is a gross fallacy. Even a brief examination will convince the reader that structurally they are phonetic and phonemic patterns probing the nature of language, and not intended for simple shock effects. When the special role of the so-called nonsense poems is recognized in the totality of Ball's poetry, then perhaps his poems in standard structure will be approached with more respect and serious consideration. Baudelaire and Mallarmé also used standard poetic structures. But adherence to standard forms does not thereby exclude these poems from the category of the avant-garde, any more than the open structures or nonstructured utterances of so many poems in the twentieth century constitute new forms of poetic discourse. Many an open-ended poem of our day is very standard and banal in its signification.

The neat compliance of Ball with form and rules of prosody belies the explosively far-reaching steps he quietly took toward polysemy and the composition of his personal epistème. After all, he was nurtured by both Rimbaud and Hegel. Like Rimbaud, Ball knew the power of transformational semantics, and like Hegel he knew the spiritual tension that two contradictory forces can create when pitted against each other. When these two conditions meet—the manipulation of language to support the existential tension—great poetry is in the making even if in small, unassuming bundles as in Ball's case.

There is a poem of Ball's called "Mallarmé's Flowers" which reveals Ball's subtle understanding of Mallarmé. This is quite a different response to Mallarmé than one finds in Huysmans' À Rebours. It is not a simulation of character, but a response to style. In the first line the first substantive, which is a composite, combines a number of the most important qualities of the poetry of Mallarmé: the word means literally "golden avalanche," metal or riches and permanence, associated with the coldness and movement simultaneously implied by the second part of the word. Then, the genitive "des," combining *from* and *of* interchangeably, introduces "alten Azur," containing the obsession with *Azur*, and the cult of the ancient that evokes Hérodiade—the name not to be mentioned until some lines later. In the next line, *star*, *snow*, and *eternity* are cohabiting with a search for beginning, and as each flower dear to Mallarmé is conjured in the next lines, the sense of *toil* emerges; Mallarmé's power to create a rose is likened to the creation of the flesh of a woman, thus directly referring to a divine maker. The verbs he uses are more applicable to the actions of a sculptor than to those of a writer, and the evocation of Christian symbols is a device whereby he transfers the aesthetic to the kind of religious terminology more likely to be understood by his readers. The short poem terminates in the celebration of the death of the poet in an atmosphere in which the immanence of flower-essence is as permeating as it is invisible.

Mallarmés Blumen

Auf Goldlawinen des alten Azur,
Aus der Sterne ewigem Schnee nahmst du im Anbeginne
Für eine, vom Weh noch unberührte, jungfräuliche Flur
Die großen Kelche deiner Schöpferminne.

Der Zynnien helle Hälse, die falben Gladiolen
Und jenen göttlichen Lorbeer der seelisch Verbannten,
Hochrot erglühend wie eines Seraphs Sohlen,
Die von der Scham zertretener Morgenröten entbrannten.

Die Hyazinthe beriefst du, die Myrthe geistern und bleich,
Gleich dem Fleisch einer Frau schufst du als Rose
Grausam jene Herodias, die noch im Gartenbereich
Vom strahlenden Blut des Propheten träumt überm Moose.

Und bildetest aller Lilien schluchzende Blässe,
Daß sie im Weihrauch verblauender Horizonte
Aufstiegen über die Seufzermeere der Messe,
Um zu verschmachten im Anblick weinender Monde.

Hosannah, Maria, in deinem Garten und Schoß,
Daß das Echo verebbe in himmlischen Abendlüften,
Wo der Heiligen Gloriolen schimmern extatisch und groß.

Selig, o Mutter, sind deiner blühenden Brüste
Erhabene Kelche voll Wein und voll Brot.
Selig der Dichter, daß es ihn siechend gelüste
Nach künftigem Leben in einem balsamischen Tod.

In view of the innumerable powers of Orpheus that had been generated during the symbolist era, it would seem impossible to expect of Ball any originality in the handling of this myth. Yet Ball's "Orpheus," written just before Rilke's *Sonnets to Orpheus*, is a small masterpiece.

> Oh, königlicher Geist, dem aus den Grüften
> Die Leoparden folgten und Delphine
> Im Tiefgeschlecht sahst du die Menschenmiene,
> Gegrüßt von allen Brüdern in den Lüften.
>
> Die Leier eingestemmt in junge Hüften,
> So standest du umbrandet auf der Bühne.
> Vom Tode trunken summte deine kühne,
> Berauschte Stimme mit den Blumendüften.
>
> Du kamst aus einer Welt, in der das Grauen
> Die Marter überbot. Da war dein Herz
> Zerronnen erst und dann erstarrt zu Erz.
>
> Durch jede Sehnsucht drang dein liebend Schauen.
> Es führten dich die Vögel und die Fische
> Im Jubelchor zum höchsten Göttertische.

If God is the doubling suggested in the image of Mallarmé, the image of the king of heights and depths is associable with Orpheus, the dialectics of position resolved in a unity of concrete brotherhood. From the depth to the heights, the recognition of the human countenance is envisioned not as an abstraction but as a composite of leopard, dolphin, and bird. In the lines that follow, the interplay between fauna, flora, and the mineral world is identified with the torture of Orpheus. The struggle ends in his resurrection in what could have been an abstraction but instead is a physical intoxication at a table (concrete object) belonging to God. If the theme of the Orpheus legend is death and transfiguration, the poem achieves it in the encounter of the most concrete objects connected by the power of Orpheus, who thus creates a unity in a divided world, one might add; but the generalization is in the reader's mind and not in the poem, for the poem has cleared a space where naming directly refers to Orpheus alone.

This concrete quality is apparent in Ball's characterizations of dreams. In view of his German romantic heritage, one would expect the dream to be a strong poetic factor in Ball's work and the techniques of veiling and fantasy to be devices of his dream transcriptions. He does indeed get from Novalis the notion of *Dursichtigkeit,* but he is not peering through veils. Rather he sees through bright and concrete entities. His dreams are, as he says, "evergreen": "immergrünen Traüme."

The process whereby dream becomes poetry, and the ordinary globe-dweller takes flight, is strikingly represented in a poem called "Like a Caterpillar." The worm collects mulberry leaves and sucks deep their juice—an image reminiscent of Mallarmé's faun sucking the grape pulp and peering through the skin. Here we see silk-foam oozing out of the worm's mouth. With the nourishment of dreams, equated here with the silk-foam, the worm weaves a net in its underground abode, and it whiles away its time in puppet shows and masquerades until it pierces the darkness of its covering and soars with wings stretched out into a new sun where death and joy converge. My paraphrase goes no further than to suggest the very concrete character of the transformation of the earthbound into a soaring being and the risks involved in the process. The linguistic movements creating the transformation are much more important, poetically speaking. The contradictions of lowly and lofty, sublime reality and delusive fantasy, are in Ball's poem verbal strategies, and the break that brings about the transformation is expressed by a verb which is generally connected with the breaking of a solid substance into particles. Equally, the spreading out of the wings is described in a word that denotes the stretching of something of a material nature rather than a spiritual one. And most notable is the fact that the dream is not an ineffable state but as real as grass and silk, and as intoxicating as champagne. The poem demonstrates once more the power of the poet to manipulate natural objects: to make them do and be according to the orders of the poet, who does not serve but is served.

Preoccupations with polysemy and polyvalences, as well as reader reception, may seem associable with the work of these three poets because of the use of similar terminologies and a common interest in the functioning of language. Astute critics, acting as heroic mediators between author and reader, decipher meaning by decoding the writer's use of language and recoding it for the new reader. But at the threshold of the century, the cult of linguistic structures as a source of creativity had as its objective a different sort of hermeneutic operation. The poet did not seem concerned with the production of a text laden with multiple meanings, intended for a reader smarter than himself, who would extrapolate them in order to create his own rational subtext. Instead, as evidenced continuously in the writings of these poets, language was a power-generator; the poet used it to provoke the imagination, primarily his own, and to release creative energy intrinsic to poetic achievement, associated in his mind with some form of divine process. The *process* of language generation—which Reverdy called "a high voltage transformer"[26]—fascinated these writers much more than did the actual production of multiple meanings for themselves or for anybody else. From artist/mirror to artist/god was the path predicted for modern times by Huidobro. The analytical exercise that fascinates literary critics, namely the transfer of a rational communication to a rational reception thereof in some modified form, is an ideological exchange, not a great concern to poets. On the other hand, the stimulation of the reader's power to create images by getting involved in the creative process of the poet is an *aesthetic* experience. Empirical criticism has encouraged the confusion between informative communication and aesthetic co-experience. In the climate of the modernism discussed here language was interesting only as a source or pool for the creative process, and hermeneutics was writer-oriented rather than aimed at reader reception. Language was important only as it illuminated the poetry; when the tables are turned around, poetry becomes interesting only as it illuminates language! For this particular set of poets, of which the current triptych delineates a model, aesthetics was much more than a preoccupation with art. Their metaphysics was encrusted with and encapsulated in their aesthetics because at that point poetry had become much more than discourse about beautiful things or unusual emotions. It was a counterproposal to ordinary living. In trying to emerge from the linguistic labyrinth, these poets thought they were leaving the poem, not as a testimony to their struggle with language, but as an opening created in the darkness, a passage to freedom. So the poem itself was not an exercise in analytical thinking but a cameo of the struggle for synthesis, not an object reflecting the writer but a system to revise the cosmos through the potentials of naming. These poets converging from three different national cultures identified a major step beyond the attribution of sign-meaning to objects or states of consciousness; they made meaning a variable in the establishment of equations between signs and between writer and reader.

NOTES

This essay first appeared in *Modernism: Challenges and Perspectives*, edited by Monique Chefdor, Ricardo Quinones, and Albert Wachtel (Urbana: University of Illinois Press, 1986), 111–127.

1. Hugo Ball, *Flight Out of Time* (New York: Viking, 1974), 68.
2. Ibid., 224–225. (I have gone into more detail of this proposition in my article, "Problems of Modernism.")
3. Ibid., 226.
4. Pierre Reverdy, *Le Livre de mon bord* (1930–1936; reprint, Paris: Mercure de France, 1948), 95.
5. Ibid., 94.
6. Vicente Huidobro, "Manifiesto de Manifiestos," in *Obras completas* (Santiago: Zig-Zag, 1963), vol. 1, 664.
7. Ball, 60.
8. Reverdy, 227.
9. Ibid., 83.
10. See Anna Balakian, "Fragments on Reality by Baudelaire and Breton," in *Fragments: Incompletion and Discontinuity*, ed. Lawrence D. Kritzman (New York: New York Literary Forum, 1981), 101–109.
11. Pierre Reverdy, *Le Gant de crin* (1926; reprint, Paris: Flammarion, 1968), 64.

12. Ibid., 47.
13. Pierre Reverdy, *Les Ardoises du toit*, collected in *La Plupart du Temps, Poèmes 1915–22* (Paris: Gallimard, 1945), 136.
14. Ibid., 164; trans. Mary Ann Caws and Patricia Terry, *Roof Slates and Other Poems of Pierre Reverdy* (Boston: Northeastern University Press, 1981), 45.
15. Ibid., 168–169; trans. ibid., 53.
16. Ibid., 170; trans. ibid.
17. Ibid., 178; trans. ibid., 55.
18. Ibid., 153; trans. ibid., 65.
19. George Yudice, *Vicente Huidobro y la motivación del lenguaje* (Buenos Aires: Editorial Galerna; 1978). In English see *The Selected Poetry of Vicente Huidobro*, ed. David M. Guss (New York: New Directions, 1981).
20. Vicente Huidobro, "El Espejo de agua" in *Obras completas*, 1:255; trans. D. M. Guss, *Selected Poetry of Vicente Huidobro*, 3.
21. Ibid., 255; trans. ibid., 3.
22. Ibid., 319; trans. ibid., 51–52.
23. Ibid., *Altazor*, canto 4, 394.
24. Ibid., "Adán ante el mar," *Adán*, 240.
25. Ibid., *Altazor*, canto 4.
26. Reverdy, *Le Livre de mon bord*, 153.

XVI

THE UNFAMILIAR LITERATURES

In the study of literature there is a consensus, long left uncontested, concerning which literatures and which literary figures are "major." The major writers generally emerge from politically prominent nations, and the chance of entering the literary hall of fame is far greater for those who write in prominent languages within powerful nations. And we can also say that the major critics are those whose critical scrutiny bears upon writers who have achieved major status in major national units.

On the other hand, the literary output of small national groups is often identified as "minor" when it would be fairer to call it unfamiliar. To bring unfamiliar works of literature to the awareness of scholars everywhere should be one of the principal functions of comparative literature.

Much of my own research and writing has gone in this direction in recent years. I spent the earlier years of my scholarly life throwing light on grossly neglected poets of a major literature. When others began to crowd that field, the challenge diminished, and I felt the need for fresher fields of discovery. Up to then I was a comparatist only in terms of digging up international sources; suddenly heritage, reception, transformation, the question of originality, the unifying elements of literary movements that transcend national literatures began to fascinate me and inevitably led me beyond the standard major literatures.

In my activities with unfamiliar literatures I encountered

two kinds of such literatures: those inaccessible because of language barriers, such as the rich literature of Middle Europe, and those hidden from us although written in universal languages, hidden because of the defaults of public relations and the politics of promotion.

The first obstacle is a difficult one to transcend. There is the problem of translation. But the problem of translation is as nothing compared to the problem of selection. If selection is left to the editorial boards of publishing houses they will inevitably decide that what is to be translated depends on what will sell widely—works such as the writings of a dissident Soviet writer—rather than what is a major text to be released to universal readership. And this is where the Comparatist should play a major role. I do not mean the Comparatist who knows English, French, German, Spanish, and Italian literatures but the Comparatist who knows some of these and in addition knows an unfamiliar language and its literature.

In this respect a project of the International Comparative Literature Association called a Comparative History of Literature in European Languages is a worthy effort to bring unfamiliar literatures into relationship with the familiar ones. Collaboratively we can do what is impossible individually. I have personally learned a great deal from my involvement as editor of the volume of Symbolism. In this connection I cannot stress enough the importance of international bibliographies, which open up writings of unfamiliar literatures both of critical and creative nature to general scholarly readers or at least to the awareness of comparatists.

As for the other phenomenon, we are seeing the emergence of a highly prolific literature in politically less powerful countries but in languages universally understood, such as the Francophone and Hispanophone literatures of developing countries. One would think that in view of their linguistic availabilities these literatures would find broad diffusion. But they have not been gaining recognition as quickly as they deserve in the world of publishing; they are not well promoted. And the literary critic, were he even to know such literature of high worth, hesitates to write a book about or even make references to an author whom his readers have not read. How often did the distinguished Canadian Northrop Frye bring Canadian literature into his archetypal studies? So the vicious circle continues, and the unfamiliar literature becomes a ghetto literature.

To promote these two categories of unfamiliar literatures there is a good method and a bad one.

A few words about the bad one. Once in a while we get conscience-stricken in comparative literature circles and we say, let's bring some of the unknown literatures into a conference! So we have a special panel on Oriental literatures or Latin American or African literatures (forgetful of the fact that these are continents, not nations, and have their own differentials). Then we find scholars qualified as critics of the single national literatures to speak about them. They in turn feel such a need to cover as much ground as possible that they fall into generalizations, and because we are ignorant of their frame of reference we become stoically and politely bored, and the literature continues to remain unfamiliar because the unknown has not been in any way brought into relation with the known. Or else those who know they will be bored stay away, and the speaker talks only to those happy few who know the unfamiliar literature or at least the language of that literature. This is what I call a ghetto conference or what others call the study of ethnic literatures.

To proceed in a more practical way in the effort to be known, as a major text, the unfamiliar work must rise above its ethnic status and come into competition with the already acknowledged major texts. This will occur only if scholars of the ethnic literature become well versed in one or more of the major literatures and are willing to bring the unfamiliar into the frame of reference of the familiar. In other words, the only way a critic will succeed in enhancing the international status of a writer of his or her native unfamiliar literature is by assuming a Comparatist perspective and bringing the said writer out of the ethnic context into the broader and more recognizable one of the limited internationalism we practice.

Some critics hesitate to do this because they see the specter of "influence" and the accusing finger of imitation threatening the unfamiliar literature. This is a false assumption. I have noted in my scrutiny of Symbolism and surrealism that although imitations may exist, the power of transformation obliterates literary colonialization. Aimé Césaire is not less significant as a writer because of his early contact with André Breton. And the fact that he read Mallarmé did not make the Hungarian Edy imitate the Frenchman's *écriture*. But discussing Césaire in the context of Breton and Edy in the context of the movement Mallarmé launched helps bridge a gap, brings the unfamiliar into an orbit of recognition, enhances the chances of a Césaire or an Edy for universal readership, makes them better candidates for publication in translation. We should not confuse ethnicity of social identity with ethnicity of literary communication. The former has a validity as a political weapon; the latter often creates a flaw in universal communication.

In this perspective translation is not the first step in bringing a major writer in an unfamiliar literature to deserved recognition. In general the translator does not have sufficient status to make this discriminative choice. Nor is the specialist in the unfamiliar literature highly qualified for this promotional task. He is apt to be somewhat chauvinistic, and national pride may make him promote the poet who sings his nation's praises rather than the one who closeted himself in his nonnational inner space. The Comparatist who is familiar with the so-called major literatures as well as with one of the more unfamiliar ones has more credibility when he or she passes a value judgment on the unfamiliar in relation to the familiar. I see this activity as one of the significant roles of the comparative dimension of literary criticism.

How will the universities of our Western Hemisphere train such scholars? Certain universities are trying to overcome national barriers and to extend the frontiers of comparative literature by establishing chairs for the study of ethnic languages and literatures. And departments of Comparative Literature occasionally appoint, often on a visiting professorship basis, specialists in one of the rarer literatures. Those who take advantage of these opportunities to study unfamiliar literatures do not necessarily create long-range resources for the broadening of the Comparative Literature base. It takes years to learn a rare language from scratch, and lectures about a rare literature are accidental and irregular experiences at most. This method is not self-perpetuating and productive in the shaping of Comparatists.

I would propose, instead, that opportunities be found and made available to encourage and seek out individuals who have acquired either through unusual opportunities or through accidents of birth into multinational backgrounds considerable knowledge of a minority literature to bring this knowledge or develop it further within the orbit of Comparative Literature and to integrate their special knowledge with what Comparative Literature departments generally offer in the relationships of literary movements, study of genres and archetypes in respect to the literatures generally "compared." These scholars would then become comparatists with a broader horizon, having added one or more new strings to the harmony of the literary harp. When they in turn go out to teach Comparative Literature, they can then include one or more other literatures within the comparison.

They will have moved toward a United Nations concept where political polarizations can be replaced by intellectual consortiums. Literature has a latent power for spiritual diplomacy, but the small cluster around which the mediations of Comparatists function must be enlarged in order to deliver Comparative Literature from its current regional and parochial character so that it may move on toward a more global comparatism.

October 11, 1978

XVII

QUALITY CONTROL IN THE TEACHING OF LITERATURE

There is at the moment a broad-scale challenge of what has long been considered "literary" in the shaping of the canon of great books highlighted in the teaching of literature. The situation has become politicized and has implicated so-called Western values. Out of the dispute there has arisen a confusion between the general concept of freedom of expression and compliance with long-established judgments about literary worth. I would like to define literature in terms that supersede considerations for quotas that aim to secure representation of ethnic and geographical differences.

Fear has been fear from time immemorial; so are anger, jealousy, ecstasy, or grief recognizable in any society and in any region of the earth. If the causes that stir these emotions vary with succeeding eras, and if the means or techniques whereby they are represented change, then the manifestations are universally identifiable. What makes literature distinct from other reading materials is its ability to convey the uniqueness of a personal experience and at the same time transcribe it in an idiom that universalizes that experience through a dimension called aesthetics.

A text in the hands of a teacher, a scholar, or even of the general reader may be subject to relative meanings; in fact, many contend that meaning is created as much by the reception of the reader as by the production of the writer. But if, regardless of its historical moment or the geographical zone from which it emerged, the writing stirs readers deeply generation after generation, then it qualifies as literature. We are told that the capacity to produce emotional response is not a gauge of literary quality. But if empathy maintains the interplay of emotion and the imagination to create intellectual pleasure for readers separated in time and space, after the impact of the initial experience, the work has achieved literary merit. Let us look at examples.

In 1989 the world lost one of the giants of this century's literature. I say "world" because Samuel Beckett was not quite sure whether he identified with his Irish origin or his French culture. He switched languages, he switched countries. He felt kinship with James Joyce, but he was also drawn to the philosophical attitudes of Heidegger and Sartre. I say "giant," yet I am referring to a scrawny, frail man who dominated no one but who in a very simple way identified with the anguish of everyman, that everyman in us who senses his mortality and still keeps hoping something will happen to change everything—which never does.

How many a comic strip, vaudeville routine, puppet show, and cartoon could embody that simple theme! But they come and go and are erased from our memory. The image of Charlie Chaplin remains rather than his script. Beckett's entire body of work constituted variation after variation of his central theme whether in narrative or dramatic form. All of it appears to be earmarked for survival in contrast with the many others about the dire fate of mankind which clutter the annals of the twentieth century that has been so prolific in the number of writers it has produced.

Many a historian, sociologist, and anthropologist will have documented the major ontological problems of man in the twentieth century and will thereby provide data for future characterizations of the human species of our time as it faltered, wavered, and struggled between the anthropocentric universe it inherited and the nonanthropocentric one that was little by little unveiled and with which it had to cope. All this shift in perception can be explained to future generations in smart expository prose; but they will need Beckett's character, Molloy, and a few other literary ones of our time to know what it felt like to be in the position stated by those who can better provide the facts.

That difference is what literature has been all about since the time of the ancient Chinese, Persians, Hebrews, Egyptians, and Greeks. They remain with us through the literature of their respective Golden Ages, but let us remember that the twentieth century and a few preceding ones constitute our golden age. André Malraux, the French writer, archaeologist, and art historian, observed the distinction between documentary writing and literature by saying that literature does not narrate history but changes it. A good example of that is the distance to note between a historical chronicle and Shakespeare's *Henry V*.

Our civilization has provided us with a great revolutionary slogan that we take pride in voicing at every opportunity to demonstrate how enlightened we are in contrast with previous civilizations: "Liberty, Equality, Fraternity." But wisdom would have us question the absolute applicability of these concepts to the structure of educational programs. Two of the three may well necessitate restrictions.

Let's look at liberty first. Of course one of the great professional privileges, nay human rights, of teachers is their freedom to choose and freedom to interpret the literary writings they convey to their young audiences. But just as teachers do not expect to be suddenly deprived of their initiative in choosing and organizing the presentation of literature by any interference on the part of the students, so also in their turn they should think twice before they indulge in a clearing of the decks in regard to the secular saints of literary history.

What have recently been termed with scorn as "privileged" texts have attained that distinction not through the whim of individuals but through a process of careful scrutiny by readers of vast experience and through vast consensus; they have earned it! Were each of us to create our own smorgasbord, the result would not be educational democracy but chaos, opening the seawalls to a total inundation of miscellaneous and idiosyncratic choices. It is of course known that many university departments of literature pride themselves on offering courses in "trivial literature," but none has been known to pressure students to take them.

Professor Richard Rorty of the Philosophy Department of the University of Virginia expressed the need for a certain degree of conformity at a conference in March 1989 entitled "The Humanities in the 1990s: Perspectives on the Liberal Arts, Research and Education." Here is what he said at this conference sponsored by the National Humanities Center:

> Reading lists should be constructed so as to preserve a delicate balance between two needs. The first is the need of the students to have common reference points with people of previous generations and in other social classes so that grandparents and grandchildren, people who went to the University of Wisconsin at Whitewater and people who went to Stanford, will have read a lot of the same books; the second is the need of the teachers to be able to teach the books which have moved them, excited them, and changed their lives—rather than having to teach a syllabus handed down by a committee.

I would add a third need—the need of the students to use their own free initiative to supplement (not abolish) the standard list with some neglected works they may have discovered under the dust of library shelves, inspired in their search by an attitude created in class that there are books out there which need to be rescued from literary amnesia. Or if the discovery is not made in the local library, it could well be something dug out of an individual ethnic heritage once the student's curiosity has been oriented toward the deplorably large mass of unfamiliar literature that awaits resurrection.

All these channels for limited freedom of choice should be tolerated and encouraged, but not the kind of do-it-yourself, self-service syllabi that are being advocated by deconstructionist scholars who, on the pretext of supporting free choice, would really be condemning students to constrictive vision and cultural isolation, in their risky effort to prove that something untested can be as good or better than what has stood the test of time.

Coming to the notion of equality, all texts are not equal,

and those who say they are—and their numbers are rising—must really be saying that they do not believe in genius. Moreover, until someone can prove that the Versailles treaty is as much a piece of literature about World War I as *All Quiet on the Western Front,* I will not be persuaded that any written document can pass for writing worthy of study in literary courses for which credit may be given by a literature department. If we break down the action of standards, we are at the mercy of capricious fashion and the law of the jungle.

But now we come to the third word, the most blessed and totally nonrestricted at the heart of the educational process: fraternity. If the sense of fraternity is instilled, there need be no worry about possible oversights in the choices that have to be made among the massive body of literary works increasing each day.

We might add that none of the current empirical approaches to critical scrutiny have come up with new measurements that would overthrow the previous aesthetic qualifications for candidacy in the literary hall of fame. The amazing thing is that the literary power of a text has proved so far to be a recognizable constant, whereas its meaning or ideology becomes a variable with the passage of time. It would then seem that the teacher's main objective is to point the way to the dramatic and imaginative qualities that prevail, as for instance in Shakespeare, rather than what is subject to changing ideological interpretations.

Recognition of the works' universal appeal is what generates the sense of fraternity. So many readers of Kafka know what it feels like to wake up one morning as a cockroach, so many share the impressions of Dostoevsky's nameless character that they are standing before a court of law to account for their mediocre lives!

Higher education's greatest demand in this age of fragmentation, caused by the divisive character that national identifications have taken, is to bring us back together to perceive beneath the political, religious, and ethnic differences the fundamental cohesion of the human species. It is that fraternal vision which makes it possible to understand

and to relate to Beckett's *Waiting for Godot* or Ibsen's *A Doll's House* in a hundred different languages, whereas the metaphysical disquietudes embedded in the former and the social problems included in the latter have been, before and since, proliferated in many other forms of documents of much less permanence.

No literature stands alone in a distinct fate; likewise no literary text can be said to be really neglected even if it is not practical to teach it in a given time and a given place. Even if we attended school our whole life long, we could not complete such a syllabus. But if the literary menu's superhistorical quality is identified and conveyed to the students, then they in their turn will be in a position to correlate the given with others which may come under their scrutiny, familiar or unfamiliar, out of which they can fashion in the course of a lifetime the personal canon to illuminate their lives.

My own upbringing reflected the period between the two world wars, and I chose my particular discipline, comparative literature, because it best implemented, as I thought, the spirit that had come out of World War I: that the only salvation for the world would be to develop a cosmopolitan frame of mind based on fraternity, so that disastrous global conflicts might be avoided. That spirit failed, and differences rather than similarities have motivated nationalist interests. As a result it becomes harder to be a literary comparatist because the survival of that optic depends on the writers and other artists who have a common pool of sensibilities from which they draw no matter what their differences may be.

I visited the former Soviet Union just before the changes in politics brought about by the Gorbachev regime; but I found the great American works of literature prominently displayed in Moscow's bookstores, and readers who probably did not understand very much about our politics understood and loved our writers' expressions of human vision and behavior. Literary works studied in relation to each other, over and above national boundaries, even when read in translations, cease to be considered as absolute selections to the exclusion of others if we think of them as part of a network of signals and wavelengths to be reached according to each receiver's set; for through wisely chosen texts it is a quality that has been transmitted along with the individual work that embodies it.

Higher education never became the integrated system for the search and determination of knowledge that I had hoped in my youth when I chose to become a teacher/scholar. If it had, we would not need to be talking about interdisciplinary studies at this late date as something unique and unusual; it would have become the rule and not the exception. The truth is that it is difficult to produce such programs because, during the decades after World War II, we did not train scholars in holistic acquisition of knowledge. If we had, that would have been the most revolutionary of all projects; other parts of the world have done a better job in integrating the various bodies of knowledge and have scholars today better equipped to man such academic programs.

Actually when spokesmen for the Humanities call for interdisciplinary programs today, they are motivated by the desire to overcome other disciplines' resistance to their own. But my own experience in recent years as head of a Comparative Literature department has shown me that the principles whereby I have lived and survived met less resistance from outside my discipline than from within. The enemies of literary studies are at work within the discipline and not without.

The philosophical saints of our currently prominent critics are not those of philosophy departments; the literary left-wing materialists who have gained attention of our academic world are perplexing to latter-day communists. The anthropologists and sociologists have grave reservations about the use of their methodologies by structural analysts of literature; political scientists would not go to the kind of literary criticism rampant today to find their truths. Freud was never convinced that he had presumably exercised an influence on literature or literary criticism, and I wonder how many psychologists put Lacan on a pedestal and how many archaeologists read Foucault.

When members of other disciplines, particularly the professional ones, suggest that it would benefit their students to have some literary training, they are not thinking of the kind of practices in literary criticism that have become imitative of the procedures of the soft and hard sciences. The nonliterature disciplines appreciate the otherness of our approach as the common denominator of whatever literature we teach. They want us to remind the students of scientific and technological disciplines of the human quality that is often lost in the process of objectification and empirical assessment at the center of so many of the other disciplines.

No matter how hard we try to simulate them, these other disciplines are better suited to search for truths and their inconsistencies. The arts are not a reflection of facts nor a verification of them. They are transformational, not to say transcendental. The challenge for the teacher of literature is to demonstrate how the world of art achieves certain degrees of unity of light in the face of the cloudy complexities of the human psyche and in defiance of the indeterminacies of ideas and of the gratuitous appearance of phenomena.

The teacher today must guard against the subversive efforts to undermine the literary community of acknowledged great works of art, that common treasure which helped shape the concept of a universal fraternity. In establishing contacts between the familiar and the unfamiliar, the teacher constitutes a continuity within the spectrum of a universal cultural history. I believe that is what society expects of literature teachers and scholars in higher education in the modest but attractive dwelling we inhabit in the human universe.

NOTE

This essay first appeared in the proceedings of the First Global Village Conference, edited by Edward R. Sunshine, Barry University, Miami Shores, Florida, February 7–10, 1990.

XVIII

CANON HARASSMENT

The notion of canon and its status in the academic establishment has acquired a very political flavor as it has deviated from strictly literary values and become compromised with multiculturalism, human rights, and gender and ethnic differentiations. The issue is no longer of the trembling of the veil of the sacrosanct canon in the normal fluctuations that occur with the passage of time but whether to rip apart completely the veils that protect its mystery. All signs forewarn that the very concept of the canon as it pertains to literature is at risk.

I used to rationalize that if our teachers became herded into political correctness, surely the publishers, who are practical men and women, would hold the line on the preservation of the canon; they have the habit of recognizing literary merit and would be loath to print and list titles as "literature" without submitting to objective scrutiny texts that smack of partisan orientation. But I am finding to my amazement that very unpredictable things are happening in the publishing world, tempted as it is by the promise of thousands of salable textbooks. Their copy editors even resist correcting grammar to preserve the authenticity of found writings. Nonbooks not only make the best-seller lists; they are also gaining entry into university bookstores as they get the seal of academic approval, inclusion in prestigious anthologies, and are taught as literature. All of this reminds one of the Dada revolution when literature got spelled for a while as *Lits et Ratures*.

But this time I am no longer behind the desk. In my late sister's library I peruse the venerable books shelved with love row upon row, the popular consorting with the classical, and I ponder on her uncanny sense of knowing which of the best-sellers might survive as literary art among all of those which reached her for forty-three years during which she scrutinized them as a member of the book review editorial staff of the *New York Times* and decided which to discard from her own shelves just so they would not occupy space. In her own library she preserved what is a real cross section of the heritage of twentieth-century society this side of the jungle.

I am not going to plead for the canon. In my youth as an enthusiast of surrealism, I was myself a canon smasher in trying to make room for surrealist texts, and in the absence of cooperative publishers I often taught from mimeographed handouts before copiers became common tools of instruction. If one pole of learning is acquisition of the known, the other is the discovery of the unknown. From my present vantage point I don't need to care how the onslaught on the canon may affect me professionally and I no longer participate in the power play. And those who would call me a conservative had better take a look at my long record as an avant-gardist.

But there is grave reason to continue to be a concerned citizen when the canon harassment becomes a philosophical and social issue. When I juggled the canon to include writers of my personal predilection in both the familiar and unfamiliar literatures it never occurred to me that Big Brother might be looking over my shoulder or that I might be harassed if I deviated from the prescribed list. What troubles me now is that the books to be taught or eliminated from courses entitled "literature" are caught up in a philosophy of multiculturalism, and additions and omissions that were signs of individualism or idiosyncrasy of taste in the midst of a plethora of possiblities have become the reflection of political stands. Changing or eliminating the canon or excluding certain texts seems tailored by ideologues who promote the sameness mentality under the dictate of the higher authority they assume.

Sometimes the clarification of a notion or of a word can be brought about by going to the source of meaning. "Canon" is a religious term, and in the context of Catholicism the power to canonize is relegated to the pope. But what is significant here is that when analogically the expression became a literary term it served under a very different modus operandi. No one single authority wielded power of judgment over the choice of the literary saints, just as the highest-powered publicists cannot control what literary works will survive that inevitable reaper, time, and determine which will disappear, after the purgatory of indecision, into a second death despite all the brouhaha of the initial promotion.

Unlike the religious practice, no literary pope or conclave of cardinals can act on the literary canon. For a time public taste, affected or driven by propaganda, can determine which books become prominent, but such popularity is as ephemeral as the clothes of yesteryear that crowd our closets but are no longer wearable. And in terms of permanence, the fads and fashions in our choice of literature will carry out their own self-regulation; the canon has its own system of triage and will not let itself be tampered with. It will leave us a balance of permanent values in its own mysterious ways. I am not so pessimistic as some about the long-range effects of canon harassment. I believe that just as sexual harassment hardly ever produces a marriage, canon harassment will not create anything permanent.

But I am disturbed by the manner of the harassment. I am shocked that the fashionable is no longer a spontaneous phenomenon but the result of contrived, manipulative forces. Changes have become as capricious as the weather and as volatile as the stock market. We have witnessed in the course of the past three decades infringements on the part of linguistics, anthropology, philosophy, and psychiatry on our discipline. Thereby Saussure, Jakobson, Foucault, Nietzsche, Heidegger, Freud, Lacan, and others in these disciplines have been put on the literary menu. But this intrusion is relatively harmless because the very abstruseness of these texts has kept the literature classroom guarded against long-term invasion. But now we are faced with a more dangerous inroad, that of sociology. It is dangerous because of its availability and easier access and because it is much less cryptic or technical and on the surface seems more associable with the literary course. Ethnographers, social historians, human rights advocates, promoters of ethnic studies and special interest perspectives seem to be manipulating our curriculum, hounding administrators who in turn pressure their faculties in the literary field to implement these maneuvers.

Now it must be admitted that many of these pressure groups are innovators and humanitarians in their own manner and domain. For the sociologist what matters most in the work of art is its *representative* character. Eugène Sue's novels about Paris reflect the Paris of his time; his works make great documentaries, so do certain slave narratives of early American writing and certain untrained women's forays into creative writing. On the other hand, reading works recognized as illustrative material is no more useful as a literary exercise than looking at a Van Gogh painting is in learning the geography of Provence.

There is such a thing as the mastery of a trade, and this verity applies to the makers of literature as well as to every other person engaged in a field of human activity from the carpenter to the sculptor, to the athlete and the actor, to the lawyer and the surgeon. One does not have to be a master oneself to recognize such mastery. It happens that in our democratic terminology we recoil from the notion of "master" in its political and social sense, but we still seek the master in his trade in every walk of life regardless of proposed quotas and compulsion about inequities; this is true in every field, except that suddenly mastery in literature is becoming an exception to be challenged.

Why impede the young from enjoying the opportunity to learn the masters of literature? May they not be exposed to human rights and all the politically correct notions in classes in History, Sociology, Civics, Ethics, where indeed the representative is more appropriate than the "great" as illustrative material? Certainly texts deserve to be discovered and to be used as documents and read as such, but in a perspective other than the literary.

There is no hegemony involved in the literary canon that has come down to us. It is a legacy of a certain flowering of civilization geographically identified as "Western" but to which every socially functioning race today has contributed and to which it is beholden. Indeed, what is more multicultural than the so-called Western culture? It is the amalgam of the offerings of a palimpsestic deposit of surviving works of the arts and sciences. Recognizing the multitudinous components of that imposing structure should not result in the need to deconstruct it so that each element may proclaim its day in the sun, but instead should result in the desire to bring greater awareness of the miraculous cohesion that has occurred with time. Let history, politics, social studies teach the current generation to respect more than in the past the individual and differing subcultures, some heretofore neglected, that constitute the achievements of the human race, but let the literature class not preach equal time for the masterful and the nonmasterful; the role of the teacher is to choose among those works that constitute an extraordinary assemblage of factors signifying "literary" and which belong to all and not to one or to an elite, and certainly it is not the business of one generation or group of individuals to determine what is to be included or excluded. Successive generations will possess the virtually genetic imprint of recognition of the best and the valuable in literary works as in art works and as in precious gems. On a more graphic level, can you persuade a purchaser of art works to buy a nonmasterful painting because "the guy needs the money" for survival? Can you coax the curator or acquisition director of a museum to hang a not-so-well-executed fresco showing the suffering of persecuted people under threat that if he does not do so he will be accused of being a heartless member of some demographic elite? It sounds absurd to ask such questions, yet that is exactly what is being done when nonmasterful writings are being shoved down the throat of innocent students in the name of "literature."

Some scholars who have gained prominence by being "politically correct" have promoted the idea that somehow political power has in the past unjustly affected the priority given to certain works over others. Walter Benjamin has been quoted as saying that the prominence of German "Kultur" was directly connected with the military power of the Nazi regime. If that was true, the subterranean forces of triage were in place to correct and undo artificial canonization. One respected American scholar has considered very vocally the proposition that Shakespeare should be less widely taught and read because of Britain's declining political power. Again, if we refer to the currently disdained discipline of History we will learn otherwise. Sometimes a defeated nation's culture is swallowed up along with its political authority, but at other times, as in the case of Greece's defeat by the Romans, the defeated imposes its culture on the conqueror. Only one law determines which way survival goes; it is based on the intrinsic impact and mastery of the cultural treasure at stake.

But whichever way it goes, a multicultural effect is created as the balance of cultural power shapes up and thereafter the resulting *métissage* creates not a polarization but a unifying factor. Perversely, multiculturalism today as a political tool is a harmful, divisive concept to deconstruct not only literary values but individual talent and fraternity among humans. The company I kept for thirty-five years as one of the builders of Comparative Literature in America was based on the principle of internationalism and not multiculturalism as that term has come to be understood. It was built on *cohesion* in bringing together the best fruits of literary merit upon which new generations could achieve an even closer union.

Now we are being offered much blindness and little insight as the basis of relevance decreases under an artificially self-imposed critical canon that practices censorship through exclusionary devices. All nations around the world today have appropriated shares of Western culture. Real multiculturalism has two sides. One side of the coin shows how these ethnic groupings are alike, the other how they differ. One does not get a focused picture unless exposed to both sides. Take the case of the English versus the American. Both countries use basically the same language, and at the beginning the germinating literature of America sounded much like the older one: it formed the Emersons and Longfellows and Whittiers. By the end of the twentieth century not only the language but also the content and resonance of American literature have moved apart from each other to such a degree that they have little to do with English literature, and it is a mystery to me why American literature is still included academically under the aegis of the English department. Why has it so widely deviated from the initial model? The reason is that it has been subjected to all the ethnic groups. The result has been an amalgamation of differences into a unity enveloping the basic human concerns, into a hue that absorbs all the separate colors of the population. And its wide success is confirmed and applauded around the world, even by those who dislike Americans politically. Why then separate these blended strains artificially? Why turn back the clock when it is naturally moving toward a new homogeneity? In the light of the current products of that literature it is fallacious to presume that it is the property of a Yankee elite. It is true that the output of that earlier Yankee elite had an impact or influence in shaping the history of American literature and is still recognizable as a surviving factor. But that early literature has not cloned itself. I don't see a single Henry James—perhaps the last U.S. writer to make an effort at English simulation—on the current market. What I see is a solid amalgam that outside forces consisting of a critical elite are trying to split into separate unicultural sectors and confine to separate catalogues.

   The truth is that there is no *pure* culture, as Hitler had to find out the hard way. We are all part of the many evolving subcultures of Western civilization. The biggest injustice has been done to blacks in applying to them the label of "minority" and thereby alienating them from the culture that has nurtured them for three hundred years (for better or for worse) and to which they have contributed their share. John F. Kennedy electrified the world when he declared "Ich bin ein Berliner." We are indeed all products of Western culture, and there are no minorities in the appreciation of what is beneficial to the human race. We are all responsible for that culture in all its strengths as well as in all its failures. To use literature to promote racial isolation or bias is nonproductive; what is referred to as racial "pride" easily turns into arrogance and is prone to violence instead of the much more desirable interracial consortium which is catalyzed by the masterful forms of literature wherever they happen to emerge. *Les Misérables* in its Broadway revitalization could be performed by an all-black cast, by an all-female cast, or by any assortment of skin colors or genders or racial orientations because none of its themes is alien to the multiple divisions of the human species. Its concerns are very much alive since the human revolution that happened in France in 1789. Historical groupings are much more important than genetic ones as determiners of universal milestones in the reception and resilience of literature.

What worries me about canon harassment is not that its intrinsic texts will get hurt but that a generation or two of students entrusted to what the French would call "oriented" instructors will be deprived of exposure to the literary treasures. In this self-destructive mood we might at least listen to foreign voices clamoring to enter our universities to acquire what we are so pressed to discard. Here are a few quotes from the many letters culled from my correspondence as Chair of Comparative Literature at New York University, written by Asian students requesting admission to the program.

"Comparative Literature may help me understand both Western and Eastern literatures better; in particular it provides me a new angle to view my native culture, literature, and language," says a prospective Chinese student.

Another one specifies: "Though I am Chinese, I can still experience the intensity of feeling in, say, poems from Whitman's *Leaves of Grass,* which has always been a source of strength and inspiration for me."

Still another, hailing from Calcutta, dreams of "having the opportunity to amalgamate my heritage with that of the Western world."

Another's goal in getting an advanced degree in the United States is to help create "the intercourse of the oriental culture and the occidental."

Unfortunately, after the Asians arrive in this country they have to modify their vision. They do read Western literature avidly, often outside of their class work, but they soon realize that there is racial division instead of "intercourse," and they are apt to be engaged not in dialogue but in collective soliloquies.

Neither ethnic studies, gender studies, black studies, nor Asian studies or Latin American studies should be subjected to blindered vision. None of them is worth inclusion in the curricula of literature unless they can give affirmative answers to several questions. Is the work studied the result of an organized mind? Does the work have any connection with, impact on, or influence over other works beyond matters of gender, race limitations, political orientations? Does it provoke aesthetic pleasure and moral upheaval? Unless all works earmarked for the literature course meet these minimum requirements there is no reason to include them in the literature discipline. Perhaps they belong in the realm of "cultural studies" but certainly not in courses in literature taught under the umbrella of the Humanities.

May 3, 1992

XIX

LITERARY THEORY AND COMPARATIVE LITERATURE

An ever-increasing dichotomy is apparent between literary history and theory. Claudio Guillén makes a point of this phenomenon in his book on Comparative Literature entitled *Entre lo Uno y lo Diverso* by declaring that they are inept alternatives. But the trend persists and is particularly confining and academically rigid in regard to Comparative Literature, whose fundamental premise is indeed the amalgamation of these two approaches to literature. Paul Valéry, in his article on the need to introduce "La Poétique"—the name he gives to theoretical considerations—at the Collège de France, stated that it should not be a substitution or opposition to the study of history of literature but that theoretical activity should give direction, meaning, and purpose to literary history. In the past, within the discipline of Comparative Literature, theoretical speculations emerged as the outgrowth of methodical sorting out of the unwieldy material. Among these methods of approach to the comparative study of literature, let us review briefly a number of universally accepted ones.

In recent years, by a certain ironic twist, the most prominent and dynamic approaches to literature developed by the Comparatists have become the foundations of theoretical criticism, but with grave mutations and generally under different names.

The first of these comparative ways of viewing, which was

in fact one of the motivating factors of early Comparatist works, is the matter of influence. Comparatists theorized, after much experience in the field, that whereas there is normal, gradual influence within a single literature from one generation to another, and even negative influence in the form of reaction—what Harold Bloom reworked into "anxiety" of influence—the cross-cultural influences from one national literature to another are more eventful, informative of differences, catalytic of transformations, signaling larger perspectives, suggesting distinctions between vague affiliations on a transnational level. In its revelatory functions there is no better way of studying the interaction of two or more cultures, two or more traditions.

But through misuses and downright sloppiness in the handling of this kind of methodology in recent years, "influence" has become a bad word, confused with "imitation," and has even been viewed as a threat to ethnocentrism. It has been replaced by the theoreticians with the concept of "intertextuality," which is random, idiosyncratic, resulting in a free play of inter-referentiality that displays the virtuosity of the critic-manipulator rather than the fruits of scholarly research in the form of deep-sea plunging into literary works. The current theoretical version of influence study has become a major feature of what could be called "aleatory criticism."

Connected with "influence" was the category of "literary fortune," or what some early Comparatists called "doxology." The purpose of taking inventory of the literary fortune of a writer abroad was on the one hand to become more cognizant of the gravitations of literary works toward each other over and above geographical barriers to suggest universality, and, on the other hand, to gauge differentials in cultural mentalities—in sum to test permeability versus impermeability of ideas, tastes, and the capacity of a particular writer to enjoy reception beyond certain obstacles of time and place. It was an excellent exercise in determining the relativism of such concepts as "great" and "minor," in defining originality within literary modes, in noting the interaction between social and literary impacts.

Now we have reception theories geared primarily to empirical maneuvers, whose essential purpose lies in the knowledge of the process of popularization, and which are systematized in the perspective of quantitative gauges of favor and disfavor leading to breakdowns of the barriers of literariness. Whereas the study of the mechanism of reception aimed at an understanding of the work itself or of the shifting standards of the perception of the qualities of the work, now the evaluation of reception becomes a pretext for the formulation of theories of the *act* of evaluation itself based primarily on sociological factors and concerned more with the receiver than with the author's work received.

Another important framework that circumscribes literatures on a comparative level is classification, better known currently as taxonomy. For the Comparatist, periodization helps to codify the group qualities of a writer and the development and direction of genres. It encourages the perception of refinements between linguistic and zone groupings, between epochs, currents, and literary movements. All these considerations are motivated by an inclination to form clusters over and above national separations and even of diverse nomenclatures used by historians of national literatures, meaning the same thing in the perspective of the Comparatist historian. But in the practice of many theoreticians today, taxonomy is viewed pejoratively and taken into account primarily in efforts to extract works from their normal clusters to draw them into nonhistorical and nongeneric orbits which transform an organization of associable readings into a self-destructive device.

One of the most fruitful types of Comparatist activity has been the study of literary conventions in the context of the standard trajectory of beginnings, peaks, and declines of literary movements. These conventions involve themes, stylistic devices, figures, and paradigms distinguishable like a physiognomy, comprehensible like a Morse code over and above the needs of verbal translation from one literature to another. The current theoretician's version is tropology. The gleaning of tropes without historical grouping often runs wild in time and space and may be reduced to familiar mythic stereotypes; so imitative is this type of study of the primordial scrutiny of Northrop Frye or of Claude Lévi-Strauss that the literary interest of the trope is stifled. For in the process an oversight occurs of the deviations which mark an original author from the conventional; there results a loss of concern for individualism—a loss which is not compensated by the discovery of some neglected components of a trope-cluster. Nor is there an attempt to determine frequencies and their meaning or the levels of quality of works emerging from such myth, image, type, or theme developments. Racine's *Phèdre* would quietly take its place in the alignment of all other *Phèdre*s, and T. S. Eliot's *Cocktail Party* would matter only in terms of whether it obeyed "the rule of three" or of "two." The purpose in these recent studies of tropologies, thematologies, or typologies is either to construct a model applicable to an infinite number of cases not exclusively of literary works and with disregard of their connection with conventions linked to literary movements, or to be limited to short selections of interreferentialities.

Most dramatic of all is perhaps the mutation that is occurring in the study of zeitgeist. The delineation of a "couleur du temps" reflected in literature or created by the literature of a certain moment in time has been one of the favored pursuits of comparatist scholars. This study of zeitgeist is being transformed by the perception currently rampant that literature is a source of information about society having distinct "truth" claims. Whereas the very association of "zeit" with "geist" implied the transcendence of literary spirit over the quantitative inventory of sociological data, data processing in literature may be useful to the student of history or sociology, or even psychology, but it rarely contributes to a unifying composite delimited in time from composites of another era. Comparative use of the device of "zeitgeist" is to construct and connect, over and above national histories and political events, the impact of ideas and mores on literature, i.e., on the *creative* interpretation of the preponderant philosophical attitudes of the era, rather than to define zone enclosures. Indeed, sometimes several zeitgeists are present synchronically, such as the scientism of the latter part of the nineteenth century coexisting with the spiritual decadentism of the "fin de siècle," each based on a different set of factors or phenomena within a shared universe. Perception of these conflicting currents does not give proof of the divisiveness or disjunction of Man and is not cause for the denigration of history or justification for transhistorical reception of literature nourished by or nourishing parallel zeitgeists.

The theory of deconstruction and deferred meaning, on the other hand, devalues the strongest of all constructive activities of Comparatists while seemingly engaged in the same type of study. The notion that a work of art is to be viewed in terms of "truth in our time" rather than as "truth in its time" through a so-called disengagement of words from static meaning may be a reflection of our own zeitgeist, or, let us say, of the postapocalyptic vision of some recent theoreticians, but by the same token, it undermines the study of literature in its own context. In so doing, this theoretical orientation devalues the notion so dear to Comparatists that there are unifying forces that bind literatures together, that help establish norms of judgment in the appreciation of individual works in the context of historical clusters, that create a basis for comparison and interpretation not wholly left to the mercy of individual appraisers and manipulators. The notion of excellence is like a pyramid, a slowly constructed monument; one of the projected achievements of the comparatist scholars is to attain a level of consensus of relative artistic merit beyond the whims of politics, national or international. Extracting certain writers and/or their works from a particular zeitgeist or aesthetic atmosphere and subjecting them to so-called hermeneutic processes may have therapeutic value for critics in search of kindred spirits, but if taken too seriously they turn the personal relevance factor into an exaggerated determinant of favor or value.

The exercise of deconstruction which moves the meaning of a work from solid to soft ground may well give a sense of power to the reader-theoretician but can threaten the integrity of the work it has transformed into a text by separating it from its group significance. Yuri Lotman worries in *The Structure of the Artistic Text* about "a theory of enunciation that is being constructed as an immanent presence in speech, outside of historical or social reality." It is an exercise that can be dangerous, for it dilutes a work of art of its complexity and can turn it into a tool useful for functions other than the literary.

Finally, we are facing the dichotomy between analysis and synthesis, whereas it was previously assumed that analysis led to synthesis. The current concept of textual analysis appears to lead to fragmentation and anomaly. Out of the isolation of a work from its era or geographical point of origin and from the establishment of disjunction arises the presumption of irony and paradox. In fact, a sudden proliferation of venerable works vested with "irony" has become noticeable. But what has really occurred is that a personal disposition toward irony in many theoretically oriented scholars has been carried into the works studied by changing the order that led from analysis to synthesis and substituting an order whereby a priori theories are substantiated by analytic data. In their revised *Qu'est-ce que la littérature comparée?* Pierre Brunel, Claude Pichois, and André Rousseau phrase it very aptly when they discern that the Comparatists question the texts, whereas the theoreticians question themselves about the texts (113). Wolfgang Iser confirms the stance of the theoreticians in *The Act of Reading* when he says, "The significance of the work, then, does not lie in the meaning sealed within the text, but, in the fact that that meaning brings out what had previously been sealed within us" (157). The practice of analysis without synthesis seems to flourish in short-range studies but precludes the development of comprehensive and unified scholarly works.

To these decoding devices, the essential Comparatist responds with encoding systems. Synthesis as practiced by Comparatists can be the harvesting of the prerequisite activity of decodings. An open and unprejudiced mind utilizing the inductive method does not tell you at first what it will find and then proceed to select weighted examples to prove the point, but freely questions the work and justifiably related works, peruses literary domains for what they contribute to a universally recognizable body of aesthetic values, and only at the end, on the basis of an a posteriori association of components concludes to a theory as the stunning reward of the powers of detecting not paradox and disjunction but cohesion and conjunction. We must be reminded that Mallarmé's theoretical work emerges *after* he has written his major poems. It is an a posteriori "art poétique" in contrast to the many a priori manifestos that sprinkle the history of literature.

The confrontation between theory and praxis highlights the duality of our profession: learning and teaching. The function of the scholarly activity is a learning process that presupposes having been taught. The current breed of eminent theoreticians of the French school were superbly taught; one wonders how their disciples, not blessed with the same kind of rigorous training, will fare. The discovery of the plurality of meaning is a power bestowed upon a sophisticated reader. In other words, it takes the guilt of wisdom to discover the so-called innocence of language dear to Roland Barthes. To disentangle the underbrush of connotations, to return to denotation, is a fascinating game made possible for scholars who were subjected once upon a time to the instruction of cultural codes, linguistic structures, and aesthetic principles. Recognition of innocence is one of the dubious pleasures that can be derived from cultural maturation.

In this sense methodology is the counterpoint of theory. In following a methodology one accepts rules instead of making them as one goes along. Methodology is to teaching what theory is to learning. In the function of teaching, the scholar—and particularly the Comparatist—sets unilateral, unproblematic boundaries to the profuse complexity of literature to be presented in proposed and planned units. Whatever meanings are found are coordinated into a centrality, and the interrelationships of authors, thoughts, or behaviors are presented in the context of the writers' orientation before they are surrendered to counterinterpretations. The notion of plural is not possible without the presupposition of single. The ignorant cannot appreciate the notion of innocence. A scholar in the guise of teacher has to deal with the condition of ignorance. The complexity of the function of the Comparatist arises from the fact that the plurality of his teaching materials establishes typologies involved in several cultures. He has to establish some kind of unity of readerly optic before he can indulge in sharing with his student-readers the processes of writing which seem to hold for current theoreticians the pleasure of the text.

Fascination with theoretical speculation does not relieve us of the more intrinsic needs of the profession. The pooling of our specialized resources toward the writing of a Comparative History of Literature is one of them. Another is our continued search for a common language of criticism. We keep borrowing the terminology of seventeenth-century rhetoricians, nineteenth-century philosophers, and twentieth century anthropologists and psychologists. The existing labels of literary criticism such as realism, modernism, and postmodernism have become contradictory, ambiguous, meaningless, distorted in their nonhistorical applications.

We have failed to resuscitate neglected writers of familiar literatures or to incorporate in our interrelationships important writers of unfamiliar literatures. Instead we participate in the faddish rehash of certain writers who have been squeezed dry of meaning and have become downright boring. We rework the standard mythopsychiatric paradigms in hermeneutic readings in shocking neglect of the body of analogical patterns and images that link so many literatures in a verifiable hermetic code through the ages. We talk so much about the importance of language to the creation of literature but have not yet made any headway in the exploration of the nature of language groups which predicts their ability or failure to embody certain types of literature.

Theory is a formidable and erudite discipline to be respected for the coordination it brings among various branches of knowledge. Its function in relation to our discipline should be referential. I am apprehensive of lightweight theoretical activities serving as an easy escape for literary critics from the hard and challenging work that is their main task. It seems to me that those who highlight rather than integrate, juxtapose rather than interrelate, use the text out of context as a pretext for theory, are dubious fellow travelers in the discipline of Comparative Literature until they learn to use theory as a means and not an end in the study of literary relationships which regards literature as a holistic entity.

NOTE

This essay first appeared in *Toward a Theory of Comparative Literature: Selected Papers Presented in the Division of Theory of Literature at the XIth International Comparative Literature Congress,* edited by Mario J. Valdés (New York: Peter Lang, 1985), 17–24.

INDEX

Abraham the Jew, 118*n*
Aldridge, Owen, 45
Apollinaire, Guillaume, 83–84, 151, 193, 194, 218; in Aragon, 200, 203; on the cubists, 38, 39, 49; on the poet, 29, 45, 187; and Romania, 178
Aquinas, Thomas, 185
Aragon, Louis, 64, 78, 87, 118*n*, 199–212, 212*nn*
Arenas, Braulio, 223
Aristotle, 187
Arnim. *See* Von Arnim, Achim
Arp, Jean (Hans), 31, 50
Artaud, Antonin, 64, 199
Augustine of Hippo, 194

Bachelard, Gaston, 11
Ball, Emmy, 227
Ball, Hugo, 49, 80*n*, 227–34, 234*n*; on language, 33, 69, 214, 218, 220; and modernism, 29, 30, 214–16, 218
Balzac, Honoré de, 56, 82, 98, 153
Barthes, Roland, 11–12, 14–15, 21, 22*n*, 74, 98, 115–16, 118*n*, 179, 264
Bataille, Georges, 64
Baudelaire, Charles, 64, 153, 182, 184–85, 194, 219, 227, 228–29; on the critic, 54, 181; and interartifactuality, 47; and modernism, 24, 25, 31; and Poe, 138–39; and symbolism, 141
Beardsley, Monroe C., 102
Beckett, Samuel, 12, 34, 94, 110, 117, 242–43, 246
Bedoin, Jean-Louis, 126
Benjamin, Walter, 254
Benveniste, Emile, 11, 15
Bernard, Claude, 82
Bessière, Jean, 81, 84–85
Blake, William, 141–42, 143, 153
Block, Haskell, 135, 136
Bloom, Harold, 147*n*, 259
Bloy, Léon, 182
Boileau-Despréaux, Nicolas, 30, 215
Boucher, François, 46–47, 205
Brauner, Victor, 125
Brémond, Abbé, 183, 194
Breton, André, 90–91, 99, 105, 118*n*, 139, 140, 159, 182, 190–91, 194, 195, 217, 239; and Aragon, 200, 205, 208, 210–11; on the artist, 92, 93; on beauty, 86, 200, 205, 210–11; and Freud, 142–43; and Hegel, 65, 73; and modernism, 25, 36–37, 38, 39, 115; and multiculturalism, 121–26, 128–31; and mythology, 175–76; and surrealism, 50, 67–71, 73, 75–78, 79*n*, 80*nn*, 87, 114, 156, 178, 199, 211, 213*n*
Browning, Robert, 173
Brunel, Pierre, 263
Burnham, Jack, 116, 118*n*
Burroughs, William, 12, 30

Calinescu, Matei, 25
Camp, Maxime du, 219
Camus, Albert, 6, 94, 110, 154
Carrington, Leonora, 125
Cavalcanti, Guido, 173
Caws, Mary Ann, 80*n*, 170*n*
Césaire, Aimé, 126, 239
Champfleury, 219
Chassé, Charles, 165
Chateaubriand, François, 124, 150, 173–74
Chaucer, Geoffrey, 172–73
Chazal, Malcolm de, 125
Chefdor, Monique, 234
Claudel, Paul, 94, 182
Clément, Catherine, 75, 80*n*
Cocteau, Jean, 202
Cohen, Gustave, 182
Coleridge, Samuel, 138
Cortázar, Julio, 87
Courbet, Gustave, 219
Cournot, Antoine, 85
Craig, Harding, 147*n*
Craige, Betty Jean, 117, 118*n*
Cravan, Arthur, 139
Crevel, René, 95
Croce, Benedetto, 172, 174

Daix, Pierre, 213*n*
Dali, Salvador, 38, 50, 58, 59, 66, 80*n*, 105, 125
Dante, 172–73, 174
Danto, Arthur C., 61, 103, 118*n*
Darío, Rubén, 25
Darwin, Charles, 147*n*

267

Davis, Garry, 129
Delacroix, Eugène, 47
Delescluze, Louis-Charles, 77
Derrida, Jacques, 17–18, 23nn, 52, 64, 75, 116; his *différance*, 19, 74, 86; and modernism, 29, 42–43
Descartes, René, 18, 99, 122, 215
Dickey, James, 89
Diez, Friedrich, 161
Domingez, Ernesto, 125
Donato, E., 23n
Donne, John, 178
Donoghue, Denis, xiv
Dostoevsky, Fyodor, 36, 94, 192, 245
Duchamp, Marcel, 20, 30, 100, 105
Duras, Marguerite, 34
Durkheim, Emile, 82

Edy, 239
Einstein, Albert, 32, 85
El Greco, 107
Eliot, T. S., 53, 172–73, 261
Eluard, Paul, 50, 51, 57, 59, 92, 105, 127, 156
Emerson, Ralph Waldo, 138, 255
Ernst, Max, 38, 50, 59, 77, 80n, 125, 217
Escarpit, Robert, 142
Esclarmonde, 77

Faulkner, William, 110–12
Festugière, A. J., 177
Feuerbach, Ludwig, 65
Flamel, Nicolas, 118n
Flaubert, Gustave, xii, 5, 6, 99, 194
Ford, Charles Henri, 139
Foucault, Michel, 13, 18–19, 52–53, 60, 71, 95, 96, 128, 247, 251; and Magritte, 56–57, 58, 93; and modernism, 29, 42–43
Fourier, Charles, 77
Freud, Sigmund, 14, 32, 65, 85, 87, 95, 190, 251; influence of, 75, 142–43, 247
Frye, Northrop, 238, 261

Garber, Frederick, 48
García Lorca, Federico, 175
Gauguin, Paul, 48–49
Gautier, Théodore, 142
Gautier, Théophile, 154, 158
Genette, Gérard, 15–16, 22n
Ghil, René, 158, 159–60, 162–64, 167
Gide, André, 140, 141, 154, 192
Giraudoux, Jean, 154
Goethe, Johann Wolfgang von, 139, 142
Goldmann, Lucien, 179

Gorky, Archile, 126
Goruppi, Tiziana, 170n
Grass, Günter, 34
Greuze, Jean-Baptiste, 205
Guillén, Claudio, 135–36, 137, 258
Guss, D. M., 235nn

Hassan, Ihab, 27
Hatzfelt, Helmet, 48
Hausman, Raoul, 32
Havel, Vaclav, 121
Hawkes, John, 30, 34
Hawking, Stephen, 33
Hazard, Paul, 145, 181, 182
Hegel, G. W. F., 65–67, 73, 87, 223, 229
Heidegger, Martin, xi, 22, 87, 95, 223, 242, 251
Heisenberg, Werner, 85
Hemingway, Ernest, 12
Hertz, David, viii, ix
Hofmannsthal, Hugo von, 154
Hopkins, Gerard Manley, 178
Hugo, Victor, 137, 141, 153, 158, 199, 223, 226
Huidobro, Vicente, 33, 69, 214, 216, 217, 220, 223–27, 233–34, 234n, 235n
Huizinga, Johan, 87
Husserl, Edmund, 87, 95
Huysmans, Joris-Karl, 159, 229

Ibsen, Henrik, 246
Iser, Wolfgang, 10, 22n, 263

Jacob, Max, 182, 204, 206–207
Jakobson, Roman, 68–69, 80n, 251
James, Henry, xii, 5, 255
Janet, Pierre, 85
Jarry, Alfred, 141, 199, 203
Jean, Marcel, 50, 127
Jean-Paul, 151–52
Jolas, Eugene, 139
Josephson, Matthew, 148n
Joyce, James, 12, 25, 31, 33, 84, 86, 105, 242

Kafka, Franz, 5, 6, 36, 94, 245
Kandinsky, Wassily, 29, 49, 215, 216
Kant, Immanuel, 99, 191
Kleist, Heinrich von, 13, 65
Kristeva, Julia, 64
Kritzman, Lawrence D., 234n
Kuspit, Donald, 101, 118n

Lacan, Jacques, 13, 14, 42–43, 92, 247, 251

Index 269

Laforgue, Jules, 154, 178
Lam, Wilfredo, 126
Lamartine, Alphonse de, 139
Lautréamont, le Comte de, 50, 87, 182, 206, 217
Lawrence, D. H., 25
Leiris, Michel, 64, 70
Lenin, 65–66
Levin, Harry, 138, 148*n*
Lévi-Strauss, Claude, 12, 128, 182, 261
Littré, Emile, 161, 165–66, 170*n*
Locke, John, 18
Longfellow, Henry Wadsworth, 255
Lorca. *See* García Lorca, Federico
Lord, Georgianna W., 118
Lotman, Yuri, 52, 60, 263
Lyotard, Jean-François, 26

Macksey, R., 23*n*
Maeterlinck, Maurice, 48–49, 182
Magloire, Saint-Aude, 126
Magritte, René, 38, 53, 56–57, 58, 73, 88, 93, 109, 127
Mallarmé, Stéphane, xii, 5, 12, 64, 77, 107, 117, 184, 191, 195, 222–23, 227, 239, 264; and Ball, 228–32; influence of, 141–42; and language, 58–59; and modernism, 32, 217; and mythology, 175; and nature, 88; and symbolism, 46–47, 112–14, 139, 140, 154, 155–56, 158–69, 170*n*, 177, 178, 211–12
Malraux, André, 243
Man Ray, 126
Manet, Edouard, 46–47
Mann, Thomas, 31
Marinetti, Filippo Tommaso, 178
Maritain, Jacques, 16, 104, 150, 181–98
Maritain, Raïssa, 182
Marx, Karl, 6, 82, 129
Masson, André, 127
Matthews, John H., 79
Mauriac, Claude, 17, 23*n*
Mauriac, François, 108–109, 192
Mayoux, Jehan, 127
Meissonier, Jean-Louis-Ernest, 205
Ménard, Louis, 177
Merrill, Stuart, 139
Mezei, Arpad, 87
Michaux, Henri, 50
Miller, Henry, 25
Miller, J. Hillis, 110–12, 118*n*
Millet, Jean-François, 205
Milton, John, 174

Miró, Joan, 50, 58, 59, 92, 105
Mistral, Gabriela, 161
Moreau, Gustave, 49
Murry, Middleton, 172
Musset, Alfred de, 139

Nabokov, Vladimir, 154–55
Nelli, René, 160, 170*n*
Nerval, Gérard de, 219
Newton, Isaac, 28, 215
Nezval, Viteslav, 126
Nietzsche, Friedrich, 31, 251
Nougé, Paul, 127
Novalis, 65, 142, 153, 232

Ortega y Gasset, José, 29–30, 97, 172, 174, 182–83

Paalen, Wolfgang, 125
Pascal, Blaise, 114–15
Paz, Octavio, 33, 36, 125, 172, 173, 178
Péret, Benjamin, 74
Peyre, Henri, 135, 136
Picabia, Francis, 32
Picasso, Pablo, 47–48, 50, 51, 56, 100, 178, 182, 203–204; Apollinaire on, 38, 39; Aragon on, 87; Maritain on, 187–88
Pichois, Claude, 263
Pissarro, Camille, 205
Poe, Edgar Allen, 178
Poggioli, Renato, 24, 41
Ponges, Francis, 94
Pope, Alexander, 30, 215
Pound, Ezra, 25, 53, 172, 173
Proust, Marcel, xii, 5, 6, 86, 94, 95, 194; and memory, 105–106, 118*n*, 190; and modernism, 25, 31; and time, 35–36
Pythagoras, 176

Quinones, Ricardo, 234

Racine, Jean, 6, 7, 174, 179, 261
Ray, Man, 126
Reverdy, Pierre, 178, 182, 194, 214, 216–24, 227; on language, 33, 69, 156, 233–34, 234*nn*, 235*n*
Rexroth, Kenneth, 139
Ricardo, David, 82
Ricoeur, Paul, 74, 80*n*, 106
Rilke, Rainer Maria, 47–48, 49, 98, 175, 178, 227, 230

Rimbaud, Arthur, 14, 64, 69, 107, 141, 161, 218, 223, 227, 229; Aragon on, 206; his "letter of the seer," 103, 152, 204; Maritain on, 182, 184–86, 192, 194; and modernism, 28, 29, 87
Ristich, Marco, 126
Robbe-Grillet, Alain, 30, 34, 35, 38, 87, 94–95
Romains, Jules, 94, 182
Rorty, Richard, 244
Rousseau, André, 263
Rousseau, Jean-Jacques, xii, 92
Roussel, Raymond, 199

Sabatier, Robert, 4
Sade, Donatien-Alphonse-François, Marquis de, 154–55
Sage, Kay, 126
Saint Exupéry, Antoine de, 182
Sainte-Beuve, Charles, 13, 146, 161, 166, 170n, 191, 193–94
Saint-Pol Roux, 156, 178, 220
Sappho, 153–54
Sarraute, Nathalie, 31
Sartre, Jean-Paul, 94, 110, 116, 154, 222, 242; on Mauriac, 108–109, 118n; and modernism, 30, 36; on the work of art, 146
Saussure, Ferdinand de, 251
Schlegel, Friedrich von, 138
Sears, Sallie, 118
Seligmann, Kurtz, 126
Senghor, Léopold Sédar, 125
Shakespeare, William, 243, 245, 254
Shapiro, James, 91–92
Simon, Claude, 5, 35, 95
Soupault, Philippe, 105
Spenser, Edmund, 173
Staël, Madame de, 137, 138, 150–51, 153, 173–74, 176–77
Stein, Gertrude, 25
Steinbeck, John, 82
Stendhal, 137
Stevens, Wallace, 44, 98, 218
Sue, Eugène, 252
Sunshine, Edward R., 248
Supervielle, Jules, 89
Svanberg, Max Walter, 126
Swedenborg, Emanuel, 147n, 153, 189
Swinburne, Algernon Charles, 141, 173, 178
Symons, Arthur, 139

Takiguchi, 126
Tanguy, Yves, 38, 58, 182
Tanning, Dorothea, 126
Tasso, Torquato, 174
Tetel, Marcel, 212
Thirion, André, 65
Tieck, Ludwig, 142
Todorov, Tzvetan, 11, 64
Toyen, 126

Vaché, Jacques, 201, 210, 213n
Valdés, Mario J., 67, 68, 80nn, 266
Valéry, Paul, 106, 178, 258; Aragon on, 203, 210–12, 213n; on Baudelaire, 138, 139; on language, 160, 168, 170n; and modernism, 89
Valle, Rosamel del, 89–90, 127
Van Tieghem, Paul, 136, 137
Vercors, 4, 5
Verlaine, Paul, 70, 159
Verne, Jules, 83
Viélé-Griffin, Francis, 139
Villiers de l'Isle-Adam, Philippe de, 154
Villon, François, 172–73
da Vinci, Leonardo, 47
Voltaire, 209, 217
Von Arnim, Achim, 65, 142

Wachtel, Albert, 234
Wagner, Richard, 159
Wald, Susana, 52
Warren, Austin, 147n
Weimann, Robert, 52
Weisgerber, Jean, 26
Weisstein, Ulrich, 44–45, 47
Wellek, René, 136, 147n
White, Hayden, 102, 118n
Whitman, Walt, 129, 178, 257
Whittier, John, 255
Wimsatt, William K., 102, 118n
Wittgenstein, Ludwig, 33
Woolf, Virginia, 25
Wordsworth, William, 153

Yeats, William Butler, 31, 107, 112, 175
Yudice, George, 223, 235n

Zeller, Ludwig, 52, 127
Zola, Emile, 82

ANNA BALAKIAN first gained international recognition as a critic and scholar with the publication of her *Literary Origins of Surrealism*. She has lectured widely in American universities and abroad, and her writings include a number of books and more than a hundred essays on literature and literary history. Professor Balakian's critical attention has focused on Mallarmé and Breton, the poetic movements of Symbolism and Surrealism, and the poets and painters of the avant-garde. Responding to recent critical theorists, she proposes new theories, giving the Comparatist perspective on the values and destiny of literature.

 Professor Balakian is the former Chair of the Department of Comparative Literature at New York University, and she has served as President of the American Comparative Literature Association.